Simon Rattle

The Making of a Conduc

NICHOLAS KENYON

*To Betty
with best wishes
for Christmas 1987
Simon Rattle*

ff

faber and faber

LONDON · BOSTON

First published in 1987
by Faber and Faber Limited
3 Queen Square London WC1N 3AU

Photoset and printed in Great Britain by
Redwood Burn Limited Trowbridge Wiltshire

British Library Cataloguing in Publication Data

Kenyon, Nicholas
Simon Rattle.
1. Rattle, Simon   2. Conductors (Music)
—Biography
I. Title
785'.092'4   ML422.R/

ISBN 0-571-14670-8

Contents

	Introduction	vii
	First impressions	I
ONE	'What a great Mars Bar of a piece!' Turangalîla in Birmingham: January 1986	14
TWO	'Monomaniacal about music' Early years: 1955–74	24
THREE	'It had to be hard sometime' Professional start: 1974–80	53
FOUR	'Making the orchestra play better' Recordings and television: May 1986	72
	Interlude	97
FIVE	'I didn't realize how important it would be to be here' Birmingham: 1980–6	102
SIX	'London has some absolutely great players and that's about it' Around London: May–October 1986	137
SEVEN	'On the whole I'm in favour of monogamy' Guest conducting: November 1986	162

EIGHT '300 per cent committed to the future'
               Development in Birmingham: 1986–   174

Last impressions: January–March 1987   203

Appendix 1: the CBSO Society Ltd
    development plan   214

Appendix 2: a chronology of major
    appointments and debuts   220

Appendix 3: a conductor's diary:
    January 1986–August 1987   222

Discography   237

Index   241

Introduction

The first thing Simon Rattle and I agreed on when this book was suggested was that it would be absurd to embark on the full panoply of an 'official biography' of someone aged thirty-two whose work was only just beginning. He didn't want it written and I didn't want to write it. But it might be of interest to have a provisional book that tried to answer some of the most immediate questions about a conductor who is without question one of the most brilliant musicians of his generation. What is his background? What has formed his musical tastes? How does he approach the problems of conducting? What is his attitude to today's highly competitive and commercialized musical world? Why has he thrown in his lot so decisively with the City of Birmingham Symphony Orchestra? What is behind their much-publicized plan for the future?

This is a musical portrait rather than a star biography. You won't find much here about what Simon Rattle has for breakfast, or where he buys his clothes, or how many girlfriends he had before he was married. (I don't actually know the answer to any of those questions, though I do have a few clues about the breakfasts.) And perhaps 'portrait' sounds too finished. This is more of a jigsaw – a collection of facts, impressions, concert programmes, opinions, reviews and recollections which may add up to a provisional picture of the man and a pointer to what it is that orchestras and audiences find so compelling about him. I have preferred to let the material stand in a slightly unfinished form rather than give the impression that anything written at present on this subject is fixed or final.

The question I most frequently encountered when writing this book – besides 'Why?' – was 'Why now?' The initial stimulus came in November 1985 when Rattle signed on to continue as principal con-

ductor and artistic adviser of the City of Birmingham Symphony Orchestra until 1989, with an option (the significance of which was not
perceived at the time) to extend to 1991. The announcement stated
that 'it is, indeed, the hope and wish of both Mr Rattle and the CBSO
that this successful association will be continued even beyond 1991'.
Here was a quite extraordinary circumstance: that the leading conductor of his generation, who could be travelling the globe fulfilling
prestigious guest engagements while perhaps being music director of
a couple of glamorous orchestras a couple of thousand miles apart,
had instead committed himself for another four years to remain outside the centres of the world's music-making and to build up his own
orchestra in Birmingham, England.

So 1986 seemed to be a good year to look at what one American
newspaper had termed this 'Young Phenom with a Baton', and to
look, too, at the musical relationship between Rattle and the City of
Birmingham Symphony Orchestra, which was bound to have international implications in the coming years. The fact, of which I was
not aware when I started, that the CBSO was seeking over half a million pounds in extra funding for ambitious plans for extra development only added to the interest of events in 1986 and 1987, for it
raised publicly the whole question of how orchestras in Britain are
funded and run in ways I could not have foreseen.

My method in the book is to take the year 1986 – an exceptional
one, even by Rattle's standards – and use it to illustrate different
strands of his work. I visited him conducting Messiaen and later
Beethoven's Ninth in Birmingham, recording Mahler in Watford,
filming Berio in Northampton, guest conducting in Amsterdam with
the Concertgebouw Orchestra, appearing in London in the Sinfonietta's Britten–Tippett Festival and in the Philharmonia's *Après
l'après-midi* series, and knocking Glyndebourne for six with Gershwin's *Porgy and Bess*. It was an exhilarating but also a difficult year
for Rattle: his wife, Ellie, was taken ill during the CBSO's visit to
Paris in February and he cancelled all his work over the following two
months to be with her following a gall-bladder operation. That
characteristic placing of family first (which should be understood as
the background to all his musical activities explored in this book)
makes his achievements in 1986 all the more remarkable.

Interspersed between these sections about his work in 1986, and
breaking up the year's chronology, are chapters on his background
and earlier musical life. The story of the past advances as the year

1986 advances, and I hope that the perspectives are in some way complementary. I have let his own words, and those of his friends and colleagues, speak for themselves; where my questions appear in the interviews quoted they are set in italics. I am grateful to those interviewees who judiciously, but not too judiciously, corrected the text of what they said.

I would like to thank Donald Mitchell and Patrick Carnegy of Faber for suggesting the project in the first place and sustaining its progress; Martin Campbell-White and Rona Eastwood of Harold Holt Ltd for unearthing all their records of Simon's work and for much help and advice; Ed Smith, Beresford King-Smith, Julianna Szekely and the players and administrators of the CBSO for their enthusiastic cooperation; and all the many friends of Simon's who gave their time to talk candidly and honestly about him. They would all want me to say that such critical remarks as they make come out of a deep friendship for him and a knowledge that he knows it all anyway; in particular, John Carewe hoped that any criticism he made of the young conductor would only help those who are to follow in his path. Jane Ruthven and Clare Ellis gave much help in transcribing the tape recordings of the interviews.

With the publishers I would also like to thank all those who supplied illustrations, and especially Alan Wood who took most of the photographs. The other photographers and sources are, wherever possible, credited in the relevant captions.

I could not have written this book without the help of Simon himself; I know it made too many demands on his time in a hectic year, and am grateful for the patience and constant openness with which he answered all the many questions. I had much help too from Simon's parents, Denis and Pauline, and from his sister, Susan, who all cheerfully withstood some probably intrusive questioning and supplied many details and press cuttings from the early years which Simon had (already) forgotten about. Denis Rattle read the book and made many helpful suggestions, as did my wife Ghislaine, Ed Smith, Beresford King-Smith and Rona Eastwood. My special thanks go to Ellie and Sasha Rattle, who appeared not to mind being disrupted at unsocial hours for conversations with Simon which always lasted longer than planned; and to my own family, who were equally disrupted at unsocial hours by my presence at the word-processor.

NICHOLAS KENYON
April 1987

Hope and Glory: Rattle enthusing orchestra and audience at the last night of a
CBSO Proms series

First impressions

I first encountered something I gathered was called Simon Rattle in 1973, the first year I was in London. I was standing in the queue for a Covent Garden Prom performance with two friends, one of whom was a cellist at the Royal Academy of Music. Suddenly a small whirlwind bore down on us, and my friend was being cajoled, persuaded and bullied in the nicest possible way by a bright-eyed, intense, utterly entrancing young man with a shock of unkempt hair and an unavoidable stare to take part in his forthcoming performance of a Mahler symphony at the Academy. The whirlwind flew on down the queue. 'That', she said with an air of finality, 'was Simon Rattle.'

It was a scene that, I was to discover, had occurred literally hundreds of times during the years in which Simon had to use every possible ploy to get people together to play for him. It was typical of his sheer energy and of his determination to make things happen. Now, little more than a decade later, things certainly have happened: instead of begging and pleading, he turns down the world's great orchestras who want to play for him and tells them to wait until he is ready. Even the Berlin Philharmonic cannot be sure he will run to them; if he misses one opportunity, there will surely be more in the future. He is in no hurry. What has happened in those years? How has he reached a position where he can choose exactly what he does and when?

I first got to know him a little at the Dartington Summer School of Music where I pushed pianos around and put up music stands; he arrived in 1975 (with his parents and his sister who were regular participants there) to do *The Soldier's Tale*, and he returned in the following years to try out some of the choral works which were to be his staple diet: Janáček's *Glagolitic Mass*, Britten's *War Requiem*,

Mozart's C minor Mass and Stravinsky's *Symphony of Psalms*.

It was his utter unpretentiousness combined with his complete professionalism that was so astonishing: there was not a trace of prima-donna nonsense, but rather a total dedication to the musical job in hand. He always knew the right thing to say to people at the right time, a word of encouragement or appreciation or even mild but firm complaint, and it always had whatever result he wanted. Not that he was calculating or smooth: it all just came naturally. Some of the performances worked, and others didn't. Sometimes he smothered the music with enthusiasm, and sometimes that enthusiasm brought results so stupendously good that no one would have thought it possible. One thing above all stood out: for all his hilarity and wild good humour, he loved the music with a keen and deadly seriousness. Making it live was his first priority: the rest followed.

Since then, I have watched him often – and by chance was at his first-ever concert with the City of Birmingham Symphony Orchestra, given by the English Bach Festival (for which I then worked) in Oxford Town Hall in May 1976. As time went on I puzzled more and more that he was so untypical of other good conductors I'd met: no bloody-mindedness, no shows of temperament, no underlying condescension towards the rest of the human race. (Of course one meets conductors who are very nice chaps, but by some law of nature they tend not to be the very best conductors...) Our paths rarely crossed, but when they did – for a newspaper interview or just a chance encounter – he was open, approachable, and always refreshingly frank.

So much for one view of Simon Rattle. What of those who know him far better than I do, and who have worked with him over the years? For some first impressions I turned to a pianist, a composer and a conductor each of whom have known him for some time. They can set the scene with some brief pictures of Simon Rattle at work.

                    *   *   *

Down a little alley-way in Mile End, London, in an unprepossessing part of the East End which nevertheless contains some superb little Georgian squares, there is a converted printing works. It has become a studio for the pianist Philip Fowke, far enough away from the neighbours for there to be no problems with practice at any hour of the day or night. A larg. high room houses two grand pianos, and the walls are lined with pictures, photos and mementos ('Claudio Arrau is indisposed; the recital will be given by Philip Fowke' is his favourite, from the Edinburgh Festival).

Philip Fowke and Simon Rattle met at the Royal Academy of Music in London, where they both had the same piano teacher. Rattle's piano-playing career came to an abrupt end. Fowke's has flourished: he has become one of the best established of all the younger generation of English pianists. His appearances with Rattle include a Rachmaninov Second Piano Concerto in the first concert Rattle gave as conductor of the Merseyside Youth Orchestra in 1973, the John Ireland Concerto in a televised Prom with the BBC Scottish Symphony Orchestra, and Rachmaninov's Third Concerto in Rattle's first concert with the CBSO as principal conductor. In the 1986 Henry Wood Proms in London they did Rachmaninov's Fourth Concerto together. Fowke is dapper, precise, and thoughtful; he weighs his words carefully.

PHILIP FOWKE: If you ask me which of all the conductors I've worked with I enjoy best, then Simon is right there at the top. When you're out on the platform with him you have a feeling of complete security. It's like playing with a safety net, and when little things happen, as they invariably do, you know you'll be OK. If you want to

'You feel you know him best through the music': Philip Fowke rehearsing Rachmaninov's Fourth Piano Concerto with Rattle and the CBSO in the Royal Albert Hall, 1986

take a little time over something, he's with you. He makes you be with him as well, of course: it's a complete collaboration. Musically he likes all the things I like – time to breathe, flexibility. He's a very passionate conductor: there's no holding back. And he's a superb accompanist: I remember Rach. 3 in Birmingham, and the televised Prom when we did the John Ireland Concerto: the beginning of the slow movement sounded glorious...

We both studied the piano at the Academy with Gordon Greene, and Simon was brilliant at slashing his way through an orchestral score at the piano, but couldn't play a C major scale to save his life (or so I heard). I used to go up to Liverpool for lessons, so it seemed natural we should do something together there. I remember Simon's complete professionalism even from the first Rach. 2 I did with the Merseyside Youth Orchestra. He knew exactly what he was doing. There was a lot of movement, and a certain cockiness in his manner – I have always wondered how that went down with orchestras where the players were much older than him. But I'm sure people put up with it because he was just so glaringly gifted.

I never feel I've got to know Simon as well as I could wish. We've had some very nice times, and a couple of years ago I bumped into him quite by accident in the Piazza San Marco in Venice, and had a marvellous time with him and Ellie and Sasha. But there's something about him which overawes me, and I can't quite work out what he's thinking. You can be terribly friendly, but you feel you are only really communicating when you're actually playing. Yes, that's it: you feel you know him best through the music.

＊   ＊   ＊

In the middle of the floor in Oliver Knussen's tiny study in his West Hampstead flat there is mound of cassettes. 'Sorry, I'm just about to sort them out,' he says resignedly, and we find space among the piles of scores and records (a fascinating collection, which continually diverts my eye to the shelves) to sit down and talk. Knussen is more than a composer in Rattle's life: he is also a catalyst, provoker and planner. Both are closely involved with the London Sinfonietta; both are artistic directors of the Aldeburgh Festival (though Knussen is more active there than Rattle, see p. 137); and both have worked at Glyndebourne. Rattle took up Knussen's Third Symphony with the CBSO and performed it widely; so far a new Knussen piece promised for the orchestra has not materialized. Knussen's enthusiasms are infectious, his knowledge of the contemporary music scene alarmingly wide and discriminating.

Oliver Knussen (*photo* John Carewe)

OLIVER KNUSSEN: Simon was asked by Michael Vyner [director of the London Sinfonietta] to do the première of my *Coursing* in one of his Sinfonietta concerts. So I took the first twenty or so pages of the piece, which was all that was ready a month before, round to him when he lived down on the Marylebone Road. It was rather early, and he answered the door in a dressing-gown and absolutely nothing else, which was, I thought, refreshingly un-conductor-like. That piece eventually got terribly stuck, and I was for giving it up, but it was Simon who insisted: 'Put a temporary ending on and let's do it.' It's a horribly difficult piece, but he understood it at once; he had no apparent difficulty at all. That's the thing I like most about him as a composer: you don't actually have to spell out what the piece is about or what to bring out; he knows.

He did my Third Symphony in Birmingham – the first conductor in this country to take it up. I did some preliminary rehearsals with the orchestra (because he characteristically felt that they should have more time on it than he had). When he began his own rehearsals a few weeks later he said, 'Well, of course I had to start from scratch!' I know he can't stand composers who bounce up in the middle of rehearsals and ask for things, so I volunteered – and he accepted – a rather funny arrangement. I sat in the control room with the sound turned off and read a book while he rehearsed next door. We left it that he would come in if he needed to ask anything, which of course he didn't. I just went in at the end and it was fine.

He has a terrific sense of style, he knows the twentieth-century literature very well, and he will know the antecedents of any piece he is dealing with (and is quite merciless in pointing them out!). He instinctively knows what you are aiming for. There are a few people who can perceive things that quickly, but there's virtually no one who can also communicate them in rehearsal, as Simon does, without ever putting a player's back up. Of course there will be minor moans, like there are about any conductor, but I've never seen him irritate players with his sharpness, and that *is* a gift.

Once every six or nine months we have a sort of listening orgy. He will bring me things – he brought the Debussy *House of Usher* fragments, which we then worked on together for South Bank Summer Music, or tapes he's been sent by unknowns – and I will play him things. That was how he got on to Takemitsu, for instance. The most recent time, last year, he rang up and said he was feeling terribly out of touch with the younger generation of composers (the ones now in their twenties) and could he come round for a 'crash course'. Now the point to make here is that when you fling a bunch of stuff at most people they might say 'very interesting, very promising', but Simon knows at once what he likes and what he doesn't, and can say why, too. When something does strike his fancy there is a quite wonderful spontaneous warmth in his response, and he usually goes into action on that composer immediately.

Writing an opera and rehearsing it at the same time is not an experience I recommend to anyone. In 1985 I was at Glyndebourne working on my *Higgelty Piggelty Pop* and was in a terrible state, obsessed with the knowledge that this piece could not be finished in time and that it might not hold up. Simon came into a rehearsal, a particularly bad one for me. I saw him quietly sitting there, and I was rather nervous – I don't think he'd seen me conduct before. So I came out of the pit at the end and everyone was worried by what they'd seen, about whether the thing was going to happen – the actual music was the last thing on anybody's mind. Simon just came up and said, 'Well, I think that music is beautiful, some of the best you've done, and I can't wait to get my hands on it!' I don't know whether he really felt it, or sensed that I was very low, or whatever, but it was so unexpected for someone at that moment to comment on my music instead of all the problems that I just burst into tears. It probably embarrassed him terribly, but I'll never forget that sensitivity or that moment.

Of all the influences on Simon Rattle's career, that of the conductor John Carewe has been probably the greatest. From a master–pupil relationship they have become close friends, and one senses that of all the people with whom Rattle is able to discuss music and conducting, with John Carewe he can be the most frank and open. Now the relationship has changed so that Carewe will often come to Rattle for help and advice: when I was chatting to them both, the day before Simon left for America in February 1987, John Carewe was about to have a session from Simon on his conducting technique. Rattle has no reservations about what he owes to John Carewe.

> SIMON RATTLE: The meeting with John Carewe was the most vital of them all. Working with Boulez, listening to Furtwängler, yes, those things were important, but the truth is that it was Carewe: 90 per cent of what I know came from him. It's extraordinary for us to have turned the corner now and just be friends and colleagues.

John Carewe is sharp, intense and perennially youthful; quick to enthusiasm, quick to praise, and equally quick to rule out of court anything he regards as unworthy or unmusical. He was a pupil of two Schoenberg pupils, Walter Goehr and Max Deutsch, and later studied in Paris with Olivier Messiaen and Pierre Boulez. He has been one of the most active conductors in Britain in the field of contemporary music, giving many premières especially for the BBC during the 1960s and 1970s. He was principal conductor of the BBC Welsh Symphony Orchestra for five years, and now conducts extensively abroad. He has been a regular teacher and coach of conductors. When I was a teenager (I never admitted this to him while we were talking!) I once went on one of his conductors' courses. It was, perhaps above all else, the experience which made me respect professional musicians and made me realize quite how impossible conducting is.

> JOHN CAREWE: I first heard of Simon when I went to conduct a summer orchestral course in 1972 at a place called Burton Manor near Liverpool, run by the Liverpool Mozart Orchestra. It was great fun; we were doing pieces like the Goehr *Little Symphony* and Gerhard's *Alegrías*. People were talking about this young percussion player called Simon Rattle who, although he was only seventeen, had already done some concerts and was attracting attention as a conductor.
> I discovered he was going to rehearse a Mozart symphony during one of my free afternoon periods, so I dropped in. I'd heard a lot about how talented he was and sure enough it was clear that this boy had real talent as a conductor. But I was horrified because everything he was

'The meeting with John Carewe was the most vital of them all'

doing was absolutely dreadful. I had a long internal tussle with myself, wondering whether I should interfere, and then I thought I must. So I said to Simon, 'I'm going for a drive, come with me,' so we got in the car and I had him there as a captive audience! I told him exactly what I felt, which was basically that he was obviously intensely concerned with what he heard inside himself but had absolutely no idea of what the orchestra was actually playing. And equally, I said to him, he seemed to have little idea of what the music really required.

Now the interesting thing, which is so typical of Simon, was his response; this is really the touchstone of the whole business. He was instantly aware that I was trying to tell him the whole truth and he was so grateful to have someone who didn't just tell him how marvellous he was. And so our relationship clicked immediately, I think. We came back after the car journey and sat down on a settee in the big room at the manor and took out the Mozart, No. 39, and went through it in the way that I understood it. I explained it to him and analysed the harmony and phrase structure and talked about how a good performance should reveal these things. From that moment he was hooked on my teaching, or rather the teaching I had inherited from my study with

Goehr and Deutsch. The main principle behind this is the idea that the conductor must have clearly grasped all the harmonic and tonal implications of a piece and must use these to organize the phrasing, the tempi and the nuances. When he has these things clearly in his mind, then there are relatively fewer difficulties physically. Young conductors either respond to this or they don't, and Simon was absolutely intrigued.

Was the next time you came across him at the Royal Academy?

Yes. He was there as a student ostensibly doing percussion and piano, and I started to conduct an ensemble for twentieth-century music which Simon got involved with as a player. We didn't discuss conducting at the Academy but he asked to come to me privately, so he used to trek down to Haslemere and we would go through scores and he would play me things and he would eat us out of house and home!

The next thing was that in the summer of 1973 I asked him to come along as my assistant to the Glasgow Schools Symphony Orchestra and play the Stravinsky Concerto for piano and wind. Now I suspect this reinforced a lot he already knew about rehearsing. We had lots of sectional rehearsals, and we would really pull pieces apart and put them back together again. It's not unique – any good conductor does it – but perhaps this is where Simon saw how you can build up with quite poor players to a very high standard of performance. Simon is a great sectional rehearser now and he knows just how useful it can be.

Then in the December of 1973 he did Mahler 2 at the Academy, getting everyone together for it. I didn't go for some reason so he brought me a tape of it down to Haslemere and he was very, very proud of it. I remember sitting in the living-room there listening to it and wondering what on earth I could say about it that would be useful and not hurtful. In the end I decided to put on the old Klemperer recording. And of course he was rather devastated. But from there we were able to move on and discuss the shortcomings of his performance positively.

Can you specify what you thought was bad about it?

It lacked character and understanding. It was a young man's Mahler, very exciting but very bland. That was a problem Simon had to fight through, to give the music its 'nose', as Max Deutsch used to describe it, its own unique quality. There was another example around that time: he put on a Bruckner 4 somewhere in north London in memory of a horn player who had drowned, a typical gesture of his. I went to hear the rehearsal and in the break I said to him, 'Look, you're not doing anything, you're just letting it roll by without giving it any shape; I mean, it's all very well just standing there looking very beautiful and getting everyone to play very beautifully but in actual fact it comes out terribly bland.' Well, he was very quick, and he immediately focused on the phrasing, tightened the whole thing up and it was much better. But that was the basic problem with the Mahler. Very intense and superficially very exciting, but he had not dug deeply into the essential musical content.

Given the depth of lack of musical understanding you felt he had, what was it convinced you that he was a born conductor?

Well, I didn't use that exact phrase but I'm not going to contradict it. You could tell that he just had this tremendous ability and tremendous enthusiasm and a desire to communicate. He had all the natural attributes you could hope to find in a young conductor. He could always make it happen, and get players to give their best for him. In that Bruckner symphony I was mentioning, at the back of the fiddles I met one of the better players in a London orchestra and he said, 'This is marvellous; we really want to play for him.' That's the point.

But he realized and I think he still realizes to an extent that his intellectual understanding of music is not what he would like it to be. Unlike certain other conductors I could think of, though, he's very conscious of that and does everything he can to overcome it. I think that was why he responded to my teaching, because I wasn't telling him about stick technique and that sort of thing – I do regret, incidentally, not having interfered with his actual technique until much later! – but about how to analyse scores. We were analysing them from the point of view of performance: not as a musicologist might, or Maxwell Davies might from the point of view of the composer, but just from the point of view of understanding how the notes on the page are supposed to work.

We studied the implications of tonality, what makes a movement stand up as an arch-form. It was a question of understanding the harmony and its implications, the fact that tonality is the outcome of very particular chord formations and their use. We did study some music outside this basic diatonic tonal system, but we mainly concentrated on Beethoven 1, 2, 3, 5, 6 and 7, Brahms 2, several Mozart symphonies, and we must have done the *Tristan* Prelude.

What's interesting about that list is that it is not at all typical of Simon's repertory...

No, that's true. He has always been conscious of how deep one's intellectual understanding of those pieces has to be, which is why he's steered away from most of them since. But he did Brahms 2 at the Academy: oh yes! In his last year he did it in his final exam and I'm sure everyone fondly hoped he would run away with the conducting prize. The other two judges would probably have been overawed by his ability and given it to him, but I had to stand up and say it was awful and I absolutely refused to give him the prize. At that stage the music just wandered for him – lovely sounds, but no appreciation of how it was actually built up.

Simon's first big break came when he won the John Player Competition in Bournemouth in 1974. Did you know he was entering for it and did you try to put him off?

He asked me for a reference for the competition and I said I would give him one but I hoped to God he didn't win because he wasn't ready for it. I told him to go in for it by all means because it would be good experience conducting a professional orchestra. And I suppose we all like to claim foresight but I did write in that reference that whether or not this boy wins, he is a born conductor. It's all history from then on!

When I heard he'd won I was very pleased for him but worried too. He did have a difficult time in Bournemouth but he survived. I suppose I underestimated how quickly he could learn. That's one thing about Simon: I've given him various pieces of very considered advice at various times in his life, and always he's ignored it and always he's been right. I suppose about six years ago, after things had really taken off for him, I told him what he should be doing was just twenty-five to thirty-five concerts a year with the greatest orchestras in the world. He chose the opposite, which was to go to Birmingham and do masses of concerts a year. And he was dead right.

Did he continue to come to you for advice while he was at Bournemouth?

Oh yes, and afterwards too. We moved in 1975 from Haslemere to Guildford, with my first wife, Rosemary, and my daughters, and he came there a lot, was marvellous company for the girls and still ate an enormous amount. There was a period when we drifted apart. This too was interesting about him, because it was when he was having his first big successes and getting lots of offers, and I think he was genuinely embarrassed about it because at that stage my career wasn't so hot. I don't think he quite realized that I was very, very proud for him and didn't mind in the slightest. We saw each other but not so regularly.

I remember he brought me a tape of Beethoven 7 which he'd done with the BBC Scottish and he said, 'John, I know you're not going to like this,' and I didn't like it one little bit. It was from this point, perhaps, that I began to learn from Simon, because I had never realized consciously that one of the essential things about the analysis we had been doing together was that once you had done it and it had guided your instincts then you had to forget everything and let it come through your subconscious. You're not teaching the orchestra or the audience what you've learnt in analysing the piece! Your analysis tells you how the music goes, and then you've got to put it across. But by this time it was a fault in the right direction.

When did you start to get at his conducting technique?

That was much later; I was back living in London, he had started in Birmingham, and we had established the very different sort of relationship we have now. He would want me to go to concerts, and tell him what I thought. I must admit I must have been very rude on occasions. But he did have a certain tension and stiffness in his right wrist which is a drawback with a big orchestra. You must be flexible and I told him very severely about that and over a period of two or three years he did put this right: he now has a beautifully flexible technique.

I remember when he did *The Rite of Spring* with the CBSO at the Festival Hall in 1981 I was very disappointed. This is a piece which we'd talked about ever since he'd done it with the NYO and recorded it – not one of his best records at all – and we had a long talk in a BBC canteen about it. (There's still one bar I'm convinced he beats wrongly!) After this CBSO performance I said straight out, 'I never expected *The Rite of Spring* to sound like Rachmaninov and I don't think I can survive this culture shock.' It was very lush and rich and stripped of all its brutality; he did it from memory and glossed over lots of things. He was trying to make it sound good. This is something he had to do with the CBSO: he had to work hard at making them *sound* fine, and this was a case where it got right in the way of the music. About six months later he did it again, this time with the Philharmonia, and it was exactly as I felt it should be. I was over the moon, because it had all the sound but that was secondary to the musical character. Very exciting and musical, with a real punch.

Do you think Simon will continue to mature as a conductor?

Oh yes, because Simon never stands still. I remember him saying to me once, 'My greatest danger, John, is that I could become too lazy. It could all be too easy.' I suppose in a sense he was asking me to keep him on his toes, but he would have done it himself anyway. We now have the most thrilling forty years in front of us because his repertory and his perception are just going to expand. I feel absolutely confident in predicting that he is well on the road to becoming one of the greatest conductors, in the line of the very best conductors of the past.

*   *   *

If Simon Rattle is well on the road to becoming one of the greatest conductors, the question that arises is: what is he doing in Birmingham, out of the London limelight, conducting an orchestra which was not, say twenty years ago, thought to be among the country's best? Rattle himself would dismiss the question with irritation as an example of London arrogance, which assumes that everything important in the musical life of the country must happen there. Nevertheless, the road he has chosen – to build up an orchestra at the same time as he develops himself as a conductor, to work out of the limelight, and to eschew for the most part glamorous guest conducting dates around the world – is an unusual and individual one.

To some, Simon Rattle may seem stubborn. But he knows what he is doing. That is one central fact about him which those who long for

The audience of tomorrow: Rattle meeting children after a CBSO family concert

him to travel the world, to conduct in more great opera houses, or even to create a new orchestra in London, do not take fully into account. There is only one place to start to understand what makes Simon Rattle work, musically, and that is Birmingham.

CHAPTER ONE

'What a great Mars Bar of a piece!'

Turangalîla in Birmingham: January 1986

Crater No. 357 on the Moon is officially entitled Birmingham Crater. There are towns named after Birmingham in Saskatchewan, Canada; Jefferson, Alabama; Los Angeles, California; New Haven, Connecticut; Miami, Indiana; Jackson, Kansas, Oakland, Michigan; and in many other American states. No one could argue that the city's reputation does not extend far afield. But it is a reputation that, over the last couple of decades, has taken some hard knocks. In the industrial recession that hit Great Britain in the 1970s, Birmingham and the West Midlands slumped; with declining productivity, high unemployment and a lack of economic prosperity it became the poorest area in the United Kingdom outside Northern Ireland.

Such a decline was, perhaps, inevitable for a city that had been built on the boom of the Industrial Revolution in the nineteenth century, and that was wholly dependent on manufacturing and trading industries for its early prosperity. 'The City of 1000 Trades', they called it, and among the many testimonies to its success came one from the composer Antonín Dvořák, who visited Birmingham in 1890: 'I'm here in this immense industrial city where they make excellent knives, scissors, springs, files, and goodness knows what else and besides these, music too. And how well! It's terrifying how much these people here manage to achieve.'

There was indeed a remarkable history of achievement in Birmingham dating back to the late eighteenth century, when its prosperity first took off. Lying as it did at the heart of the country's canal network (it still likes to boast that it has more miles of canal than Venice) it became a centre of communications, and the place where scientists, men of ideas and entrepreneurs gathered: Joseph Priestley, who discovered oxygen; James Watt, who invented the steam engine; Josiah

The city's ambassador: Rattle and the CBSO in the Town Hall, Birmingham

Wedgwood, the potter; William Murdoch, inventor of gas lighting; John Baskerville, the printer; Matthew Boulton, the industrialist – all these lived and worked in Birmingham. Soon, too, it was at the heart of a railway system, and there seemed no limit to what it could achieve. Large food and drink companies such as Cadbury's originated here (the Utopian village of Bournville was the centre of the Cadbury operation), and brewing, metal-working, engineering, car manufacturing and all kinds of light- and medium-scale industry became important parts of the city's economy.

So it was scarcely surprising that when industrial decline hit Britain it should hit Birmingham hardest. But although economic circumstances are still extremely hard for many, there has been a determined effort to adapt to changed circumstances and find a new role for the city. The foundation of the 350-acre National Exhibition Centre ten years ago marked a turning-point, and that complex now houses a large percentage of Britain's major exhibitions. Birmingham is now promoting itself heavily as a venue for new business, offering 'a total workforce of around half a million with experience and skills in every type of industry ... [and] some of the lowest industrial rents and rates in the country.' There is a major science park at Aston devoted to the emerging 'sunrise' industries in the fields of electronic, computer and precision engineering which it is hoped will replace the traditional industries now in decline. The Science Park has close links with Aston University, and can call upon advice from its scientists and technical experts. The biggest step forward for Birmingham – and one that closely involves the City of Birmingham Symphony Orchestra – is the plan for the massive International Convention Centre supported by European Economic Community money, which is planned to open in 1991 (see p. 200).

But for all this determination and resilience, it still cannot be argued that Birmingham is a remarkably attractive city. In interviews Simon Rattle has had to fall back on the assertion that 'It's not a pretty city; on the other hand, it's not as ugly as Cleveland or Detroit.' A long-time observer of the Birmingham scene is Beresford King-Smith, the deputy chief executive (as he was newly styled in February 1987) of the CBSO, who has worked for the orchestra for many years.

BERESFORD KING-SMITH: Birmingham is the spider in the middle of the motorway web and people come here because of their jobs. There was a strong civic pride in the nineteenth century – that's where all those big Victorian buildings come from – but then after the war something went wrong, and the planning was I think a disaster. We're not the only city that's suffered from it but it was very bad here. Somehow the city got cut in two by the ring road and there's us up at this end and them at that end, and that is a bad thing in any city.

But those things are now gradually being healed. Some good buildings are going up; architecturally it is still not anything to write home about but the feel of the place is improving. A few open spaces are being created – that's something we lack in the middle of the city, a bit of grass, a few trees – which make a tremendous difference. But the really encouraging thing has been to see the political parties working together on all this. In the past a change of power from Socialist to Conservative in Birmingham, or *vice versa*, was a very serious thing for us because

Birmingham has always been a hung parliament. But now the industrial decline and the effort to get the Convention Centre on the map, the influence of going for the bid for the Olympics, and the influence of the present city chief executive himself, have been a great asset; they've produced very different attitudes locally. There's a feeling now that we need to cooperate to survive, and that is very healthy.

It has been very healthy too for the City of Birmingham Symphony Orchestra. As Birmingham's reputation as an industrial centre declines, the city has been anxious to find other roles, other areas where it can show its expertise. And in the partnership of the CBSO and Simon Rattle it has found an outstanding export. George Jonas, chairman of the CBSO, likes to tell a story:

GEORGE JONAS: I arrived in San Francisco a couple of years ago, and got into a taxi. The taxi-driver started talking: 'Where are you from?' 'England.' 'What part of England?' 'Birmingham.' 'Oh, Birmingham. Would you know a guy called Simon Rattle?' He'd conducted there, you see. Birmingham was known in San Francisco by Simon Rattle. The orchestra is as good an investment for the name of Birmingham as anything here, and we can be the city's ambassador abroad.

Still, the CBSO's importance to Birmingham could not have been as great as it is had it not established its remarkable artistic success within Britain, and had it not established its even more remarkable relationship with the local community. How has this extraordinary, alchemic brew been mixed?

*   *   *

JANUARY 1986: Birmingham Town Hall is an imposing Roman-style temple just a short walk from the busy Broad Street railway terminal. It was designed by Joseph Hansom, better known for his invention of the hansom cab, and was styled on the famous temple of Castor and Pollux in Rome. The building is faced in Anglesey marble, and you can see fossils still standing in the marble. It stands with one side to Victoria Square, a welcome open space which is also, incongruously, enclosed by the Italian Renaissance-style council house, built in 1879, and the French château-style General Post Office of 1910 – an imposing trio of public buildings. Behind the Town Hall a new piazza has been created around an old memorial tower outside

Hansom's Hall: Birmingham Town Hall, designed by Joseph Hansom, the home of
the CBSO. The newly-created piazza leads directly to the orchestra's offices in
Paradise Place, and the Adrian Boult Hall

the big new Central Library of 1973, one of the largest libraries in
Europe. Just round the corner, in what is known as Paradise Place, the
CBSO have their offices next to the Birmingham School of Music
which houses an excellent small rehearsal and concert hall named
after Adrian Boult, one of the orchestra's most distinguished principal conductors.

Birmingham Town Hall has been the CBSO's home since its
foundation. Any drawbacks in the acoustics, of which the orchestra
are acutely conscious, do not seem to worry the audience. The place is
packed to bursting for a programme which, were it put on by any of
the London orchestras in London at any time (except possibly during
the Proms), would empty the house at a stroke: Messiaen's *Turangalîla Symphony*, a post-war classic, sensual and accessible. The Philharmonia Orchestra's most recent *Turangalîla* in London, the
previous November in the Royal Festival Hall, under the young conductor Esa-Pekka Salonen, had drawn a miserable 40 per cent house.

Why does the audience come in Birmingham? To answer that
question would be to pinpoint a magic formula on which every con-

cert promoter would love to get his hands, and the answers are not simple. But a couple of points stand out. Unlike in London, many people buy their tickets as part of a subscription scheme, which predisposes them to come. Messiaen's *Turangalîla* is a work that the Birmingham audience knows: Rattle and the CBSO have programmed it before with great success. There is a confidence that the orchestra will play it well. But more important than these things is the long-term relationship which, over five years, Rattle and his players have built up with the audience. They have come to trust his taste. If he wants to give them Messiaen, it's probably worth having. There is an evident loyalty which suggests that the audience feels it's worth the risk. That is not the situation in London, where there is constant competition from the one-off, hand-me-down programmes of popular classics undertaken on very little rehearsal. And there is no competition in Birmingham. Who is to say whether the CBSO's Messiaen audience might not have been much smaller had a promoter chosen to bring another symphony orchestra for a Brahms and Tchaikovsky concert in a tent down the road? But in any case, there are few conductors in London or elsewhere who use their direct pulling power over an audience in the way that Rattle has done to promote the contemporary repertory. He is an exceptional enthusiast in that regard, and his tactics have paid off.

In fact the CBSO's programme this January is even more adventurous than the last time they programmed *Turangalîla* back in 1981. On that occasion they offered Mozart's *Prague* Symphony as a sweetener; this time they have decided to take the contemporary bull by the horns and are offering one of their new commissions, the latest in a long and fruitful line of works premièred in Birmingham with the financial support of the Feeney Trust, a work by the young French composer Tristan Murail. This points up another aspect of the Rattle revolution in Birmingham. Audiences no longer regard twentieth-century music as a medicine which has occasionally to be taken for the good of their souls. They enjoy it or, if they don't actually enjoy it, they are happy to experience it and discuss it. Listening to the Birmingham audience talking in the foyers during the interval of this Murail–Messiaen concert, far more of them seem to be talking about the music than would be the case in London (where the sort of remark you overhear tends to be about the new Volvo). 'It sounded like sort of outer space music,' said someone of the Murail. 'It didn't mean much but I liked some of those noises,' said another.

One vital reason why contemporary music is now more readily accepted in Birmingham than it is in London has to do with the purposeful shape of the programming and its grounding in the early twentieth-century repertory. A London audience which listens to Beethoven, Brahms and Mendelssohn as a staple diet simply doesn't have the apparatus to understand Messiaen when it comes along. There is a similar problem in New York, where the Philharmonic tends to programme new works by Xenakis with nineteenth-century Romantic works beside which they seem nonsensical. But in Birmingham, where the staple fare is Sibelius, Stravinsky, Schoenberg, Bartók and Debussy (all composers close to Simon Rattle's heart), the musical language of the early twentieth century is uppermost in the audience's ears. Against that background Messiaen makes sense. And against the background of Messiaen, Murail makes sense. Birmingham is not unique in this, but it is rare: London Prom audiences in the Pierre Boulez era had something of the same experience, and Rattle points out that as a child in Liverpool he had the same experience in that enlightened period with the Liverpool Philharmonic when Stephen Gray was general manager and Charles Groves was principal conductor.

Tackling *Turangalîla*: a session with Messiaen's score. Tristan Murail (ondes martenot), Simon Rattle, David Murray (EMI producer), Peter Donohoe (piano)

And the final reason the Birmingham mixture is so successful is that the orchestra itself is now fluent in this kind of repertory. This is something Rattle himself draws attention to when I catch him after the morning rehearsal – itself an unusual event, since rehearsals on concert days outside London usually take place in the afternoon.

SIMON RATTLE: We thought there's no way you can play a piece like this twice within two hours, so now we've got a chance to rest. Usually it's a desperate panic between the end of the afternoon rehearsal and the concert to grab a veggieburger or whatever it may be ... We've done *Turangalîla* a good deal together now: five times altogether, including the Welsh première! We sent Messiaen a copy of the big poster all in Welsh which is quite some curiosity. We very much hope he'll be able to come over when we do the piece later in the year for the Bath Festival. [He did, and orchestra members recall his visit as a highlight of the year: 'as if Mozart walked in when you played the *Jupiter*!']

One of the things I remember about all the performances has been the incredible response of the audience: here in Birmingham there was something that sounded like an Indian war whoop at the end. The orchestra know it very well now, so it's more like rehearsing a very complicated big-band arrangement by Stan Kenton – actually it sounds like one too, I'm glad to say! – than putting together a 'difficult' piece of modern music. It really is like falling off a log for them now, which means we can concentrate on just getting it perfectly dead on, absolutely accurate, rather than having to start from square one.

It staggers me to think that when the Philharmonia played it in London last year they did it on two rehearsals. When we first did it we had seven rehearsals, spread over some time. The thing that surprises people about the piece is that the orchestra is not huge. It's nowhere near as large as the orchestra for *The Planets* though it makes as least twice as much sound (and at least ten times as interesting a collection of sounds). There is obviously a huge percussion section but I think it's really the use of the brass section that makes such a difference. In fact we use a trumpeter who's playing in the show *Cats* to do the piccolo trumpet part and it's marvellous: he can play any note at any volume, any time, and so he'll be blasting out Lloyd Webber one night, and by ten o'clock in the morning he'll have driven up the motorway and be slamming out *Turangalîla* for us. One needs that, one needs a jazzer's nerve to go for it.

I first heard the piece in Liverpool in the 1960s, done by Charles Groves who did so much there for contemporary music, which we tend to forget. *Turangalîla* was done when I was ten or eleven, and I'd seen the score but never heard it, so I bullied and badgered my parents into letting me go and it was one of the most thrilling experiences I remember. I nearly jumped out of my seat in the way I see audiences doing today. What a great Mars Bar of a piece!

The performance in the evening is a knockout, with a sustained accomplishment and commitment on the part of the orchestra which is unhappily not very frequently found in London. One or two bits of playing are perhaps not as skilful as you would hear from a London orchestra, but the cohesion and drive of the whole more than makes up for that. And even more striking for a visitor from London is the concentrated attention the audience gives the piece: there's a real feeling of constant communication, not only between Rattle and his players but between them and the audience. The tension is palpable and the electricity generated is remarkable.

The CBSO puts on only one performance of the Murail–Messiaen programme in the Town Hall even though most programmes can now sell out there for two performances during the week; then they take it to Nottingham, to the new concert hall which provides a valuable regular outpost for the orchestra's work, where they are engaged by the local authority which is prepared to take what is offered and not bargain for Brahms; and then, riskiest of all, on the Thursday they take the same programme down to London for one of a series of four concerts they are presenting in collaboration with the London Symphony Orchestra in its resident season at the Barbican Hall. It draws a 60 per cent house, which is good, the audience is alert and the performance is only slightly less fine than in Birmingham. But the feeling of absolute identification of an audience with its own orchestra, the palpable bond of communication that came across from the packed hall in Birmingham, is missing.

That suggests one major question to me for the year 1986: is Rattle creating a new environment for music-making in Birmingham which could not possibly exist in London, or is he showing London a possible way forward for concert-giving in the future?

A nice postscript to this Messiaen experience indicates how far the orchestra's reputation outside the city is valued within Birmingham. At the annual banquet of the Birmingham Chamber of Industry and Commerce the following month, the president, Francis Graves, delivered a speech entitled 'Don't Undervalue Birmingham' in which he picked up on a piece written in the London papers about Rattle's concert: 'I don't know if Joe Chamberlain still sees the *Observer* each Sunday. If he does he would have read about reactions to a certain

piece of twentieth-century music. I cannot even trust myself to pro-
nounce the composer's name, and I doubt whether the name of the
piece would mean a great deal to many of us here. But the *Observer*
noted that ... Simon Rattle and the CBSO achieved a full house for
it at Birmingham Town Hall, unlike in London. So much for Birmingham as a cultural desert...'

One thing that is clear from even the briefest visit to Birmingham is
that the success of the CBSO at present owes much to the personal
charisma of Simon Rattle himself: it is because Rattle is there to conduct them that promoters will accept adventurous programmes from
the CBSO, and that the orchestra is welcomed more and more
abroad. Yet the CBSO has a strong and characterful past of its own,
just as Simon Rattle has a past, with many sides to his musical personality. And he, like so many others in this cosmopolitan city, is not a
local lad. To find out his musical background involves a trip further
north to another troubled area of British inner-city life, Liverpool.

CHAPTER TWO

'Monomaniacal about music'

Early years: 1955–74

First notes: Simon at the piano in Liverpool (*photo* Denis Rattle)

I

1955–70

Simon Rattle's home was full of music, but he made it even fuller from an early age.

His father, Denis Rattle, was for many years the managing director of an import–export company which dealt with the Far East in a wide range of major items such as industrial machinery and medical equipment, as well as such minor, unromantic items as plastic flowers and bras. But he always had a passion for jazz, and when he was reading English at Oxford he joined the university dance band which was called The Bandits (whose members included Frank Taplin, a future chairman of the Metropolitan Opera in New York, and Desmond Dupré, the lutenist). He considered a career in teaching, and then toyed with the idea of career in jazz, but put both aside when the war broke out. He joined the Navy, and it was from that point that his future moved in the direction of business rather than teaching. He met his wife, Pauline, in Dover, where he was on mine-sweeping duties and she was running a music shop. ('I had to wangle a second year in Dover,' he recalls, 'which wasn't really allowed because it was supposed to be so dangerous. I spent every penny I had as a sub-lieutenant on records, just so that I could talk to her.') It was their mutual love of music that brought them together. They married in 1941 and went up to Liverpool where he was sent to recover from his arduous duties, arriving on the night of the famous 1000-bomber raid which destroyed so much of the city.

Through contacts he met in Liverpool he was asked to help set up a company shipping goods to China immediately after the war, though the Communist takeover soon put paid to that and the focus of activity shifted to Hong Kong. For many years the work proved challenging and exciting, but it became increasingly irksome as he found himself dealing mainly with creditors and debtors, and his mind turned back towards the idea of a teaching career. It was not to be until he was fifty, however, that he made the break, left the company, went back to college and re-emerged as an English teacher – at a considerable salary drop – at a school where he also became involved in music, teaching the recorder, guitar and piano.

Denis Rattle had always played jazz on the piano at home, and Pauline Rattle also played from time to time. Their first child, Susan, born in 1946, had a major influence on the family's development because although she is highly intelligent she is slightly disabled, with muscular problems which caused her parents to worry for a long time as to whether she would ever be able to be fully independent. She trained as a librarian, however, undertaking the demanding three-year course at home and obtaining a librarianship degree. She has for many years now been extremely happy working at the Central Library in Liverpool. She too has a passion for music: she plays percussion and from her early years she was bringing home records and scores which were to have a profound influence on her younger brother.

Simon was born nine years after Susan, on 19 January 1955. In an interview several years ago he spoke very candidly about the early influence of his mother: 'Because my father's business took him away a great deal when I was a child my mother was the more dominating force. I remember particularly that she never smacked me. Discipline in our house – which has always been a very gentle place – was always administered verbally. The worst punishment you could have was a really sharp word and my mother was always good at that ... She's always said I was a good baby and didn't cry much. When I was a bit older I was too fat, though not from the diet my mother served me but because I was a sort of food kleptomaniac, relentlessly pilfering food from the fridge ... Right from childhood she influenced my reading tastes considerably. I was encouraged to read George Orwell and H. G. Wells. My mother used to leave books around in the hope that I would try them ... As a person my mother appears very quiet on the surface, but underneath that calm exterior there is a good deal of turbulence and intensity. I know she is proud of me but she keeps it to herself. It's rather more obvious in my father.'

Simon, from the family album

It was certainly Simon's father who first led him towards music. Playing his Gershwin songs and jazz numbers on the piano, he noticed that the two-year-old Simon would tap along on whatever was handy with a distinct and firm sense of rhythm. It was definitely jazz and not classical music that made the first big impression on Simon, and he remembers reacting strongly against some of the classical records Susan brought home to listen to. By the time he was four he had a small drum kit, bought for him by his father who thought 'Ah, a real jazz partner at last!' Simon managed to break it up within a short space of time. However, he had a real aptitude for percussion, and it was this that led to his first public appearance.

An early thirst for words...   ...and music

FRITZ SPIEGL: My daughter Emma went to the same kindergarten as Simon, and we knew the family well. I remember that whenever Simon came round for a party he would always perform; it was difficult to get my children to play anything but he would immediately leap up to the piano, harpsichord, organ or whatever. In 1961 I'd been asked to put together an entertainment for the anniversary of the Bluecoat School. There was an old Victorian Bluecoat march of which I had the music, so I scored it up and we had Simon aged six as the drummer. He was real extrovert, but I can't honestly say that I spotted him then as someone who would go this far.

DENIS RATTLE: Simon had never had a lesson at this point, but I taught him the piece Fritz arranged. I'd played some percussion in my school orchestra very roughly, so I took him through it. At the end of the performance Fritz lifted him up on to the table and Simon got his own round of applause. I think that made a big impression, the applause! That was what decided us to go to John Ward, who was playing percussion in the Liverpool Phil., and asked him to teach Simon seriously. Another thing which very much influenced Simon just around this time was that I started to take him to Merseyside Youth Orchestra rehearsals on a Sunday morning; he must have been six or seven. And when he saw the chap up at the back playing the timpani Simon knew that he was the king – he was obviously in control of everything – so I think his attitude was 'never mind the conductor, that's where I want to be'.

By this time it was clear that Simon had real musical talent. He was beginning to learn the piano too, with ten-minute lessons at his prep school, Newborough. He had developed a great interest in twentieth-century music – Schoenberg's *Five Orchestral Pieces* he distinctly recalls as a piece he found 'just wonderfully beautiful' at that time. Among the pieces Susan Rattle recalls bringing home from the library around this time are Bartók's *Miraculous Mandarin* and Violin Concerto, Schoenberg's *Gurrelieder*, Tippett's *A Child of our Time*, Mahler's First, Fourth and Sixth Symphonies, Shostakovich's First, Fifth and Tenth Symphonies, Walton's *Belshazzar's Feast*, and Rimsky-Korsakov's *Capriccio espagnol* and *Sheherazade*, a fascinating list which includes pieces that are still among Simon's favourites. Moreover, Susan gradually taught him to read the scores of these pieces. Denis Rattle recalls this happening 'very casually and normally. When listening to Proms or records at home he would borrow scores. But it was not long, with Susan's help, before he could sit and read a score, just as other children would read a comic.'

SIMON RATTLE: Having a sister who was handicapped put me in the very unusual position of having someone who was nine years older, and intellectually nine years older – which is a huge gap – but who was willing to play with me the whole time. I think I was very much affected by what she would bring back from the library; that's why I started with twentieth-century music rather than anything else (I remember at the Academy, when I was seventeen, realizing I was hearing Brahms's Third for the first time, which was a real shock).

The thing I most loved to read, which is pretty scary now I think of it,

was the great green bound copy of the Berlioz *Treatise on Instrument-
ation*, and that must have been when I was seven or so. I think if I found
a child doing that I'd think 'God, how ludicrous' ... I really don't
remember how Susan taught me to read scores, but she did. I just
needed to know everything: I was absolutely monomaniacal about
music in a way I'm not any more, thank God. That changed around
puberty, but I still see it in some of my colleagues, and it's frightening.

DENIS RATTLE: Simon listened to all sorts of music on the radio in
these years. He must have listened to virtually every Prom during the
summer for years from the age of eight or nine, and our household was
organized round getting supper in and the homework done in order for
him to be upstairs with his radio by 7.30! He must have absorbed an
incredible amount of music then, and he knew it really well and would
often be following scores.

Some of the most remarkable events in those years before Simon was
eleven must have been the Sunday afternoon concerts in the Rattle
household. At the weekend Simon would go with his father and Susan
to the local library where they would choose records and scores of
some twentieth-century display pieces, usually those which involved
a lot of percussion. During the week, Simon would copy out all the
percussion parts and build the pieces into a programme. With a neigh-
bour, Sally Loader, and Susan, and occasionally with his parents as
well, he would give a concert on the following Sunday which consisted of playing the records with 'live' added percussion.

DENIS RATTLE: He would have the plum part, of course, and we
would chip in and he would tell us off if we did anything wrong. We did
all sorts of pieces – Shostakovich 5, Mahler 4, Respighi's *Pines of
Rome, Fountains of Rome*, you name it, we were in there. We even did
A Child of our Time, and bits of *Rosenkavalier* ... The programme for
each concert, written out by Simon, would be pasted on the drawing-
room door.

SUSAN RATTLE: Simon would always write on the parts not only the
kind of percussion instruments but the size of instruments he would
have wanted to have played it. This was a result of John Ward, who was
always very precise about which exact instrument was to be used: if
there was a single gong in a piece he would line up a whole row of gongs
and would choose which it was to be ...

Simon's first experience of playing in a live group was with a small orchestra of very young musicians under the direction of Raymond Mulholland. He played violin and percussion, and made his very first attempts at conducting as well. When he went to Liverpool College he was entitled to play in the Liverpool Schools Junior Orchestra, where he played percussion, but since rehearsals were on Saturdays, and the college worked on Saturday mornings, he was rarely able to attend. Dennis Rattle explained the situation to Bill Jenkins, conductor of the Merseyside Youth Orchestra (which was run under the aegis of the Royal Liverpool Philharmonic), who allowed Simon to join the percussion section there even though he was below the usual age for the orchestra. He was ten and the usual entry age was fourteen, but he was so keen that Bill Jenkins allowed him to start playing with them at once, and he formally joined the orchestra in March 1966, at the age of eleven, using some new drumsticks which his father brought him back from Hong Kong. 'People still have vivid memories of Simon as a chubby boy playing cymbals nearly as big as he was,' recalls his father. One of the other percussionists in the orchestra was Annie Oakley, who now plays percussion in the CBSO. 'She used to say that she always looked at the stairs to see if they had been soaped before she walked down because she knew that Simon's greatest wish was to take over the timps!' says his mother. And so he did, by the end of the following year.

Simon describes playing with the Merseyside Youth Orchestra as his most important early musical experience:

SIMON RATTLE: I think I was a very solitary kid, probably rather strange because I was so obsessed. And I had very few friends of my own age until I was eleven and was playing in the MYO. That somehow opened me out, and made me a bit more normal. Bill Jenkins was a wonderful Welsh character, and he gave me many of my ideas, and many of my opportunities, too.

I used to listen to concerts on the radio, and badger my father to take me to Philharmonic concerts. I think my parents' expectations of me were enormously strong, especially having had a handicapped child. They very much wanted me to succeed.

Simon Rattle is remembered well at the Liverpool Philharmonic. From the age of eight or nine he would be at concerts: a performance by Charles Groves of Mahler's Eighth Symphony at Liverpool Cathedral in 1964 had Simon (in short trousers) and his father in the

Principal timpanist: the Merseyside Youth Orchestra in 1970, with Simon
surrounded by percussion (*photo* Royal Liverpool Philharmonic Orchestra)

front row. By the time he was nine he would be going round backstage to get conductors' autographs, and to discuss with them – with
some persistence, recalls his father – features of their interpretations
with which he agreed or disagreed.

SIMON RATTLE: When I first started going it was really only pieces with percussion instruments in them which interested me: so it was mainly twentieth-century repertory, and especially anything contemporary. I remember being thrilled to bits by Henze's Second Symphony, but more because it had percussion than for any other reason. I liked violent, garish music – *The Miraculous Mandarin*, that kind of thing. But I was so lucky growing up in Groves's time there because we really heard a lot of adventurous music. There was the tradition of John Pritchard's *Musica viva* series, which was so enterprising. Gerhard's *Concerto for Orchestra* I think was the last piece I remember there. It just wouldn't happen now because the climate has changed so much. And when people give me credit for what I'm doing in Birmingham it's all because of what I was able to hear in Liverpool.

DENIS RATTLE: A week before his tenth birthday he went to hear Arthur Fiedler at the Philharmonic. He was one of the most interested in Simon and had a really long talk with him and Simon queried some of his tempi, not in a critical way but asking 'Why did you do that?' Just a week later I was off to America on a foreign leadership programme, with real red-carpet treatment all the way. I found myself at a dinner in Boston and at my table were Anthony Eden (by then Lord Avon), Adlai Stevenson, Walter Cronkite, the mayor of Boston and his wife, and on my left a white-haired man, very distinguished, and I knew I recognized him. So I whispered to the mayor's wife 'Who's that?' and she replied with all the surprise in the world, as if everyone knew him, that it was Fiedler. So I turned to him and did the usual 'You won't remember me, but...' thing, and suddenly he stood up and silenced the table, Anthony Eden and everyone, and said, 'I'd like to introduce you to the father of a remarkable boy I met in Liverpool called Simon Rattle, whom you will be hearing of again.' And the sad thing is that Fiedler died just six months before Simon made his début with the Boston Symphony Orchestra in 1983. That was typical of the kindness with which people listened to Simon at that time.

It was at one of those Liverpool Philharmonic concerts, Simon recalled, that he had the musical experience that really set him on the road to conducting:

SIMON RATTLE: I remember the Mahler 8, yes, and was extremely impressed by all the noise, but I didn't really know what it was about (and I still don't understand the piece at all: if I could take my favourite fifteen minutes out of the second part I would be happy never to hear the rest of it again! The more it tries to carry conviction the less successful it is.).

But when I was eleven my father took me to hear George Hurst conduct Mahler 2. And that was it. That was a completely transfiguring experience. It was the road to Damascus and it knocked me for six. I couldn't get the impression of it out of my mind for days, and I think that in serious terms that is where the seed was sown.

Meanwhile Simon's piano-playing really took off. From the age of nine he studied seriously with Geoffrey Arnold, music master at Liverpool College, who subsequently went to Australia to become chorus master at the new Sydney Opera House but has since died.

SIMON RATTLE: We always felt he was a very remarkable musician. I think he has to have a lot of the credit for pushing me through, making me learn other instruments – it must have been around then I started the violin – getting me into other orchestras, forcing me at the pace he knew I needed to go. It's only looking back that one realizes how important teachers are in that way. It's not necessarily what they teach you, it's just what they put in your way, what's set up by them. Then to be taught by a Godovsky pupil, Douglas Miller, that was really extraordinary. He knew Rachmaninov really quite well, he'd met all sorts of musicians, and I remember when I took him the Grieg Concerto to play and he said, 'Yes, when I met Grieg . . .' – that was really one of the climaxes for me! Godovsky I knew about through Miller, and I learnt the *Java Suite*; once in Glyndebourne during the summer someone said, 'Mr Godovsky would like to meet you,' and it turned out it was a relative of his who would have been about forty, who had subsequently married into the Gershwin family.

The violin I eventually gave up, though I played a good deal for Bill Jenkins and I remember leading the school orchestra for a while. I'm very grateful I learned the fiddle, but I think the problem really was not hearing what I was actually playing. One of my violin teachers, the one who made me give up, said 'You have to stop playing Rattle and hearing Heifetz!' which was true but a tiny bit hard as I was only twelve or so!

When he was eleven he won a music studentship which was offered by Liverpool Education Authority to young musicians of great potential. The prize consisted of lessons with the most outstanding teacher available on Merseyside. Simon had the good fortune to go to Douglas Miller (who was eighty-four when he began to teach him) and within a couple of years he was playing his first Mozart concerto, K488. Denis Rattle recalls questioning Miller about Simon's interpretation of a piece by Rachmaninov and being told 'Rachmaninov

Prize student: Simon at twelve, winner of the Merseyside Student of the Year prize; he was awarded 100 per cent marks for his performance of Moeran's *Windmills*

was quite young when he wrote it: I have no doubt Simon has a better idea of how it should sound than we have. He seems to have a direct line to the composers.' In 1967, when he was twelve, he was elected Student of the Year by the Liverpool Youth Music Committee, in competition with instrumentalists aged between ten and twenty-two. He played Moeran's *Windmills* and all three adjudicators gave him 100 per cent. As a result of that he played Gershwin's *Rhapsody in Blue* with the Liverpool Concert Orchestra, a piece and a composer both of which were to remain close to him in the future.

DENIS RATTLE: He was invited by the Birkenhead Music Society to play that Mozart concerto, and they had the nerve to ask him as well to play a short recital in the first half of the concert! So of course he did, and I remember one of the pieces he did was the Scarlatti *Cat's Fugue*, and to my absolute horror, half-way through the fugue he went back to the beginning and I thought 'God, this is going to go on for ever, he's never going to get out of it!' But I think the third time round he found his way home. The band in the Mozart was extraordinary: no bassoon, so they used a trombone, who was brilliant, played every note.

When Simon was eleven he went on the first of a series of annual European Summer Schools for Young Musicians, with the encouragement of Bill Jenkins of the Merseyside Youth Orchestra, and under the watchful eye of a couple of players, Bill Overton and Wesley Woodage whom his father had known at school, both trumpeters in the BBC Symphony Orchestra. The school that year was in England, but subsequent ones were in Salzburg, and then Mödling, outside Vienna near the Czech border. Rattle recalls: 'Whether it was wise for my parents to send a kid off to Europe I think they've been wondering ever since.' The critic Geoffrey Norris remembers Rattle playing K488 'impeccably', with Anthony Lewis conducting, at Mödling in 1967. A year later they were there when the Russians invaded Czechoslovakia. Rattle remembers that as an extraordinary experience, 'having people coming in and saying "How much German do you know, do you realize what's going on?"' But politics rarely impinged on the summer schools:

SIMON RATTLE: We had a wonderful time. In Mödling we were conducted by Malcolm Arnold: it was my first experience with a real live composer conducting his own music and discussing it with me. He was incredibly helpful, and we had all sorts of adventures, and played jazz

The fifteen-year-old conductor: press cuttings of his first charity concert

too. I had some very important musical experiences on those courses. I met Maurice Miles who taught conducting at the Royal Academy, and had some of my own first chances to conduct. I suppose I was fourteen and just before I went off to Vienna again that summer I thought, 'I'm going to take some music and get some people together,' and true to form, ever ambitious, the first piece I tried to do was Ravel's *Mother Goose*.

The first symphony concert Simon Rattle conducted in this country took place when he was just fifteen, in April 1970. This was the beginning of some extensive press attention for the young prodigy, in Liverpool: 'MAESTRO SIMON DRUMS UP AN ORCHESTRA JUST FOR CHARITY. A charity gave fifteen-year-old Simon Rattle the go-ahead when he asked if he could put on a musical evening for them. But they got a shock five weeks later when Simon came up with a seventy-piece symphony orchestra. "We thought he had a small concert in mind," said one astounded official of the Liverpool Spastic Fellowship. "He has shown tremendous enterprise."'

> SIMON RATTLE: I had with a couple of my schoolfriends the hare-brained scheme of doing a concert for charity with what was originally going to be a chamber orchestra. The thing mushroomed and ended up being a full-scale symphony orchestra! I remember the Vaughan Williams *Tallis Fantasia* which I couldn't conduct, and the Schubert *Unfinished* which I nearly could. I asked people from the Liverpool Phil. to play, and I think they were so astonished at the cheek that they agreed. Anthony Ridley, who is now a conductor in his own right, led the orchestra and gave me a few tips on how to conduct at the same time – my first teacher – and John Ward played the timps and Robert Braga played the wonderful viola solo in the *Tallis Fantasia*.

The concert was quite an event. Rattle rehearsed for five and a half hours, and at one point the four-year-old son of one of the players disrupted the proceedings. Rattle quipped, 'I see our leader has arrived,' and the incident helped to break the ice with the mixture of amateur and professional players. Among the packed audience in Liverpool College Hall that evening was Charles Groves, principal conductor of the Liverpool Philharmonic. As well as Schubert and Vaughan Williams there was also Malcolm Arnold's *English Dances* and Mozart's Clarinet Concerto. There was a great deal of 'young star' coverage, but Rattle also had the benefit of his first critical review, from Neil Tierney in the *Daily Telegraph*. It was extremely prescient:

The poise and dignity of fifteen-year-old Simon Rattle compared favourably with the ballyhoo publicity which preceded his advent as a conductor with his own orchestra, the Liverpool Sinfonia, at Liverpool College last night. He has a demonstrative but very discerning beat, a pleasing personality and a genuine gift with the baton which survived even the absurdity of having two flashlight photographs taken at the very start of the performance. There is a future conductor of real insight here and his development is not helped by the atmosphere of the circus ring...

After that Simon did not look back. A month later he was directing a percussion group he had got together, called Percussionists Anonymous, in a concert which included a work by his teacher John Ward. In June 1970 he was asked to play one of his piano party pieces, Gershwin's *Rhapsody in Blue,* at short notice in Philharmonic Hall with the Merseyside Concert Orchestra after the scheduled pianist, Eva Warren, fell ill. In November that year he and a colleague from the MYO, the oboist Denise Burrows, received an award, worth fifty guineas each, under Pernod's Creative Artists Awards Scheme. The Pernod Award was presented at a Philharmonic Hall concert by the youth orchestra in which both of them took part. She played a piano solo as well as the oboe with Simon accompanying. He played three solo piano pieces: one of Rachmaninov's Op. 32 Preludes and Ravel's *Le Gibet* and *Scarbo* from *Gaspard de la nuit.* He was also allowed to conduct the orchestra in the suite from Britten's *Gloriana.* Afterwards he immediately went out and spent his fifty guineas on a new gong.

The Merseyside Youth Orchestra subsequently took part in an International Youth Orchestra Festival in 1972. The young assistant manager of the Liverpool Philharmonic, who had the responsibility of running the MYO and who was later to become general manager and then chief executive of the CBSO, was Edward Smith.

ED SMITH: The first thing I ever remember him conducting was the Britten *Gloriana* Suite in a little church in Brig, Switzerland. Simon came as a percussionist and a conductor and he was allowed to conduct that one piece and also played timps in the Vaughan Williams *London Symphony.* But you couldn't hold him back, even then: on the same course in Lausanne Simon decided to get together an international big band to play Henry Mancini arrangements. That made the biggest impression of all, and he really began to acquire a reputation.

Gong money: Simon receiving a prize of fifty guineas alongside the oboist Denise
Burrows, which he immediately spent on acquiring a gong. Next to him is Raymond
Mulholland of the Liverpool Youth Music Committee, who gave Simon his first
chances to conduct (*photo* Simpson's)

In October 1970 we gave him his first job as an extra percussionist
with the Liverpool Phil. In fact I think my first formal contact with him
over that was to write to his games master at school asking for him to be
given the afternoon off sports so that he could attend the rehearsal of
Gerhard's Third Symphony!

Simon's strictly professional career had perhaps begun a little earlier,
for Fritz Spiegl, who had first asked him to play percussion publicly
as a very young boy, again engaged him to play percussion in a massive account of the Handel *Fireworks Music*; his father certainly
remembers that the modest cheque Simon received on that occasion
was regarded as a landmark. Meanwhile, at Liverpool College,
Simon's academic career proceeded by fits and starts:

SIMON RATTLE: I really didn't enjoy school – I think I was too much
of a misfit – until the last years, thirteen to sixteen, when I began to
enjoy things and I was concentrating on the things I loved doing. It still
felt as if there were two separate lives, the musical and the working life.

There was a bit more of a synthesis towards the end, but at the beginning I was completely isolated. I am glad, though, that I didn't go to a specialist music school. I know so many people from them and I've seen the problems they cause. After all, we musicians have to spend our lives with real people in the outside world, not just with other musicians. And we're a strange race.

PAULINE RATTLE: It wasn't a musical school, more a rugby-playing school, but of a very high academic standard. Simon did have the good fortune to have a house master who was very interested in him and interested in music, and an English master who was also interested in music, and so he came through. He was talented but the academic work never meant much to him. We did think at this time that he would go to Oxford, and the Latin master at Liverpool College gave him extra tuition. Simon was eventually to go, but in his own way!

He applied to go to the Royal Academy, and was accepted, and then I think for the first time in our lives – because you know how hard it is to persuade Simon to do anything he doesn't want to do – we did insist that he get his A levels if he wanted to go to the Academy. He knew if he didn't get them, well, sorry son, but you'll have to stay at school another year. And that had a remarkable effect on Simon. For three months he didn't go to any parties or anything – of course we couldn't stop him going to the Phil., and as usual we all went as a family on those occasions – but apart from that he just worked and worked because he was absolutely determined to get them and go to the Academy. Although he was only sixteen he got four grade As at A level, in History, English, Music and General Studies.

(Susan Rattle added that during the period he was preparing for his exams he was also conducting the Merseyside Concert Orchestra on Monday evenings, preparing for a concert that she was playing percussion in.)

Another feature of these years was that Simon began to compose seriously. There was a modest piece for strings, an Elegy Op. 2, which was performed in Liverpool. There were sketches for much more ambitious pieces, such as the Mahlerian *Episodes*, which included extensive parts for carefully-specified percussion, but petered out after the first few energetic pages. And there were some songs, mostly written for friends. Nowadays he is quick to dismiss the whole thing as a passing phase and is hard on the pieces themselves:

SIMON RATTLE: They were duff. The sort of thing that's quite impressive when you're twelve, I suppose, but far less so by the time you're fifteen or sixteen. The songs I wrote for a singer I was very fond of. But I didn't have any application, and I didn't have any original ideas – I just rehashed other people's stuff. I did do some orchestration exercises, which I'm glad I did. And composing taught me that it's just as laborious to write impossibly bad, derivative music as it is to write masterpieces!

The summer before Simon went to the Academy he played for the only time in the National Youth Orchestra. ('On the whole I preferred the international gatherings; there was more sex, which wasn't a great feature of NYO courses.') The major attraction which drew Simon that summer was the presence of Pierre Boulez. They rehearsed in Croydon during August, and then appeared at both the Proms and the Edinburgh Festival. At the Proms Simon was given the solo piano part in Bartók's *Music for Strings, Percussion and Celesta*, while in the Edinburgh concert, which was televised, he played the cymbals in Debussy's *La Mer*. Simon was able to meet Boulez and have some consultation sessions with him ('I've never actually claimed to have been taught conducting by him') but it was not until 1977, when Rattle returned to conduct the NYO that he really learned from Boulez (see p. 64). In particular he had a scheme to mount with his Liverpool Sinfonia a performance of Boulez's *Le Marteau sans maître*. 'Madness! What a thought! In the end I couldn't do it because the singer was ill, but it would have been wonderful to have a try.' In the NYO Simon made many friends among the players who were to remain friends after he went down to London, and some of them played for him in the various orchestras he got together. And while he never managed to do the Boulez he did mount one more ambitious programme of twentieth-century music which included Peter Maxwell Davies's *Antechrist*, the Milhaud Percussion Concerto (with his teacher John Ward as soloist) and the Falla Harpsichord Concerto.

There was one final Liverpool ensemble which was to prove vital to him in those hectic years before he went up to London to the Academy – the Liverpool Mozart Orchestra:

SIMON RATTLE: Very important to me was a Liverpool family by the name of Dutch. David Dutch formed the Liverpool Mozart Orchestra and I very regularly played a lot of Baroque music with him and his wife at their house which we nicknamed The Baroqueries. I played continuo, or sometimes violin when we had a string quartet, though they had to be very tolerant! There was a long-distance lorry driver who played

Baroque violin so beautifully, David was a marvellous oboe player, John Grove was the bassoonist and Elspeth, David's wife, played the flute. The experience of playing really fine chamber music was vastly important to me. And it was on a course organized by David Dutch with many of those people involved that I first met John Carewe.

That meeting proved to be a turning-point, a first step on the road to conducting maturity. But John Carewe's lessons were not learnt quickly or easily: meanwhile London, with all the excitement it had to offer, beckoned. Simon arrived at the Royal Academy of Music in September 1971. He was still only sixteen.

II

1971–4

SIMON RATTLE: It seems like a gigantic arrogance now, but I didn't apply to anywhere else; and it didn't occur to me that I wouldn't get in. There were very good teachers there and lots of people I knew: Maurice Miles for conducting, Jimmy Blades for percussion, Gordon Greene for piano, Fred Grinke, Sidney Griller for strings, John Gardner for composing – these were all people I'd met. So it was the obvious place.

I decided quite soon that whatever I was meant to be studying, I would pick the brains of every professor in the building. I went and saw them all. And what was astonishing was the range of levels of teaching, how shocking the worst teachers were and how remarkable the best teachers were. I must have learnt as much from that as from anything.

In the first year you couldn't do conducting as a first subject, but quite soon I was getting twentieth-century things together, and I realized I obviously had to fix the players myself if anything was to get done. I soon got involved in the conductors' course, just playing the piano, and then someone dropped out, so I got in . . . It all happened fairly quickly.

Gordon Greene and I parted company. We always ended up talking about politics and he said, 'You don't practise,' and I said, 'I do: an hour a day,' and he said, 'Well, an hour a day isn't practice; promise me you'll devote five hours a day to it or it's really not worth it.' So we parted amicably. There was always a problem with my piano-playing. People used to be very impressed that I could play so many notes, and it didn't matter if some of them were wrong ones. It never really occurred to me to practise to make it a lot better, and by the time of the Academy I was really playing no better than I had when I was twelve or thirteen. I was a very good faker.

So I transferred to John Streets, who then ran the opera school. He was a person who had the speed of musical responses that I needed. He is one of the most complete musicians I've ever come across. I did still play the piano: I remember four of us took the Messiaen *Quartet for the End of Time* to him, and I realized I had no range of colour at the piano; if anyone played like that for me today they'd never be asked back...

JOHN STREETS: There was this little person racing round the Academy with stars in his eyes; someone like that always sticks out a mile, and one soon heard about this chap Simon Rattle. I think the first time I actually met him was when he came in to accompany a singer, some bits of Stravinsky's *Rake's Progress* or something, and I thought, 'Heavens, this is good.' He always accompanied a bit like a conductor: you know, he set the tempo! But quite soon I asked him if he wanted to come on to the opera course and do some playing and he leapt at that. At that time Steuart Bedford was my right-hand man, and I think the first thing Simon was involved in was Donizetti's *Belisario* at Sadler's Wells, where he was assistant conductor, doing all the off-stage bands and so on. That was March 1972, pretty early, in his second term. Then in November 1972 he did an opera workshop with all sorts of things: bits of *Così*, *Louise*, and Michael Head's *After the Wedding*, which we commissioned. But he did all that himself, with a rather nice cast: Felicity Lott was there, and so was David Rendall. And then a Stravinsky *Soldier's Tale* in December that year.

In 1973 he worked on Janáček's *The Cunning Little Vixen* which Stu Bedford was conducting, and this was much more important because he did a lot of the coaching and a lot of the preparation. He was very involved in it and I think that gave him a love of Janáček – and then of course that was an opera he did at Glyndebourne very early on. Later in the year, in December, it rather surprised me to find that he actually conducted one performance of Offenbach's *La jolie Parfumeuse* which David Lloyd-Jones conducted. So that must actually have been his first official appearance in the pit. He wasn't reviewed in the press, because it's always rather difficult for us to get you people in except to first nights!

The first thing that was really noticed was the double bill of Ravel's *L'Enfant et les sortilèges* and Stravinsky's *Pulcinella* in November 1974, because that was after he'd won the competition, and after he'd left the Academy. He was intending to do a further year – I don't know what he would have got out of it – but the competition changed all that. Then we subsequently invited him back to do the Poulenc *Mamelles des Tirésias* and Vaughan Williams's *Riders in the Sea* with John Copley.

What would you and he talk about in your sessions?

He would bring in whatever he was working on at the time, and then we'd go off into long discussions about French music, style in Debussy and Ravel; it's very close to me and at that time Simon didn't know as much about it. I remember those occasions far more than the times he brought Beethoven sonatas. I did encourage him to bring Mozart in the hope of broadening things out a bit. We used to talk tremendously about literature: I had met Pound and talked to him, and Simon was fascinated by that. We talked about Joyce and poetry, and I think that may have influenced him towards the idea of taking a year off and going to Oxford. He was always interested in theatre and film at this time, and realized how much you needed to know about these cultural things in order to do the music well.

Was his operatic conducting technique always assured?

Right from the word go; there was never any problem at all. And what he also had besides the technique was this marvellous thing of communication right to the back desk of the second fiddles. They always looked at him, and that didn't always happen with some of our staff conductors ... And he was happy in the pit; there were never false leads; the singers wanted to sing for him. He was always very patient with directors or lighting people and would just put down his baton and wait for it all to happen.

Has it surprised you that Simon has not gone into an opera house on a permanent basis?

That's an interesting one. As he's probably told you he wasn't very happy at Glyndebourne initially and that possibly soured things. Would he perhaps have found the repertory a bit restricting? And the business of doing ten or twelve performances in a row? Now he is in complete control of an orchestra in a way that you can't possibly be, completely, in an opera house; there are so many other things to consider. He may come to it in the future. Perhaps we're all surprised that he's stayed so long in Birmingham, but delighted, too, because it's worked in exactly the right way.

By the end of his first term at the Academy he was already associated with the conductors' course and the opera course, doing a great deal of accompanying, and gathering ensembles together for twentieth-century music. In an end-of-term concert that December he even took over from an indisposed conductor at twenty minutes' notice and did Beethoven 8 with one of the Academy orchestras. But he was not getting on as quickly as he could have wished through official channels, so he began the most ambitious of his activities to date by forming the New London Chamber Orchestra, a forty-strong band aged up to twenty-two, which drew on several people he knew from the National Youth Orchestra course the previous summer, including the first violin, the first cello and Philippa Davies as principal flute.

Then just before he came back to London after the Christmas break he was offered his first semi-professional work. Leon Lovett, the conductor, asked him to be repetiteur and chorus master for a modern double bill which the New Opera Company was putting on at Sadler's Wells Theatre: Elisabeth Lutyens's *Time Off? – Not a Ghost of a Chance* and Anthony Gilbert's *The Scene Machine*.

One of the people who took part in that production recalled: 'Leon Lovett was having a lot of trouble dealing with the Lutyens, which was a very tricky score, and so in came this sixteen-year-old boy wonder and immediately made sense of it at the piano. He could play the piano like a complete orchestra, could tell the singers what to do, and gave everyone confidence. In the nicest possible way he took over.' Lovett subsequently passed on to him another fun job: conducting for the Alvin Ailey Dance Theatre when they visited London: 'the first serious professional thing I did,' Rattle recalls. 'But it was never followed up; those years were full of things that led nowhere.'

He was busy everywhere with rehearsals and going to other people's rehearsals. He says he rarely had the time or money to go to concerts, but would often go in to BBC rehearsals at Maida Vale or the Festival Hall – especially when Boulez, who was then chief conductor of the BBC Symphony, was conducting. 'When I think about what I was doing each day in those years ... I'd be hospitalized if I tried it now. Burning the candle at both ends in every possible sense!'

In 1973 the conductor of the Merseyside Youth Orchestra, Bill Jenkins, who had so greatly encouraged Simon and given him so many chances to play piano, violin and percussion with the orchestra, retired. Simon was given the chance to succeed him, and he eagerly embraced the opportunity. It was the beginning of his long-term collaboration with Ed Smith who ran the MYO – they have worked together ever since, first when Simon became associate conductor of the Liverpool Philharmonic, and then when Ed Smith became general manager of the CBSO.

ED SMITH: The first concert he did as conductor of the MYO was during his second year at the Academy: the programme had Philip Fowke doing the Rachmaninov Second Concerto, Shostakovich 10 and Tchaikovsky's *Marche slave*. You don't catch him conducting much Tchaikovsky these days! I think that's the first and last time he conducted that piece. And it was as vulgar as it always is! He would come up from London every Sunday for rehearsals, and would often be around at concerts. What he really wanted then was to go on one of the

conductors' seminars which we'd arranged very successfully in the previous years: in 1970 we had Howard Williams, Tim Reynish and Colin
Metters, and the last one was in 1972 – Mark Elder, James Judd, Anthony Beaumont and Barry Wordsworth – a good line-up. Simon was
always after me and I had to sort of hide behind pillars because I knew
he would say 'and when's there going to be another seminar?' But sadly
the Gulbenkian who funded them weren't able to continue so '72 was
the last.

I had to be quite strict about some of his activities, because I was
assistant manager of the Philharmonic so I had other responsibilities. I
remember him using one of the RLPO players' xylophones without
asking: there must still be a letter from me somewhere saying 'Please
note that you are not under any circumstance to touch instruments
belonging to members of the Liverpool Philharmonic without permission.'

But the Merseyside Youth Orchestra with Simon was a great success,
and we decided to try some ambitious pieces: the next concert was
November 1973, and we did the Berlioz *Symphonie fantastique*, and
the Shostakovich Second Cello Concerto with Roderick McGrath.
Then there was *The Rite of Spring* in 1974, and that was historic
because it got tangled up in the Bournemouth Competition...

The first MYO concert was well received in the Liverpool press: 'a
resounding success', one paper called it, while Neil Tierney continued
his advocacy of the conductor in the *Daily Telegraph* by praising his
'definite beat and expressive left hand. Conducting from memory, he
showed a splendid grasp of the music.' Another paper, which referred
to the Rachmaninov Second Concerto as 'Rachmaninov's Brief Encounter', reported that 'superlatives were tossed around the audience
afterwards, and people were clearly amazed at Simon's conducting
the Shostakovich [Tenth Symphony] without a score'. It has
remained one of his most powerful performances.

Meanwhile, in London, he was stirring things up at the Royal
Academy. As well as gathering together small groups for contemporary music, he started on his biggest project: performing Mahler symphonies with an orchestra he fixed himself.

JOHN STREETS: It wasn't much done at that time, students actually
getting their own people together to put on a concert. Maybe there was
the odd Beethoven orchestra, but not a Mahler 2 orchestra and chorus!
It was frowned on slightly, and I don't think there was any real cooperation; you know what these places are like if you try something unusual, especially if it turns out to be rather better than the official

activities! But I don't mean to say that he ever had had any real trouble with the authorities.

SIMON RATTLE: Some ways they tried to stop it, other ways it was just gently ignored. And sometimes they would actually help and lend me parts and occasionally print a programme. But basically they just let me use the hall, and sometimes I had to hire the parts myself.

If there was a single occasion which put Simon Rattle on the map in London it was the performance of Mahler's Second Symphony which he conducted at the Royal Academy on 6 December 1973 at 2.45 p.m. Among other things, and quite apart from the success of the event itself, in the audience that afternoon was someone who was to have an incalculable effect on his future – the agent Martin Campbell-White from Harold Holt Ltd, one of the most prestigious agencies in London. The agency handles an impressive roster of artists: among the conductors Campbell-White looks after in Britain are Claudio Abbado, Andrew Davis and David Atherton. Like any good agent, Campbell-White had heard about Rattle on the musical administrators' grapevine:

MARTIN CAMPBELL-WHITE: Stephen Gray, the manager of the Liverpool Philharmonic, came in to see me at the time when Andrew Davis was principal guest conductor there. We were chatting away and he said, 'There's this fantastic boy we've got working with us conducting the Merseyside Youth Orchestra and he's going to do *The Rite of Spring*.' And I said, 'That's interesting,' and as a passing comment while I thought about the next hard negotiating point for Andrew Davis I said 'How old is he?' And Stephen said he was seventeen. He told me a little more about him, and I was sitting there thinking seventeen? *The Rite of Spring* with a youth orchestra? He told me he'd been in the National Youth Orchestra with Boulez and had played percussion with the Liverpool Phil. since he was fifteen as an extra, and that he'd left school and gone straight to the Academy.

So I did a little research and found out that Simon was doing this performance of Mahler 2. I made contact with him and found out that he'd asked permission of the lords and masters there if he could do it officially and they said no, probably because he wasn't in the right year or something. But he was determined to do it and had got his orchestra and chorus together. I went along to the performance and he had quite obviously galvanized them beforehand in the rehearsals. The performance was somewhat raw but, my God, it was fantastic. It really was, and I don't even think the technique was limited. The impassioned

approach that is a hallmark of Simon's style was already there, and the
ability to get those people to play with him, which is something very
special.

It was tremendous. So I said to him at once that I thought we would
love to do something for him at Holt's but that clearly he was much too
young, and I wondered what he wanted to do. He said he wanted to
study more and learn more repertory and so on. But I did begin to mention his name to one or two people and said that I thought there was this
incredibly talented youngster around. And word began to spread: Nick
Tschaikov, who was then chairman of the Philharmonia, heard him
and said he wanted to offer him a Festival Hall début. Brian Dickie
from Glyndebourne came to an opera Simon conducted at the Academy
and offered him work there. Michael Vyner came to the Ravel–
Stravinsky double bill at the Academy and that opened up the London
Sinfonietta, and so on.

Martin Campbell-White's prudent scheme for Simon Rattle was to
develop·a very small amount of work, carefully paced and planned,
with high-quality organizations in London. But the best-laid schemes
... Simon had never been content to do things by halves, and in 1974,
towards the end of his third year at the Academy, he entered for the
newly established John Player International Conductor's Award in
Bournemouth. This was part of a scheme established by the Bournemouth Symphony Orchestra to provide opportunities for young conductors and soloists. Unlike most conducting competitions, which
guarantee only a few engagements, this one carried a substantial opportunity: to work for two years with the Bournemouth Symphony
Orchestra and its smaller Sinfonietta alongside their regular conductors Paavo Berglund and Kenneth Montgomery. The competition
was to be held in May 1974 in the Guildhall, Portsmouth, and there
seemed little hope that Simon would not apply.

He got references from John Carewe, from Charles Groves, who
wrote a letter asking them to accept him in spite of his youth, and
from Norman Del Mar, who was conducting the Academy Chamber
Orchestra at the time. Martin Campbell-White was not aware that he
had entered:

MARTIN CAMPBELL-WHITE: I didn't know, and if I had known beforehand I would most certainly have discouraged him. I would have
thought he had everything to lose and nothing to gain. By then he
already had the Philharmonia début fixed and there were a number of
other things in the pipeline – the right progression for someone who
was still only nineteen and a half. Anyway, I went down to the compet-

Competition winner: having received first prize in the 1974 John Player
Competition, Rattle most untypically dons a tie for his portrait.

ition and there were a number of conductors who were as they say in
America 'concertizing regularly', but Simon was head and shoulders
above the rest. It was absolutely clear that he had the talent to bring it
off, and he did!

Of the 200 conductors who applied, ten were selected to go to Portsmouth. Simon was surprised that he had been chosen purely on his
paper qualifications, because the upper age limit of thirty-five meant
that many of the other entrants would have had far greater experience
than he had. His parents had not stopped him entering because, they
said, they knew he was not going to win it. Interviewed before the
competition Simon said, 'You have to be 50 per cent lunatic to want
to be a conductor. It's such hard work and there are so few opportunities, but it's a bug, and once you have been bitten there's really
nothing you can do except allow it to lead you forward.' Looking
back on it now he finds the whole thing even more amazing:

SIMON RATTLE: If there was any proof needed that I didn't take it
very seriously, I lived in a flat with a cellist called Cathy Giles and I was
about to go off to the competition and she said, 'Simon, you haven't
packed your tails,' and I said, 'Well, I'm not going to need them, I won't
get past the first round, and in any case, I can't because I've got the last
rehearsal of *The Rite of Spring* with the MYO in Liverpool so I
wouldn't be able to do it anyway.' And she said, 'You really should take
them...'

The line-up in the competition was impressive, and included plenty of
conductors who have made professional reputations since: Richard
Hickox, Ronald Zollman, Geoffrey Simon (who came second), Colin
Metters and a fine Japanese conductor, Hikotaro Yazaki. In the first
round of the competition they had to conduct a variety of pieces,
including Shostakovich 5, and accompany a Chopin piano concerto.
At the end of the second day four of the ten were chosen to go forward
to the finals, and Simon was among them. This was 28 May. In the
final round all the four conductors had to direct Strauss's *Don Juan*.
Simon conducted one of the fastest and brashest performances in
living memory. George Hurst, artistic adviser to the Bournemouth
orchestras, came up to him afterwards and said, inimitably, 'Simon,
that was thrilling. And the other thing about it was, it was terrible.
Don't ever do anything like that to me again!' The orchestra applauded.
Denis Rattle recalls: 'It was a splashy old show, but tremendously exciting and he was the star turn of the evening, no doubt. I
think some of the others who were more experienced might have won
it, but perhaps in their minds was the fact that this chap had to work
with them for two years, and some of them were not so bright at
English. Anyway, Simon got it.'

ED SMITH: This was the weirdest situation, especially in view of the
later Birmingham connection. We'd done *The Rite* with the MYO in
Liverpool, but we were due to go down to Birmingham and do a concert in the Midland Youth Orchestra's series including *The Rite*. We
knew it overlapped with the competition but Simon said that as there
was no way he was getting further than the first round it didn't matter;
there was no question he'd be back for the rehearsals. We had a deputy
conductor in Liverpool and every half day Simon was ringing me saying
'Don't worry, I'll be back tonight,' and of course he wasn't. So we
rehearsed in Liverpool on the Friday night without Simon and travelled
down to Birmingham on the Saturday and he travelled straight up from
Bournemouth having won the competition. So the first concert he ever

Young Phenom With a Baton

By Heuwell Tircuit

EVEN AS ROCKET careers go, English conductor Simon Rattle's rise has been phenomenal. Barely 25, he can boast a host of important posts, recordings and reviews, an American debut with the Los Angeles Philharmonic at age 24, followed by the Chicago Symphony and this week leads the mountainous Mahler Tenth Symphony with the San Francisco Symphony.

And this, mind you, after a major success at last week's subscription series.

Rattle began his career at age 15, as percussionist with the Liverpool Philharmonic. By age 19, he won the International Conductors Competition in Bournemouth and was named an assistant conductor with the orchestra and Sinfonietta of that city.

That, however, was way back in 1974.

He has just been appointed principal conductor of the distinguished City of Birmingham Orchestra. In addition, he is assistant conductor of the BBC Scottish Symphony, with standing commitments to London's Philharmonic and Sinfonietta plus the Glynde-

Mozart — especially Haydn. I would gladly conduct a Haydn Symphony every night. And I love Berlioz. Between, there is something of a pause in my repertory. As much as I admire Beethoven, I

the conductor can make his own, alternate decisions. Each of us who conduct it, in effect, does his own version. I, for instance, don't feel the xylophone is appropriate. So I took it out."

From Birmingham With Brio

In Los Angeles, the name of Simon Rattle has been celebrated by music lovers ever since the British wunderkind first conducted there in 1976, at the age of 21. In England's West Midlands, where Rattle has been principal conductor of the City of Birmingham Symphony Orchestra since 1980, he can do no wrong. In most points in between, however—including New York, where musical careers are traditionally launched—Rattle has been more talked about than heard, with a reputation aglow from a small but spectacular recorded repertory. His career so far has been a series of object lessons: in how to make great music exciting on its own without a spurious lather of self-serving promotion, and how to preserve the integrity of a career against all the temptations of the jet age.

Last month, during a tour

holding a short baton at a curious downward angle, pokes and jabs to define the brilliantly clean rhythmic outlines that are the earmarks of Rattle's work. They are a reminder, too, that his early musical training was as a percussion player.

Born in Liverpool and educated at the Royal Academy of Music, Rattle made his professional conducting debut at 19, with a

RATTLE: GUTTY CONDUCTOR WHO 'LIKES TO TAKE RISKS'

By ELIZABETH VENANT

Simon Rattle sat in the maestro's dressing room of the Dorothy Chandler Pavilion, clutching a mug of steaming tea. The young Englishman, who with Michael Tilson Thomas is principal guest conductor of the Los Angeles Philharmonic, had just finished rehearsing Beethoven's Third Symphony, the majestic "Eroica." All Beethoven symphonies are difficult to conduct, plus with the "Eroica" there was a particular hitch. It was a specialty of two former Philharmonic maestros, Carlo Maria Giulini and Zubin Mehta. Rattle was doing it in Los Angeles for the first time, and he was determined to do it his way. Commented one Music Center staffer "That takes guts."

Rattle makes the podium roar

English conductor makes it to the BSO — at last

By Andrew L. Pincus

SIMON RATTLE says you can call him anything, but don't call him "maestro" or "mister." Members of the London orchestras that he guest-conducts call him "Baby" Rattle.

The baby in the family is no longer the gifted 28-year-old English conductor, but his 2-month-old son, Sasha, the first child born to him and his wife, the American soprano Elise Ross. Mother and son flew to Boston with the conductor when he made his Boston Symphony Orchestra debut in two sets of concerts last

suit, are dwindling. In Birmingham, he said, "we can play whatever we like. We have full, enthusiastic audiences."

The challenge is greater than an American might suspect. For one thing, the Birmingham's hall, where the orchestra plays in the round and

Gathering laurels: the American press discovers the Rattle phenomenon

conducted in Birmingham Town Hall was *The Rite of Spring* with the MYO the day after he'd won the competition! And Peter Donohoe was one of the timpanists!

Rattle's engagement in Bournemouth began in September 1974, so there was no question of his returning to the Academy for a fourth year. Thus it happened that what was to have been his first major official undertaking at the Royal Academy, the double bill of Ravel's *L'Enfant et les sortilèges* and Stravinsky's *Pulcinella* in November 1974, took place after he had left. Both pieces were to become firm favourites: *Pulcinella* became one of his first commercial recordings, and the Ravel opera he returned to on a number of occasions, notably at Glyndebourne in the summer of 1987 (See p. 160). For the first time he received widespread attention from the London critics. The production was given on the open stage of the Duke's Hall because the opera theatre was out of action for renovation: perhaps he was in luck, as usual, for as conductor he was much more visible in this set-up. Summing up a remarkable year's progress, Alan Blyth wrote in *The Times:*

> Stories of the formidable talents of Simon Rattle, the conductor, who is nineteen, have been spreading widely in musical circles over the past few months. They were confirmed in no uncertain terms on Wednesday at the Royal Academy of Music [when] he showed talents of command and understanding beyond his years. Obeying Sir Adrian Boult's prime rule of leading with his right hand and letting it give all the important directions, he drew uncommonly sensitive playing from the Academy's orchestra and saw to it that they and the singers made the most of the scores...

Other press comment was equally favourable:

> Much of the musical success must be due to Simon Rattle, a young conductor of distinct promise, whose performance is remarkable not only for delicacy (he must be careful, though, not to slacken the pulse in slow music) but for the precision with which the off-stage voices were handled. There was some most creditable playing from the orchestra, and if occasionally the singers were overpowered (hardly surprising with a low stage and no pit) it was enjoyable for once to hear detail that an experienced conductor would firmly keep down! [Ronald Crichton, *Financial Times*]

> I wish more audiences could have witnessed another young conductor, Simon Rattle. His assured and delightful handling of student forces in Ravel's *L'Enfant et les sortilèges* probably produced on a shoe string, was nevertheless one of the Academy's vintage efforts... [Felix Aprahamian, *Sunday Times*]

> ... greatest praise must go to the gifted young conductor Simon Rattle, who had his student orchestra playing like seasoned professionals. His attack, sense of rhythm, and ability to control large forces in the orchestra and on stage indicate an outstanding natural talent for opera. One can safely prophesy a future for him in his chosen profession so long as he does not go dashing ahead too quickly. [Harold Rosenthal, *Opera*]

Everything looked set for a glittering future. But far from dashing ahead too quickly, Simon Rattle was just about to hit his first major obstacle.

CHAPTER THREE

'It had to be hard sometime'

Professional start: 1974–80

'I faced the whole difficulty of coming to terms with the limits on one's ability':
Rattle in action in his early professional years

I

1974–7

Simon Rattle did not need to win the John Player Conductor's Competition. He was already known in London, and with Martin Campbell-White of Harold Holt as his agent he would have begun to receive some high-quality work. There were already possibilities in

the offing, as he recalls: 'Maurice Handford asked me to go as his
assistant to the Calgary Philharmonic, and I seriously thought about
that. John Streets saw the possibility of getting me into Glyndebourne. I might have gone abroad to study, but though I might learn a
lot from Celibidache or Franco Ferrara now, it might not have been
so then. People went too early and got submerged, especially by Celibidache. I toyed with the idea of going to university then, but after the
competition all that changed.' Had he not won the competition he
might have stayed at the Royal Academy of Music for a fourth year.
He would have continued to conduct the Merseyside Youth Orchestra, and would have been invited by Stephen Gray to conduct the
Royal Liverpool Philharmonic Orchestra. His London début with the
New Philharmonia Orchestra was in place for the start of 1976, and
interest had been shown by groups such as the Nash Ensemble and
the London Sinfonietta. There is no reason to doubt that the rest
would have followed naturally.

But Rattle had a problem. He was a young, brilliant, already technically expert conductor without a repertory. Though he knew a
great deal of music, the sort of thing he was good at conducting –
Mahler, Stravinsky, Shostakovich – was only a part of the staple diet
of most symphony orchestras. So the chance to spend two years with
the Bournemouth Symphony Orchestra and the Bournemouth Sinfonietta was an important one: a chance to learn the repertory away
from the London limelight, and to deal for the first time with a professional orchestra. It encouraged him to turn down work in London
and concentrate on learning. But it was a struggle, and it is possible
that he might have learnt more easily in other circumstances, with
more sympathetic orchestras. Instead he went through what he
admits now was the worst period of his professional life:

SIMON RATTLE: The Bournemouth orchestras were the first professional orchestras I had conducted. And that's really why I went in for
the competition, for the experience of conducting professionals. But I
remember standing there at the beginning of my first rehearsal with
them in the autumn and wondering what on earth I was going to do. We
did eighty or so concerts a year and I'm sure they, who were incredibly
nice about the whole thing, would say that seventy of them were bad.
  There was a problem in that they were staggeringly unimaginative in
repertoire and couldn't for financial reasons do anything which
involved extra players. So I sent them a list of what I would like to do
and I knew when at the end I slipped in Dvořák 7 and Schubert's *Unfin-*

ished that they'd choose them for the first concert! It wasn't their fault: Bournemouth was a place where they'd had protest letters about the Walton First Symphony. But it had the effect that, for instance, when the Sinfonietta was faced with Stravinsky's *Rake's Progress* they thought it was modern music.

In Bournemouth I faced the whole difficulty of the young professional coming to terms with the limits on one's ability. I'd done a certain sort of conducting, but I didn't realize that when you conduct professionals you have to start again completely. And the problem was that I wasn't good enough to conduct them, I know, but I wasn't bad enough for them to ignore me completely! It was the worst of all possible worlds: if I'd been worse they probably could have played better.

But it was a worthwhile experience. It had to be hard sometime, and you have to learn; in this case I just learned the conductor's problems very fast. Some of the times were very difficult, especially with the Bournemouth Sinfonietta. They had a set way of playing, and I don't think they liked someone who wanted to interfere with that. They were rather distant and they didn't want to give the immediate emotional response to the music that I wanted.

I'm certainly glad that I didn't stay in London and take whatever things people were silly enough to offer me. I was offered four concerts with the London Philharmonic that year when Fischer-Dieskau cancelled. It didn't cross my mind to accept. If I had I wouldn't be here talking today; I would be a bitter percussionist somewhere, because I couldn't have done it and they would have seen through me in an instant.

I can look at it fairly dispassionately now, but during the Bournemouth period I very seriously toyed with the idea of giving up altogether. What partly saved me at the time was working on some of the same repertory with the Northern Sinfonia and finding that actually it was quite easy with them; and the fact that straightaway, in the autumn after the competition, I was working with the Nash Ensemble, and found that I could give them something to chew on and I wasn't completely out of my depth. It was so refreshing to work with people like the clarinettist Tony Pay, and I think perhaps I didn't realize that everyone in the musical world doesn't work that way...

TONY PAY: Martin Campbell-White had mentioned Simon to me, and the Nash were looking for someone to conduct *Pierrot lunaire* for us on a tour to Spain. So I suggested Simon to Amelia Freedman who runs the ensemble. And the word came back that he'd like to do it but that he wanted two or three rehearsals. We were all incredibly busy and the piece was in our repertory and I really didn't think it was necessary to do more than one rehearsal. But he insisted and so we did them. He really had something to say about the piece and he wanted to change

the way we played it. He had a view about it, and so it really was worth
rehearsing it. That was the first of many times, with the Nash and with
the Sinfonietta, where having Simon conduct made a difference.

Meanwhile Rattle was getting to grips with the Bournemouth Symphony Orchestra and the Sinfonietta. His programmes with them
were uncharacteristic in that they included almost none of his favourite works or even music by his favourite composers. Some of the restrictions on him were explained in an interview he gave at the time: 'I
was amazed at how much thought it takes planning the programmes:
I spent three or four hours with David Blenkinsop, the concert manager, one day just sorting out four programmes. Of course it helps me
that the Sinfonietta repeats programmes in different places. It means
that the idiocies I do on the second night I don't do on the third. At the
moment I'm learning the standard repertory because I've never really
had time to do that. It's interesting to discover the limitations of programming for the orchestras. For instance, we can't do Mahler
because we can't afford it, and we can't do Maxwell Davies because
they say it'll send the audience away.'

There is a note of frustration here which is amply echoed in the programmes themselves, although in the education concerts he did for
schools some of his favourites do turn up: Janáček, Bartók, Milhaud,
Stravinsky. For his formal début with the BSO, in Aldershot (which
even the local paper admitted was 'not perhaps the most inspiring
place to make a début'), the programme consisted of Schubert's
Unfinished Symphony, Strauss's *Four Last Songs* with Linda Esther
Gray and Dvořák's Seventh Symphony. The Schubert went back to
his very first Liverpool concert as a conductor, but has not re-
appeared in his repertory since.

With the Sinfonietta the fare was even less typical and more problematical. For the first tour around the West Country he took Boyce,
Vivaldi, Stravinsky's *Dumbarton Oaks* and Mozart's *Jupiter* Symphony to Totnes, Bodmin, Falmouth, St Ives, Tavistock and Chard.
For an important first appearance at the Brighton Festival he had an
entirely classical programme: Haydn's Symphony No. 60, Mozart's
Sinfonia concertante for violin and viola, and the *Jupiter* again. This
was desperately difficult and unfamiliar fare for Rattle at this time,
and he acknowledges that his classical performances were probably
poor. The programmes continued to be unrelentingly inappropriate:
in the following weeks he did Haydn 86 and 95, Beethoven 4 and

Mozart's Horn Concerto No. 3.

With the Sinfonietta the following summer, 1975, he had his first experience of Glyndebourne, preparing Stravinsky's *The Rake's Progress* with them for the tour. He had considerable difficulty, as John Carewe recalls him mentioning at the time, getting them to play with a sharp yet flexible sense of ensemble. This was something that was noted during the tour: reviewing the performance at the New Theatre, Oxford, Gillian Widdicombe wrote in the *Financial Times* that Rattle was 'brisk and sensible, but not yet coaxing a virtuoso performance from the Bournemouth Sinfonietta, for one reason or another'. Later projects with the Sinfonietta included a Contemporary Music Network tour for the Arts Council with a programme that must have come at least as a welcome change to Rattle in its complexity: Schoenberg's *Accompaniment to a Film Scene*, Goehr's *Little Symphony*, Dominic Muldowney's *Music at Chartres III* and Henze's First Symphony. But he recalls the experience as 'a total disaster. We had fifty-one hours of rehearsal and at the end, as someone who heard it said, it still sounded like one of the '50s recordings which convince you how dreadful modern music is!' Then in 1976 it was back to Bach *Brandenburgs* and Schubert 5, along with Gerard Schurmann's *Variants*, and then a mixture of Haydn 91 and Mozart 38 with Jean Françaix and Dvořák. Haydn 22 and Mozart 39 followed, alongside a Bach cantata – again, works to which Rattle has not so far returned.

With the Bournemouth Symphony Orchestra things were better and improved rapidly. Among the programmes were Berlioz's *King Lear* Overture (with which he was to open his New Philharmonia début concert), Bartók's *Concerto for Orchestra* and Rachmaninov's Second Symphony, a mainstream Rattle piece. At the beginning of 1976, when he turned twenty-one, he celebrated with one of the more successful of his Bournemouth series of concerts: music from Janáček's *Cunning Little Vixen*, Wagner's *Tannhäuser* Overture, and Rachmaninov's Third Piano Concerto, soon to be a favourite. That programme toured Plymouth, Camborne, Exeter and Portsmouth before ending up at Bournemouth where it was enthusiastically received. His final stint with the Bournemouth Symphony Orchestra included Kabalevsky's *Colas Breugnon*, Rachmaninov's Second Piano Concerto, Mussorgsky's *Night on the Bare Mountain* and Dvořák's Eighth Symphony (one of the works from this period it would be good to hear him do again). His last programme consisted of Schumann's Second Symphony, Strauss's Oboe Concerto with Heinz Holliger (who was to become a close friend of Rattle's) and Elgar's *Enigma Variations*, an early calling-card of Rattle's in his guest engagements around the world.

He was undoubtedly a better conductor at the end of the Bournemouth period than he was at the beginning. At one concert his father, meeting George Hurst, who had expressed his views on the performance with which Rattle had won the competition in no uncertain terms, said to him, 'Didn't they play well?' Hurst's reply was to the point: 'They had no choice.' But it is possible to wonder just how much Rattle really learnt there that would not have been acquired gradually over the years. It was a harder schooling than strictly necessary, and certainly he experienced for the first time what it is like to be an unpopular conductor.

Reactions from the players varied, it seems, from tolerance to annoyance. At one extreme is a Sinfonietta player who recalled that 'we found him very irritating indeed, rhythmically very inadequate; we didn't like working with him at all'. Another opinion is that his Haydn and Mozart were poor – 'slow movements too slow, silly bowings and phrasings; they often came out deadly boring' – but that he was obviously aware of his own failures in this area: 'He had even then a definite presence and authority which many established conductors lack; the opinion of many of the orchestra was that he was very intelligent but lacked technique and musicianship. But he knew his limitations and openly admitted in a most endearing fashion that some of the things he tried didn't work. He was down-to-earth, outgoing, direct, witty. One had the impression he had thoroughly thought out his interpretations (though sometimes with slightly absurd conclusions). He improved extraordinarily fast and at the end of the Bournemouth period it was becoming much more comfortable to work with him. He was always charming, unassuming and diplomatic.'

Rattle's own view of this period is that the problems were inevitable and could not have been avoided. It might have been even worse elsewhere, he argues, and no young conductor can avoid the problems of facing professionals for the first time. As for the repertory, he feels there was a balance of opportunities and difficulties: 'Some pieces I was scared off for life, others I began to get to grips with. My love of Haydn started here, so I have a lot to be grateful for. It was the beginning of the road with Mozart's *Jupiter* and *Prague*.

The Schubert *Unfinished*, on the other hand, I've never done since. I realized that so many orchestras play it so incredibly badly that I have to be a really very good conductor before I can make them do it better.'

It is hardly surprising that Rattle learnt fast in this period, since outside Bournemouth he had made great advances. Following his success with the Nash Ensemble he was invited to conduct part of a concert they gave in the Queen Elizabeth Hall in February 1975: this was his professional South Bank début, and *The Times* praised his 'clean and careful' conducting of Ravel with Felicity Palmer. (Later in the year he made his first recording, an all-Ravel disc, with them.) In January he had appeared at the Institute of Contemporary Arts with a section of the Royal Philharmonic Orchestra in a programme of new music which contained a pair of obscure works for brass and percussion. He knew most of the players so the engagement was not a problem for him. *The Times* noted of one of the pieces that 'there was never any real textural interest and Simon Rattle, the conductor, did well to obtain what sounded like a quite committed performance'.

Then in April he was approached at very short notice to conduct an English Chamber Orchestra tour of Spain: Pinchas Zukerman, who was to conduct, had fallen ill. Once more he took fright, thinking he would be eaten alive by these experienced players:

SIMON RATTLE: Martin warned me that Quin Ballardie who ran the ECO was going to ring and I said that I just couldn't cope with it, I was too young, it wouldn't work, and all that. But Quin rang up and said, 'You don't know me but I run the ECO and I hear you're a bit nervous about conducting us in Spain. I've told all the people you're coming and your name is on all the posters so let's just assume you're coming, shall we?' Amazing! I was completely blustered into it. But I enjoyed it, and they were tolerant of what must have been some of the worst Mozart Fortieths ever.

An orchestra with which Rattle was to try out some of his most ambitious projects around this time was the amateur Salomon Orchestra. In June 1975 he did a concert with them which included the Adagio from Mahler's Tenth Symphony (before the publication of the full score of Deryck Cooke's completion of the whole work, which Rattle later took up enthusiastically). This drew a warm notice from Stephen Walsh in the *Observer*: 'The Salomon Orchestra has a good record in bringing forward young conductors. I doubt, though, whether even they have gone much nearer the cradle than Mr Rattle... Even he wasn't quite equal to the basic difficulty of securing deft and athletic playing from amateur players in a Haydn symphony ... [but in the Mahler] he showed remarkable ability to sustain long melodic sentences and build them into coherent paragraphs. The searing climax was by any standards exciting.'

Rattle still found it valuable to be involved not only with amateur music-making but also school music-making. During the summer he went up to Aberdeen to conduct at a festival of youth orchestras there, and in September took his first course with the London Schools Symphony Orchestra. This was something that Andrew Davis had previously done, and through Martin Campbell-White Rattle was asked to conduct their autumn course and to make his Festival Hall début as a conductor at the end of it. It was a bold programme which included Ligeti's *Atmosphères*, never before heard in the hall, and Mahler's First Symphony. Ronald Crichton in the *Financial Times*, pointing out that Rattle was only seven years older than the oldest schoolchild in the LSSO, praised the Mahler: 'Nothing was funked ... Mr Rattle's secure and sensitive guidance of this tricky score was of the greatest value.'

This amateur début was followed, and naturally overshadowed in importance, by his professional début in the Festival Hall in February 1976, conducting the New Philharmonia Orchestra (which was soon to drop the word 'New' from its title). This was a landmark, an event that had been carefully planned by Martin Campbell-White to gain the maximum attention. Simon's parents came down from Liverpool, and there was a party afterwards attended by such luminaries as Sir Robert Mayer. Rattle had expressed his misgivings to an interviewer beforehand: 'What can a twenty-one-year-old have to teach Gwydion Brooke?' he said, referring to the orchestra's famous first bassoonist. But according to the orchestra's historian, Stephen J. Pettitt,* he did in the event have something to teach Brooke, because the bassoonist made a wrong entry in Shostakovich's Tenth Symphony and Rattle, conducting from memory, was able to steer him through it.

He was the youngest conductor ever to appear with the orchestra, and this inspired some faintly contradictory comments in the papers from the critics who were, however, united in their praise of the new

---

* *The Philharmonia Orchestra: a Record of Achievement 1945–1985* (Robert Hale, 1985).

Taking on a London orchestra: Rattle rehearsing with the Philharmonia in Nottingham, 1978; he had made his Festival Hall début with them in 1976.
(*photo* Gerald Murray)

conductor. In the *Guardian* Hugo Cole wrote that 'Conductors, like swimming champions, mature younger and younger, and skills which were once acquired only over many years and laborious processes of trial and error are today picked up by conservatory and university students in no time at all. Yet Simon Rattle, at twenty-one, is still something rather exceptional ... the symphony was well and seriously performed, suggesting that the New Philharmonia Orchestra were taking their conductor seriously, and giving him the performance he wanted and knew how to ask for.'

On the other hand, Robert Henderson in the *Daily Telegraph* underlined some of the problems when he noted that 'whereas brilliant soloists in their early twenties are a normal feature of concert life, the very difficulty of gaining the necessary practical experience makes the appearance of a conductor of similar authority at the same age a rare and, indeed, unlikely occurrence'. But he found the début 'strikingly auspicious', and felt that 'rarely had any apologies to be made for his youth'. Max Harrison in *The Times* wrote: 'Mr Rattle is a convinced advocate; he presented an altogether clearly thought out interpretation and obtained superb playing from the New Philharmonia.'

This was indeed, as one writer put it, a 'glittering start'. Rattle's enthusiasm for making things happen as a conductor, and all those years of gathering together amateur forces and cajoling people to play for him had paid off to the extent that it had given him the necessary experience to face an orchestra like the New Philharmonia without any qualms. Martin Campbell-White was delighted: 'The buzz started and I remember I introduced him to Daniel Barenboim and one or two other people: there was a great deal of interest in him from the right quarters from an early time.' Still, Campbell-White recalls that Rattle was very much his own master in the choice of work that he undertook, and his choices were usually right.

Later that same month Rattle gave his first account of a work which was to become central for him: Gershwin's *Porgy and Bess*. This was the beginning of a ten-year love-affair with this opera, 'one of the twentieth-century's most neglected operas', as Rattle called it. It was the first time he worked with Willard White, who was to be his Porgy ten years later at Glyndebourne as well as several times in between. The performance was put on by the Chelsea Opera Group in the old Town Hall in London's Euston Road, and it apparently had plenty of fizz: Alan Blyth in the *The Times* wrote that it did 'nearly as much justice as is possible in a concert performance of the opera'. (Only in a concert performance were non-black singers allowed by the rules of the Gershwin estate, a major factor in delaying the first staging of the work by an English company.) In a prescient review in *Opera* magazine, Rodney Milnes noted that 'the vigour and total lack of inhibition that characterized both the orchestral playing and choral singing must be put down to Simon Rattle's inspired conducting ... let us hope that more successful concert performances will inspire a new stage production of Gershwin's masterpiece'. They would, but it was to be quite a wait.

There was more opera that summer, with the newly formed English Music Theatre Company. First at The Maltings at Snape, home of the Aldeburgh Festival, and then on tour around the country before arriving at Sadler's Wells, Rattle conducted Kurt Weill's *Threepenny Opera*. He then returned to the Dartington Summer School, galvanizing the choir – which included his parents – for a performance of Janáček's *Glagolitic Mass*, a work that was to be among the first he recorded. In August there was his first Prom, or part of one, with the London Sinfonietta at the Round House conducting Lutyens's *And Suddenly It's Evening* and Birtwistle's *Meridian*: he was the youngest

Play-through: an exhilarating moment at the Dartington Summer School of Music, when Peter Donohoe and Rattle (as orchestral accompanist) played through Rachmaninov's Third Piano Concerto together. Rattle's parents, regular Dartington participants, are in the middle of the front row. (*photo* Charles Davis)

conductor ever to appear in a Prom. That success was to be followed up by regular Proms with the Sinfonietta, including his first Albert Hall appearance the following year with a Mozart, Schoenberg and Stravinsky programme in which he returned to *Pulcinella*.

But the major events of that autumn were the result of Martin Campbell-White's desire that, slowly but surely, Rattle's name should become very well known abroad. The London Schools Symphony Orchestra did an extensive and exhausting American tour which took Rattle to Carnegie Hall in New York for the first time, to Chicago (where his conducting of Elgar's *Enigma Variations* was compared favourably to that of another recent English visitor, Edward Heath) and to Los Angeles where, as Simon recalled, 'Ernest [Fleischmann, manager of the Los Angeles Philharmonic] met us off the plane and immediately started asking me to go and do things with the Philharmonic: I was scared stiff!' Meanwhile he worked with the Scottish Chamber Orchestra for the first time, establishing a good rapport which was to become important for the future when he would try out major new projects such as Beethoven's Third and

Ninth Symphonies with this group. And Martin Campbell-White arranged his débuts with a couple of foreign orchestras, starting with the Trondheim and the Sjaellands Symphony Orchestras in Scandinavia, both of which he enjoyed. The vistas were opening up rapidly.

Another important experience in this period was to be asked back to conduct an ensemble he had played in, the National Youth Orchestra; not only to perform *The Rite of Spring*, but also to record it in what was his largest recording undertaking to date. John Carewe was less than flattering about the end result (see p. 12), and Rattle is due to record the work again in the near future with the CBSO. But he remembers it as a chastening experience because the NYO recording immediately preceded a course directed by Pierre Boulez:

> SIMON RATTLE: That orchestra is a mirror: they can adapt so quickly. There were some problems with the recording because of the sheer timelag in hearing what was happening. I remember I couldn't see the piccolo trumpet player at all because he was so small, but I worked out that he was the one whose feet didn't touch the ground so I waved in that direction! Just after the recordings Boulez came to direct the orchestra. They played him what I had trained them to do, and I watched his face. I was very proud because they could produce exactly what I had done, and I wondered what he'd make of it. He spent about an hour making it worse and worse, and then a couple of hours transforming it. Mainly he worked on the 'Danse sacrale', and I learned a hell of a lot seeing him mould that in his own image – going for a feeling of weighting, his insistence that you could hear what all those chords actually were. In his work with the orchestra he was basically just pointing out my deficiencies in a very clear way!

II

1977–80

The first radical change in the pattern of Rattle's work happened in 1977. After his two-year stint with the Bournemouth orchestras came to an end in the summer of 1976 he did a modest amount of guest conducting, but he still felt the need to work himself gradually into the repertory before making any substantial commitments or accepting any major offers. So the two posts which came his way in 1977 were both very welcome: the more substantial of them was as assistant conductor of the BBC Scottish Symphony Orchestra in Glasgow, and

Hitting to win: a table-tennis session during Rattle's first fraught season at
Glyndebourne, 1975 (*photo* Greg German, *Sunday Telegraph*)

the more public of them was as associate conductor of the Royal
Liverpool Philharmonic Orchestra in his home town.

It came as a surprise to Martin Dalby, Head of Music for the BBC
in Scotland, that Simon Rattle would want to accept an assistant's
post at a time when his career was taking off so rapidly. In fact it was
ideal for Rattle, for it gave him the rehearsal conditions and the work
out of the public limelight in the broadcasting studio that he needed.
He wanted to broaden his repertory, but also to explore those areas of
it with which he felt at home, something that had been impossible
under the constraints of West Country touring.

For their part, the orchestra responded with enthusiasm and did
everything in their power to make him feel welcome. According to
John Purser's new history of the orchestra,* only their principal conductor, Karl Anton Rickenbacher, was baffled by the choice of a
twenty-two-year-old conductor for the orchestra. Martin Dalby
made every effort to accommodate Rattle's wishes, and the results
were programmes that included many of his best pieces. Dalby soon
realized that Rattle's title was the wrong one: 'He obviously assisted
nobody, so somewhere along the line we re-designated it as associate
conductor.' He took up the post on 1 July 1977, and his contract was

---

* *Is the Red Light On? The Story of the BBC Scottish Symphony Orchestra* (BBC Scotland,
1987).

renewed in 1979 for a further year to 30 June 1980. The commitment, a substantial one, was to do twenty-five programmes in the studio as well as public concerts.

*   *   *

Part of Dalby's efforts to make Rattle as content as possible in Glasgow involved finding ways to augment the orchestra in order to undertake the repertory Rattle wanted to do. His first concerts included Bruckner's Fourth Symphony, Brahms's Second and Rachmaninov's Second. Major undertakings in 1978 included Mahler's *Das Lied von der Erde*, Bartók's *Music for Strings, Percussion and Celesta*, Messiaen's *Oiseaux exotiques* and Mahler's Fifth Symphony (interestingly, a work to which Rattle has not yet returned in Birmingham). Among the few classical works he attempted was Beethoven's Seventh Symphony, in a performance in June 1978 which he was unhappy with, and he later did Beethoven's Fourth and Brahms's Fourth. But these were the exceptions: more typical were Strauss's *Don Quixote* and Berlioz's *Symphonie fantastique*, for which nothing was stinted in terms of players, and Rattle must have felt much more at home with this repertory than with what he had been used to in Bournemouth.

There was also an element of contemporary music in these programmes, but it was not extensive. Thea Musgrave's *Night Music*, Lennox Berkeley's Flute Concerto, John Maxwell Geddes's *Lacuna*, Peter Maxwell Davies's early *Five Klee Pictures* and Elisabeth Lutyens's *Echoi* were among the recent works tackled. But more significant than this for the future was the foundation repertory he developed in the early twentieth-century classics: Debussy, Ravel, Stravinsky, Berg, Prokofiev, Janáček, Shostakovich and Bartók. This was the music that he felt most at home with, and it was his skill in this area that perhaps made it possible for him to tackle contemporary works with such comparative ease.

One of the contemporary works he undertook caused something of a fuss, according to John Purser. He wanted to use the orchestra to prepare himself for the first performance of Peter Maxwell Davies's very complex First Symphony, which he had been asked by the composer to première in London with the New Philharmonia Orchestra. The Scottish Symphony Orchestra performance was to be broadcast later, but the glory of the first performance would go to Rattle with the London orchestra. Although Maxwell Davies expressed his appreciation of the Scottish orchestra's work, some of the players apparently regarded it as 'a gross and insensitive insult' that their orchestra was used in this way as back-room preparation for the achievements of a London orchestra.

Another minor controversy surrounded Rattle's determination to do *The Rite of Spring* with the BBC Scottish. In January 1980 he spent a week rehearsing and then performing the work, for which a large number of extras was needed. Dalby managed to obtain all except one (the bass tuba player) from Scotland, but word got round the BBC that the expenditure had been lavish. In an interview with *The Times* in 1982 about the reorganization of the BBC's orchestral resources, the BBC's Controller, Music, Robert Ponsonby, said that the orchestras had to rationalize their repertory to suit their size: 'When the BBC Scottish did *The Rite of Spring*, extras were brought in from the four corners of the Empire.' This infuriated Dalby, who protested vigorously that that was untrue, and that in any case such demarcation of repertory between the regional symphony orchestras was impossible to put into practice: was the BBC Symphony Orchestra going to stop playing Mozart? And in fact that policy has gradually been eroded: in an interview in the 1987 Proms prospectus, John Drummond, now the BBC's Controller, Radio 3, said 'Of course the BBC Scottish wants to play *The Rite of Spring* and the BBC Symphony Orchestra wants to play Haydn symphonies and no one's going to stop them.'

That saga produced what Rattle regards as his finest *Rite of Spring* up to the present time. 'They'd never done it before and they'll probably never do it again. We rehearsed it for five days, and we built it up chord by chord until everything had this weight and depth and richness, and then we were able to put the punch on the top of it.'

Besides that work were several others that have turned out to be Rattle favourites: Sibelius's Second and Seventh Symphonies, Stravinsky's *Petrushka* and, perhaps most notably, Shostakovich's Tenth Symphony, which he had taken to the Proms with the orchestra in 1979. Already by that time there had been strong hints that the BBC was going to attack the orchestras as part of a package of economies the following year. Martin Dalby remembers turning to Pat Ramsay, the BBC's Controller, Scotland, after that performance, and saying, 'You're not going to let them touch it after *that*.' Ramsay did not reply, and ironically it was the Scottish Broadcasting Council of the BBC, rather than the BBC in London, that in the end recommended the sacrifice of the BBC Scottish Symphony Orchestra in 1980 – and that caused the Musicians' Union strike which led to the cancellation of some of that year's Proms.

Rattle was in Los Angeles in January 1980 when he heard the news of the proposed cuts. He was outraged, and told an interviewer: 'It only proves the people who run the BBC are philistine. It's not the music department; they're fine. It's the top management's fault. It's a first-rate example of the damned bureaucratic mind. Extraordinary if you think of it in humanitarian terms. Here's eighty people, put out of a job, and in Glasgow; they don't stand a chance of finding other employment at short notice. And what happens to the area's culture? The country's?' Rattle went back and wrote a letter to *The Times*, making the same points in more measured terms.

One of his last acts before his contract in Scotland expired in mid-1980 was to take part in a gala concert in May at the Theatre Royal, Glasgow, in aid of the strike that had by then been called. It was a grand gathering of conductors: Christopher Seaman, Sir Alexander Gibson and James Loughran, with a splendidly miscellaneous programme of lollipops. Then, during the following week, Rattle concluded his Scottish work with an entirely typical collection of pieces: David Matthews's *September Music*, Elgar's First Symphony and Mahler's *Das klagende Lied* and Fourth Symphony. Rattle has said, 'I found everything that I consider to be at the centre of my repertory with the BBC Scottish, and I remember vividly the sensation of welcome ... they had amazing vitality and great warmth.' It was a fruitful time, but once again Rattle was lucky: the orchestra was much damaged by the settlement of the Musicians' Union strike later in the year (which left it still in existence but without some key players) and the post of associate conductor has not been revived.

*   *   *

Rattle's other post, which he took up in April 1977, was as associate conductor of the orchestra with which he had grown up, the Royal Liverpool Philharmonic. The post was less onerous in terms of appearances – some twelve concerts a season – but far more public and rather more problematical. It had been specially created for him as part of the change-over from Sir Charles Groves, who retired as principal conductor, to Walter Weller, who succeeded him. Rattle had already returned twice to the orchestra in 1975, the year after winning the John Player Competition, first with Shostakovich's

Tenth Symphony and Rachmaninov played by his friend Philip
Fowke, and then with a Ravel centenary concert including a complete
concert performance of *L'Enfant et les sortilèges* which was perhaps
less effective than the one he had given a year earlier at the Royal
Academy. Nevertheless, he impressed Stephen Gray, the orchestra's
manager, who had been one of the first people in the professional
musical world to notice him, and whose mention of him to Martin
Campbell-White really started the wheels rolling for Rattle as a professional conductor. He was well aware of Rattle's skills as a
programme-builder, and wanted to give him his head:

> STEPHEN GRAY: Simon is a natural entrepreneur. He was always tre-
> mendously interested in the business of putting on concerts, from his
> teenage years, and he was very shrewd, and had a terrifically inquiring
> mind. I remember very clearly discussing the cast for the Ravel opera
> and being so impressed with the maturity with which he knew who
> could do what, and who he wanted to sing which part.
>
> I think the orchestra regarded him as their son rather than their
> father, and there was a little bit of that in their attitude to him. In the
> three years he conducted us very regularly he did some fascinating pro-
> grammes, and they were such events. (I remember every one of his con-
> certs, which is more than I can say about a lot of the others...) He
> asked for a great deal of rehearsal, for example for the Strauss *Meta-
> morphosen*, and I generally agreed. Mahler 10 we didn't have enough
> time for, and it wasn't one of his best performances. But Mahler 2 in
> Liverpool Cathedral was the greatest thing he did for us.
>
> The performances were pretty rough, and little things went wrong,
> but they always hung together. I haven't had anyone to work with since
> who had that sort of flair for sparking me off with programme ideas. In
> fact I don't think I've ever met anyone quite so gifted in every way.

Rattle's associate conductorship was inaugurated with another performance of Gershwin's *Porgy and Bess*, as part of the Hope Street
Festival. Once again Willard White was Porgy. 'A triumph for all concerned,' reported a local paper. And in his first season in 1978 there
was Mahler's *Das Lied von der Erde*, Rachmaninov's *Symphonic
Dances*, Dvořák's Cello Concerto, and a symmetrical programme he
has perhaps never bettered:

Strauss	*Don Juan*
Ravel	*Shéhérazade*
Messiaen	*Et exspecto resurrectionem mortuorum*
Ravel	*Three Mallarmé Poems*
Strauss	*Metamorphosen*

In July 1978 he conducted Janáček's *Jenůfa* for the first time, in a concert performance with Pauline Tinsley: 'a triumph of closely involved, inspirational conducting', wrote Neil Tierney in the *Daily Telegraph*. Rattle has several times come near to conducting it in the opera house – in New York, at Covent Garden and at Glyndebourne – but it remains something to which we must look forward.

The 1978–9 season included Janáček's *Taras Bulba*, Walton's *Belshazzar's Feast*, Sibelius 1, Mahler 10, and a lively Bernstein–Gershwin evening. A novelty of that period was the extraordinary fantasy by H. K. Gruber, *Frankenstein!!*, which Rattle also conducted in a chamber version in London with the London Sinfonietta. This brought the national critics up to Liverpool to be amazed: in the *Financial Times* David Murray wrote that this 'pandemonium for baritone and orchestra' was 'singularly charming ... nearly half an hour long, it is a setting of wicked children's rhymes by the Austrian surrealist H. C. Artmann ... traditional monsters rub shoulders with Batman, Robin and Jimmy Bond, with lashings of simple horror ... Bright-eyed scores like this suit Simon Rattle to a T, and the performance by the Royal Liverpool Philharmonic under him evinced infectious relish.'

The 1979–80 concerts all included some Stravinsky: the *Firebird Suite* alongside Rachmaninov's Third Symphony, *The Rite of Spring*, *Petrushka* with Beethoven 7, the Mass with Mahler 6, the *Symphony of Psalms* with the Fauré *Requiem*, and the *Symphony in Three Movements* alongside Brahms's Violin Concerto.

Though there were many successes among these performances, and though the fascinating juxtapositions of works made up the first fully characteristic Rattle public concert programmes, the collaboration with the orchestra was not entirely a success. One player recalled: 'We found his rehearsal technique rather exhausting. His brain is so quick that he'd say "Two bars before A" very quickly and there would be a downbeat before anyone was ready. So he'd stop, repeat the instruction and again he'd be off before the violins had the instruments under their chins. He spoke in a clipped, jerky way which was quite taxing on the nervous system ...

'Many of us definitely did not enjoy rehearsing with Simon. But the shows, during which he couldn't talk so much, were good. He was excellent at getting good performances. I remember he spent a long time trying to get the orchestra to play one long phrase as one long phrase, not twenty short ones. Unfortunately many of us were rather unwilling to accept his authority.'

This friction caused problems when Walter Weller was suddenly snapped up by the Royal Philharmonic Orchestra in London, since it then looked as if Rattle was the obvious person to succeed him as principal conductor.

PAULINE RATTLE: [The management] were pressing him a lot, and pressing us too. We were very close to the Philharmonic at that time, and twenty or thirty people would come back home after Simon's concerts, so we knew them well. It was a great embarrassment to us: we were very happy when he was offered it but I quite saw his point that it wouldn't have been right.

SIMON RATTLE: I'm sure Stephen Gray was very upset when I didn't do it: he had given me *carte blanche* with those programmes and had showed absolute faith. But I had to say that I wasn't going to be rehearsing Stephen Gray or conducting Stephen Gray. They all remembered me as a bumptious little kid running around backstage collecting autographs and listening to every rehearsal. In some way there was a good rapport, but I never felt, as was somehow obvious with the other orchestras I was working with, that I really knew how to make that orchestra better. It was obviously not going to work.

The orchestra, for their part, decided in a majority vote that they did not wish him to be appointed. (This was something that he was unaware of until he read it here. He said he was relieved, because several members of the orchestra had said strongly to him that they did want him and he had felt bad about being so convinced it would not work.) Probably for the best, both sides of the possible marriage realized in advance that it should not happen.

In any case, other orchestras were on the scene by then and Rattle's career was racing ahead. In 1978 he had made his first visit to the Rotterdam Philharmonic, where he had been offered a music directorship in succession to David Zinman: he declined but accepted a principal guest conductorship. The following year he returned to Los Angeles for his long-awaited début with the Philharmonic, and Ernest Fleischmann again wooed him with the offer of a post. Chicago followed later that year, and Toronto and San Francisco were planned for 1980. It might have been thought certain that his future lay in that direction, in picking up a music directorship, as Andrew Davis had done, with a much-respected foreign orchestra. In fact the engagement that really mattered in this period had taken place in December 1978, when Rattle had conducted the City of Birmingham Symphony Orchestra for the first time in Birmingham.

CHAPTER FOUR

'Making the orchestra play better'

Recordings and television:
May 1986

Waiting for the red light: a break in a recording session

I

ON THE RECORD

30 MAY 1986: Watford Town Hall. It is a week after a Brighton Festival performance of Mahler's Second Symphony by Rattle and the CBSO which went exceptionally well and generated an electric atmosphere: the players seem to regard that performance as one of the highlights of the year. And last night was one of the orchestra's

concerts in London, where they were taking part in the London Symphony Orchestra's season at the Barbican. 'I can't let a concert like that go, ladies and gentlemen,' says Rattle at the start of today's recording session in a nice little formal speech, 'without saying how great it is to work with an orchestra whose playing just gets better and better.' Upstairs, in a back room which has been converted into a control room, EMI producer David Murray, who now works on most of Rattle's recordings, makes a few last notes and prepares to check the balance during the opening rehearsal.

To be recorded is the first movement of Mahler's Second Symphony, a daunting undertaking because, as Rattle says, 'only the world's greatest orchestras get to record the Mahler symphonies', and he is perfectly well aware of the competition and what the comparisons will be. But this is a work he knows better than almost any other: it was the symphony he chose to put on at the Royal Academy of Music in London, the symphony with which he opened his first Birmingham subscription series in 1980, and above all, the symphony which, when he heard it as a boy of eleven, first made him really want to conduct.

Because of scheduling problems the orchestra, soloists and chorus haven't been able to record the whole work together, as Rattle would have found ideal. Sessions have already taken place, at the beginning of this month, for the massed forces in the finale, and now the orchestra alone faces the challenge of the first movement of the symphony. But, maybe because of the exhilaration of the Mahler at Brighton, or the success of the previous evening's concert, the orchestra's playing is on a bit of a down. It's proving difficult to recapture the excitement cold. The band seems a little tired. 'Let's get the feel of this place,' says Rattle, and they launch into the first movement's opening. Watford isn't a venue to which they are accustomed: most of the recordings these days take place in the University of Warwick Arts Centre, but EMI felt that that hall couldn't quite contain the vastness of sound needed in Mahler's Second.

The rehearsal continues: there's a lot of trouble just to tune a unison E carefully through the orchestra, and at one point Rattle points out with a slight edginess that the sequence C–B♭–A 'is not all semitones; we're not all right on that one'. In that first gargantuan run up the scale by cellos and basses he is working, as so often, on getting them to play through the sound and project: 'We shouldn't ever allow ourselves to play uh–uh–uh–uh–uh ... It's so much better

Going for take: Mahler's Second Symphony at Watford Town Hall, 1986

when we *warm* the sound.' (Rattle is always careful to speak of 'we' rather than 'you' when rehearsing: a typical touch – he doesn't tell them what to do, they do it together.)

A while into the session and Rattle's red podium phone rings. 'OK, they're ready to take something; now, let's try and re-create the atmosphere of that Brighton performance for [and he peers out into the hall where I and an orchestra member are sitting] an audience of one...? Two! Thank you...'

SIMON RATTLE: For me, the important thing about recordings is that they are the most effective way to make the orchestra play better. We make great strides when we do a difficult record. The increase in confidence and technical ability, just to assimilate all the things you have to do in the course of a session: that pushes the orchestra on so much. None of these recordings I'm making now is my last will and testament. I'm afraid I'm not so interested as I should be in the finished product, perhaps, because the work has been done. I must admit I fell asleep listening to my test pressing of *The Planets*, but that was a long time ago. Some of them I've never heard again after the pressings.

The awful thing about recordings is that you listen to them afterwards and you really can't tell what were the bits that went well in the studio and everyone was thrilled and you thought 'this is a great performance', and which bits were put on with everyone feeling totally whacked at the end of the day and playing with gritted teeth. You just can't tell, and maybe there's something wrong with that. But we try now to do more and more straight performances in the recording studio, with as few re-takes as possible. That way we preserve the feeling of the live occasion. Mahler 2, for instance – well, I think you came to a session which did least to re-create that feeling; it was hard work. But the last movement with choir and everyone, we just did most of that in one long performance and it was really superb.

Do you think recordings in general are a good thing?

Oh yes. I grew up with them and I still learn a lot from listening to them. I couldn't possibly know the music I do if they weren't around. The problem is the effect they have on people's performances: everything tends to come out sounding more and more the same, and conductors seem unwilling to be really different. A conductor like Harnoncourt is an exception: he's certainly different! But on the whole there's less and less individuality, and recordings just veer towards some sort of norm. And the worst thing would be, for myself, if I ever thought that I'd 'done' a piece because it's recorded, so it's over and finished with. There's a finality about records which isn't very healthy. For me they're just a stage along the way. For the orchestra I think they're bad if it makes them think they have to play carefully without ever a wrong note. We do want the notes right, but if it stifles your sense of live music-making and adventure then recordings are not a good thing at all.

*   *   *

The CBSO's recorded output in 1986 is quite staggering. In quantity it doesn't compare with that of a London orchestra, but none of it is purely commercial work and all of it is first-rank repertory. The year is exceptional, admittedly: alongside the massive milestone of Mahler 2 are two other huge works, Messiaen's *Turangalîla* and Elgar's *The Dream of Gerontius*; then there will be Stravinsky's *Petrushka* (with the other big ballets to follow) coupled with the *Symphony in Three Movements*, and two Sibelius symphonies, the Fourth and the Sixth. That's nine recordings in a year, all of important and substantial pieces.

This situation has come about purely because of Rattle's fierce loyalty to the CBSO. As an exclusive EMI artist he records only for that company, and EMI would be happy – indeed in the earlier days it was desperate – for him to record with other orchestras with a high international profile. As someone close to him put it, 'They hear he's going to do a date with the Concertgebouw or whoever, and their

A dream of a recording: Janet Baker, Rattle, John Mitchinson and John Shirley-Quirk during the 1986 sessions for Elgar's *The Dream of Gerontius*

first thought is "What can we record?" But that isn't the way Simon works any more.'

In the early days of his contract the work was with several orchestras, with a special emphasis on the Philharmonia with whom he appeared regularly in London. He was originally going to record all the Sibelius symphonies with them. The very earliest discs were ones in which the orchestras were able to provide their services as part of their contract arrangements, so that the only cost to EMI was Rattle and marketing. That arrangement produced one of his first records, of Stravinsky with the Northern Sinfonia, as well as the record which first really alerted EMI to his potential: Mahler's Tenth Symphony in the Deryck Cooke version with the Bournemouth Symphony Orchestra, recorded in June 1980, just before Rattle went to Birmingham.

With the release of that Mahler recording in 1981, EMI made a determined effort to promote Rattle, and it paid off. The record did well and encouraged them to make more. But that was just at the time when Rattle was becoming completely committed to the Birmingham orchestra. Some other collaborations had taken place, including an unlikely one with the London Symphony Orchestra in a recording of Prokofiev and Ravel piano concertos with Andrei Gavrilov: Rattle has only ever conducted that orchestra on one other occasion. With the Philharmonia he recorded *The Planets*, Sibelius's Fifth, Shostakovich's Tenth and a splendid Janáček coupling of the *Sinfonietta* with *Taras Bulba* which the players much enjoyed making. He made Rachmaninov's Second Symphony with the Los Angeles Philharmonic as their principal guest conductor, but that was the only recording there, and it was not especially well reviewed.

Rattle's recordings with the CBSO began with large-scale choral undertakings: Janáček's *Glagolitic Mass* and Britten's *War Requiem* (a work which EMI had, coincidentally, already arranged to record with Rattle's predecessor in Birmingham, Louis Frémaux, before his abrupt departure in March 1978). They were followed by Weill's *Seven Deadly Sins* with Rattle's wife, Elise Ross; several piano concertos with Cécile Ousset; Vaughan Williams with Thomas Allen and Robert Tear; Nielsen's Fourth; Mahler's *Das klagende Lied*; and

Renewing Britten: Rattle with the soloists in his recording of Britten's *War Requiem*: Thomas Allen, Robert Tear and Elisabeth Söderström, 1983

Unearthing Britten: Rattle during recordings of some of Britten's early unpublished music, with the pianist Peter Donohoe and the soprano Jill Gomez, 1982

Simon with his wife, Elise Ross, during recordings of Weill's *The Seven Deadly Sins*, 1982

early Britten including several first recordings of pieces such as the *Four French Songs* with Jill Gomez, *Young Apollo, An American Overture* and *An Occasional Overture*. Many of these were prepared for by concert performances at the time of recording (the Britten overtures, for instance, were heard in Birmingham, one of them conducted by John Carewe in the concerts he took over when Rattle's son was born, and the *Four French Songs* were slipped into a Cheltenham programme).

Rattle will now record only works that have been most thoroughly prepared in advance, preferably by a whole series of concert performances. Mahler 2 and *Turangalîla*, for example, are both solidly in the orchestra's repertory, and were performed several times during 1986 before reaching the studio. The only exception to Rattle's present exclusive commitment to the CBSO in the recording studio is his work with the London Sinfonietta on completely different repertory, and in the first week of 1987 he was with them, taping Paul Whiteman arrangements, Milhaud, and Gershwin's *Rhapsody in Blue* with Peter Donohoe.

Rattle's EMI producer for all the early recordings was John Willan, now managing director of the London Philharmonic Orchestra. He is a good colleague and a close friend of Rattle's, and potentially a very important influence on the future direction of his career:

JOHN WILLAN: I don't think Simon would mind me saying that we had a lot of problems with the first recording we did, which was *Pulcinella* with the Northern Sinfonia. He'd done a lot of conducting by then, but not in the studio, which is a very different thing. I was surprised, for example, by his inability to match the speed of one take with the next, or to remember exactly what he'd done half an hour ago. It was fine in a sense, because what he was wanting was to do it differently, but it made it awkward for us. Then there was a problem with one of the players, and eventually we had to give up and come back for another session later. But it all came out very well in the end, and I still listen to the record!

I did a *Planets* with the Philharmonia and him at Kingsway Hall, but I'm not sure that he ever liked it. That was typical record company stuff: young star, got to do a popular piece. The orchestra played stunningly, of course, but I don't think it was technically very good from our point of view.

It's quite surprising that he wanted to make any records at this stage.

I don't think he did, really. And it was only because he was soon allowed to do the things he passionately wanted to do, like Mahler 10

'I'm not saying he hasn't got a lot to learn, but he's smart': John Willan's view of
Simon Rattle. Willan was Rattle's recording producer at EMI and is now manager of
the London Philharmonic Orchestra

and the Janáček *Glagolitic Mass*, that we got him into the studio at all.
If EMI had gone on doing what they tend to do with young artists,
saying, 'Now you listen to us, lad: make a Beethoven 7 and we can sell
that,' then I think he wouldn't have stayed in the studio long.

It was a struggle to get that repertory through EMI. They weren't so
worried about Mahler 10 because it hadn't been done properly before;
it was a big thing for us, and they hyped it up and in fact it sold very
well. But when we got on to things like the *Glagolitic Mass* . . . a lot of
problems. And that's just so upsetting and stupid because here's Simon,
he's on television and so on, and you've got a real chance there *not* to do
the standard repertory and have it compared yet again with the Karajan
version.

Were EMI worried about his lack of international profile?

Yes, very; when I was there they were extremely concerned that he
should – not my words at all – stop mucking about with a regional orchestra and get to the Berlin Philharmonic and all the other places who
were desperate to have him. But Simon was always very firm about
that, and he just said, 'What for?' There was no point for him. Records
with Berlin or Amsterdam would have sold better, I suppose, but then

you have to balance the cost against that: it's probably three times as expensive to go to Berlin as to go to Birmingham, so you'd have to sell three times as many records.

Then you have to think in the long term of your relationship with the artist, which is what E M I eventually did. They realized that if Simon had such a very clear idea of what he wanted to do, they should respect that if they wanted to be with him in ten or twenty years. The mistake with a young artist is to push him into the big-time circuit too soon.

Presumably Simon quickly became much more professional in the studio?

Oh yes, incredibly quickly, which is part of his strength. He picks up on things so rapidly. One impressive thing with the C B S O was that he knew very quickly what was possible for the orchestra: I remember I would say to him, 'It's not together there, are you worried about that?' and he would say, 'No, it's impossible, leave it.' Or if I said that the trumpet sounded a bit flat there, he'd just say, 'Have you tried to play it?' Simon is absolutely on the ball and he usually knows what's gone well. If you tell him over the phone that the trombones are too loud there, he'll adjust it. But if he then comes in to listen to the take and finds that the trombones weren't too loud, he can be quite straightforward about it!

Doing the Britten *War Requiem* was incredibly complicated because we had a very odd schedule: Bob Tear could only come on certain days, the chorus could only be there in the evenings, so we couldn't record it in order. And it was a problem for the engineers because we started with the smaller, chamber orchestra sections, for scheduling reasons. That was bad, because engineers like to get the feel of the full sound first. Mike Sheady did a great job, and he was always keyed up; some of the older engineers always tended to be a bit sleepy. Mike had a great rapport with Simon and was able to say that we ought to move the horns back or whatever, and Simon would trust him.

Some people have said that Simon's knowing what he wants does mean he can be very stubborn.

Oh, absolutely, he's incredibly stubborn. If he decides he wants a particular singer then that's the singer he'll have. So you make a straightforward choice: if you want to do that piece with Simon, you do it with that singer. And usually he's right. We did Mahler's *Das klagende Lied* in Birmingham Town Hall with Helena Döse, and Simon could tell I wasn't happy with the choice, but he would never explain. I just said, 'You're sure?' and he said, 'Yes'. And she was very good for that piece. He's pretty idiosyncratic about singers. I'm not saying he hasn't got a lot to learn, but he's smart.

It's going to be very interesting seeing what happens in the next ten years. I cannot imagine that he won't just develop and mature and get better and better. This decade has got to see him moving a little bit more abroad. But he can afford to take his time. He's got decades in front of him.

So now with the LPO, what are the conditions you can make to attract Simon to work with you in London?

The sort of conditions we want conductors to ask for. I mean, some are content with two rehearsals for a concert, and they never ask for more; but when Simon asks for extra, or for string rehearsals or whatever, I don't argue because I know he needs them. The Stravinsky concert we did in 1985 had a lot of extra rehearsals, but it paid off. Not financially, of course – it cost a bomb – but artistically it was a terrific concert. It's no secret that our principal conductor, Tennstedt, has some health problems. I hope he will stay around as long as possible because the orchestra plays wonderfully for him, but Simon is one of the people I would like to think of in the future. Not now, because Birmingham is going so well. But he may reach a plateau with them.

Since John Willan moved to the London Philharmonic, Rattle's records for EMI have been made in collaboration with David Murray, who was previously a music producer for BBC Radio 3. He told me about the typical working methods of Rattle and the CBSO in the studio.

DAVID MURRAY: He comes to a session with an incredibly precise idea of what he wants to do. He'll take suggestions, but more than once I've felt that it's us, the producer and the engineer, who are slowing things up and standing in the way of getting the thing done. The set-up is usually this. For half an hour or so he'll warm up the orchestra and go through a few difficult bits while we balance and check things. Then we will do a test take of a section of the work to see if we agree on balance. Once he's made his comments and we've made our adjustments Simon will record a complete performance of the work, or at least a complete movement. Then he'll come in and listen to that, and people from the orchestra will come in too (which is very different from the usual thing with some orchestras, where mainly wind players who are worried about their solos will come in and listen to a take). Then he'll go back, but he won't just do the bits that didn't work. He'll do another performance. And usually, as with *Petrushka*, that's the one that is the basis of the recording. Then we will do small patches for editing, but it is always better to do those small adjustments on the basis of a full performance rather than trying to stitch the whole thing together from this or that take. He hates that: he wants to get the feeling of a performance.

And does he change things a lot while the recording is happening?

They're mostly minor adjustments rather than anything radical, because remember that the interpretations are already there, and the orchestra now will have done a lot of performances of anything we record. But he is very realistic. He knows what happens at sessions, and when he comes in to listen to final tapes you don't find him asking for some other mythical performance he and the orchestra never actually gave! And that also shows up in the way he runs the sessions. One of the most remarkable things about Simon is his ability to listen critically while he's conducting. Many conductors find this difficult, and because there isn't time to play back everything they rely on the producer. But at the end of a take Simon will tell me what went right or wrong from his point of view, and then will listen to my opinion of what we have to do. And he's absolutely open with the orchestra, so that they know what went well or badly, and he'll expect that, after he's corrected it, it'll go right every time. They get better together all the time and the final 'complete' take is virtually always the master. It was like that with Sibelius 3; we'd done a performance and sorted out the difficult bits, but rather than leave it there Simon suggested we should put all the 'correction' takes back into context by doing another complete performance. And it was by far the best.

So is he realistic in what he asks for from the orchestra?

He's good at pacing them. Sometimes I think he overestimates what they'll be able to do: for *Turangalîla* he initially suggested just four sessions, but I insisted on five because we needed at least half a session for balancing, which is very complicated in that piece. But he knew which bits to do at the start of the session, or early in the morning, when

On his way? At the height of the Falklands crisis, someone suggests a long trip abroad for the young conductor

everyone was relaxed and not too tense. And some movements we actually did on one take, with a couple of patches, because the orchestra was so much at home with it. In Mahler 2 each movement was done as a continuous whole, except for the finale which had to be split before the chorus section. But there too we were building on concerts they'd just done, and there were very few takes. And I must say it was really thrilling, with all the atmosphere of a concert performance; unbelievably exciting. Even the tape editors got worked up about it!

I thought very carefully about the venues for these big recordings, because Warwick, which is our recording base with the orchestra, doesn't have much breathing space for really large works (though the Messiaen was fine there). So for the choral works we went elsewhere: for the Mahler to Watford Town Hall, which I think has turned out sonically marvellous, and for *Gerontius* back to the Great Hall at Birmingham University, which John Willan had used for the Britten *War Requiem*. There are problems in the orchestra hearing itself well enough, because the acoustic is very ambient, but we solved that by putting screens around the orchestra to focus the sound for them, while leaving ourselves with the resonance overhead. That piece we also recorded in very long stretches: for example, the whole of the first section with the tenor, right up to the top B flat. And then when we did the repeat of that, Simon said that just to give it the right atmosphere again, they should play the whole Prelude. And it worked. That's one of the things about him: you may disagree with what he wants to do at first but usually you know in the end he was right.

Does it annoy EMI that now Simon will only record with the CBSO?

I think in the beginning, before my time with EMI, there was a worry about him recording only with Birmingham and not with our other orchestras. That was to do with the perception of the CBSO abroad, and it would certainly have been easier at that time to sell records made by Simon with internationally famous orchestras. But that's changing because the recordings themselves are of such a standard that EMI now has great faith in the orchestra. Furthermore, the orchestra is touring more and is better known abroad. It's another case of Simon being right about the long-term strategy.

How do you plan what to record and how far ahead does that happen?

There was a bit of a hiatus after the change-over of producers for Simon's recordings, but things are better established now. He will suggest things to me, we will discuss them, and then I will put up a scheme which has to go through our various discussions about international repertory. For instance, EMI were at first cautious about *Turangalîla*, because we already had the Previn recording, and it wasn't thought by the marketing people to be a very popular (that is, saleable) proposition. But in the end they decided to go for it and in fact the coincidence of the CBS recording of the same piece with Salonen actually strengthened EMI's resolve to record the work. All the 1986 recordings were pretty big and there were a lot of them, so it's hardly surprising that there were some eyebrows raised in the company about all that in one year.

He now has a definite idea of what he would like to record until 1991, which says something about his commitment to the orchestra. We talked about it, I wrote lots of plans, and then he gave me a quite simple year-by-year scheme: there will be the big Stravinsky ballets, most of the major Debussy and Ravel, Berlioz's *Symphonie fantastique*, and one or two other big things which depend on sponsorship or other support, such as Henze's Seventh Symphony and *Barcarola*, which is just not a commercial proposition for us. We'd love to do the Janáček *Cunning Little Vixen*, and we very much hope to record the Glyndebourne *Porgy and Bess*.

So can he do more or less whatever he wants to do?

Well, no one has *carte blanche*, and there are always the commercial considerations. The marketing men will say what they think will sell where and what won't. But my first priority is to make good records with him.

In June 1987 it was announced that, in a major extension of his exclusive contract with EMI, Rattle would make a further fourteen discs by the end of November 1991, including much of repertoire David Murray mentions above, as well as Mahler's Sixth Symphony and Walton's First.

II

SMALL SCREEN

AUGUST 1986: The Derngate, Northampton, is one of the splendid new halls – there are others in Warwick, Nottingham and Cardiff – which in recent years have completely transformed the regional audience for orchestral music and have made the CBSO's touring activities so much more fruitful. The Birmingham orchestra is regularly heard here: the acoustic is fine, the arrangement of the seats is close and intimate, and the architectural design is striking. The facilities are good.

But today the whole floor of the hall has been cleared, and the paraphernalia of a TV recording session dominates the place: piles of

Only the jacket missing: Rattle rehearsing for a TV programme under the glare of
the cameras

equipment, masses of wires, and production assistants and assistant
producers running everywhere. It looks like chaos, but at the eye of
the storm, producer Barrie Gavin – loyally dressed in a CBSO T-shirt
– maintains his legendary calm, making sure that everything is in
place. The orchestra, with the vocal group Electric Phoenix, is about
to record one of the great avant-garde masterpieces of the post-war
years for a BBC Television documentary: Berio's *Sinfonia*, with all its
complex collage effects, quotations from earlier works and counter-
point between speaking, singing and playing.

I retreat to an upstairs box with Ed Smith and Bob Moore, the
burly, cheerful general manager of the hall, who is taking an intense
interest in the session, and I have a go at following the huge score of
the Berio as they rehearse the first movement. The television operation is a complete mystery to me: there is a continual procession of
discreet acolytes across the back of the hall, checking on this and that.
But then suddenly the cameras begin to wheel and dive. One camera is
steered back and forth across the whole front line of the orchestra,
swooping up and down in the process. Later I ask Barrie Gavin about
the precise significance of this filming method: 'Oh, I just told them to
try whatever they fancied, so that's what they did.'

In a rehearsal break, Electric Phoenix – who have almost made this piece their own property since inheriting it from the Swingle Singers, for whom it was written – are enthusing about Rattle's conducting of the score. 'It's just so clear and precise; you know exactly where you are. I can't imagine the piece has ever been better done,' says Carol Hall. Terry Edwards, the hugely tall director of Electric Phoenix, is almost apocalyptically enthusiastic on the subject: 'I just think we're so lucky to be alive at the same time as Simon Rattle.' Then they disappear to be photographed in their glitzy costumes: Barrie Gavin ponders whether to feature them all in little roundels on the screen when their names are mentioned in the piece. Rattle says something unquotable about not having Berio at the sessions; as usual, he hasn't retired to a secluded conductor's room but is chatting to the singers and taking the chance to look over some publicity photos of himself he's been handed, which seem to puzzle rather than amuse or horrify him.

The trouble with a television session like this is that it will bear absolutely no relation to the finished result in the programme, which at present exists only inside Barrie Gavin's head. 'Simon's talked about the piece: yesterday he said, "I really don't think I've got anything to say about it," and then sat down and talked for half an hour! And we'll have film of Berio in Italy ... It's coming together.'

In the event, Sinfonia is a brilliant piece of exposition. Less idiosyncratic than some of Gavin's other films with Rattle, it has a very simple format: the scene for each movement is set with talk that gives a flavour of the music, using extracts from conversations with Berio (in Italy), Simon Rattle, and Terry Edwards and Judith Rees of Electric Phoenix. Apart from an odd camera angle which almost looks down on the top of Rattle's head (perhaps to accommodate the great height of Terry Edwards) the filming is unfussy, and Rattle is able to discourse on the similarities between Sinfonia and Joyce's Finnegans Wake.

But then when the performance proper begins (and happily, Sinfonia, for all its complexity, is not a long work and so can be broadcast in full) the tricks start: pictures are superimposed; Electric Phoenix is faded into the film of the orchestra; and Rattle is often elided altogether or appears in a corner of the screen. It is a virtuosic piece of mixing and editing, and for once the format faithfully reflects the complexities and contradictions of the music.

Rattle's television work with the CBSO is, if anything, even more remarkable than his recording work. The two major projects which were recorded in 1986 and shown in 1987 both featured contemporary works which would not be a commercial proposition to record on disc, but as the focus for a pair of documentary programmes featuring Rattle they immediately grabbed Barrie Gavin's attention. The first was the Berio, and the second was Hans Werner Henze's Seventh Symphony, of which Rattle and the CBSO gave the British première in July at the Proms in London. Already recorded, and shown in the autumn of 1986, was a series of four BBC2 programmes called *From East to West*, and earlier in the year there was a major documentary on Percy Grainger for Central TV; both were directed by Barrie Gavin.

This is an unprecedented output for a single British orchestra, and there is no doubt that Rattle's exposure in this area – he was featured in colour on the cover of *Radio Times*, with its massive nationwide

Reading the composer's mind: Rattle working with Hans Werner Henze on a television programme about the Seventh Symphony, shown in 1987

sale, when *From East to West* was screened – is a major factor in the orchestra's present success and economic stability. The problem with such work is that it comes and goes and is difficult to rely on: an earlier BBC project devoted to the music of the Second World War evaporated through lack of money (though it did produce two off-shoot programmes, one on Stravinsky's *Symphony in Three Movements* and one on early Britten). But Rattle and the CBSO have now built up a remarkable tally of programmes together, especially in partnership with Barrie Gavin.

It was Humphrey Burton of the BBC, who met Rattle after the John Player Competition, who first realized that the young conductor might be ideal televisual material; he suggested various projects to him though none in the end materialized. One of them was a gargantuan plan by producer Herbert Chappell for a series called *The Glory of Music* to be presented by Rattle. This was to consist of thirteen two-hour programmes of documentary and performance, taking in everything from Gregorian chant to punk rock, interviewing artists, watching them rehearse, and finally showing them perform. But in the end Rattle couldn't face the style of the presentation. The pilot ran: 'The glory of music is the simple fact that we can all share it ... There are very few things that can match the excitement and the sheer thrill of listening to great music. And it's those qualities I want to communicate to you in this new television series.'

One thing Rattle quickly became aware of is that he is not as good talking to the camera as he is talking to someone in a natural interview format. Barrie Gavin is aware of this and yet *From East to West* included an introductory straight-to-camera piece by Rattle which was among the least successful aspects of the whole undertaking. When he is talking freely about pieces which grab his enthusiasm, particularly alongside other people, as he did with Oliver Knussen in a Stravinsky programme, the results are natural and communicative.

The local independent television station in Birmingham, Central TV (formerly ATV), has always been extremely supportive of the CBSO and Rattle and has mounted some major projects. One of his earliest TV films was a documentary for ATV, made very early in the Birmingham period, about the performance of *Porgy and Bess* which the CBSO mounted in 1981. This programme stirred up controversy locally because he was outspoken about certain aspects of the orchestra's work, about how poorly they were paid, and he questioned whether Birmingham really deserved them. Subsequently he has

Planning the shots: Rattle and his wife, Elise Ross, consulting the experts during the filming of *From East to West*, the BBC TV series about the influence of the East on the music of the West, shown in 1986

tended to confine his comments to the works in hand. Outstanding among the Central TV films was a documentary on Elgar which juxtaposed biographers talking about the more elusive aspects of Elgar's personality with some magnificent performances of his music, including Alexander Baillie playing the Cello Concerto.

Among the earliest collaborations with Barrie Gavin was a simple concert relay, recorded in Frankfurt in 1982 during the CBSO European tour, in which Rattle himself introduced the programme of Stravinsky and Rachmaninov. Then there was a film of Weill's *The Seven Deadly Sins*, with Rattle's wife, Ellie, in the leading role, which followed a South Bank Summer Music performance and which was to coincide with the EMI recording. But there were problems. Barrie Gavin later recalled one in a diary of the production: 'A scene in the back of a taxi. Two freelance directors (Derek Bailey and myself) are on our way to the BBC. "What are you doing next?" says Derek. "*The Seven Deadly Sins*," I reply. "So am I," says Derek, "for Granada." General consternation. Each of us goes to our respective production chief to report this coincidence. Neither of us wants a kind of horse-race between the two productions. The BBC and Granada decide that the two productions are totally different in style and concept. We can both go ahead. Like two schoolboys taking an exam, Derek and I keep our eyes henceforward firmly fixed on our own work.'

This was the most adventurous of the Gavin–Rattle collaborations in dramatic terms, but for the next project they attempted something more ambitious musically: a four-part series of performance and discussion about the music of 1911. The programmes were based around two favourite Rattle pieces, Mahler's Tenth Symphony and Sibelius's Fourth, each of which had a programme to itself. The last programme was a straight performance of Mahler's Tenth, but the first was the most ambitious: a panorama of the music of 1911, bringing together all sorts of pieces written in that year, and juxtaposing them with paintings of the period. It was an extremely ingenious programme which captured a good deal of interest, though some felt that the approach was too kaleidoscopic and not sufficiently explanatory.

But the kaleidoscopic approach pleased Barrie Gavin, who set about the next series he conceived with Rattle in the same way. *From East to West*, 'dreamt up in a Chinese restaurant', was an exploration of the impact of the East and its music on Western culture, which grew out of a conversation about Debussy but was quickly extended to include Mahler's Eastern-influenced *Das Lied von der Erde*. That work became the focus of a major documentary with the Mahler scholar Donald Mitchell and a complete performance recorded at the 1985 Proms with Jessye Norman and Jon Vickers.

The most original programme in the series was the first, an uninterrupted sequence of music and images which pointed up all sorts of connections between the music of the East and that of Western composers as diverse as Ravel, Debussy, Steve Reich, Holst, Messiaen, David Matthews, Koechlin and Henry Cowell, returning at the close to Ravel's evocation of *Asie* with which it started.

The second programme was very different: an exploration of the sound-world of Toru Takemitsu, whose music Rattle had performed for the Aldeburgh Festival when Takemitsu was composer-in-residence there. It featured a single work, *The Flock Descends into the Pentagonal Garden*, which Rattle and the CBSO would bring to the Proms in 1987. This was beautifully organized by Gavin into 'thirteen steps around Toru Takemitsu', in which different aspects of his work were matched with the corresponding sections of the piece.

Barrie Gavin's collaboration with Rattle is very close: they have made fifteen programmes together and after Berio and Henze will embark on another, on Berlioz.

BARRIE GAVIN: It's a Mickey Rooney–Judy Garland act, though I won't tell you which is which! 'Let's do the show right here,' that sort of thing. Simon is incredibly practical and he thinks fast. He's good at deciding 'OK, let's do it,' and then getting his players to respond. And he's able to communicate the enthusiasm. He's so stimulating to plan things with, like the first *East to West* programme, where we chipped in with all our favourite pieces and then created the patchwork; that's a very enjoyable aspect of working with him. For television, I also need to have absolute confidence that he'll produce the goods on time. With everything there is riding on it, there's no point having a conductor who says he needs an hour to rehearse and three and a half hours later you're still waiting. Simon is absolutely efficient and he knows exactly what's needed.

One of the most attractive things about him is that he doesn't want to appear centre screen, talking about 'Me and My Music'. He talks very quietly, and like all inexperienced broadcasters looks at anything but the camera. He sounds rather like Neil from *The Young Ones*, apologizing for 'A lot of heavy music'! But he has a gift for the apt metaphor, and his directness with the musicians makes him a marvellous communicator.

One of the other Barrie Gavin programmes shown during 1986, Central TV's film on Percy Grainger, was a superbly made film, with footage for *The Warriors*, for example, which ranged far and wide in its search for visual images to complement Grainger's bizarre music. Rattle's ability to hit on the memorable phrase which sums up the composer under discussion was once again in evidence:

> I think he hated a lot of his most successful music. In fact, I think he hated most of what he did ... He was a firecracker among musicians. Something to do with his temperament made him explode into new ideas and something in him made them self-destruct.
>
> There are certain strands of his personality that are deeply unappealing. Something that was perhaps less unusual at the time but now seems loathsome was his very strong concept of race, the feeling that only blonde, blue-eyed people could be trusted.
>
> Grainger was an enormously practical person. He would re-make his music in any way that would mean it could be performed ... [he had] a concept of elastic scoring that says this piece may be played by any combination, from three instruments up to 300. And it's true, you really can do this.

To a large extent the Gavin–Rattle programmes have begun to tackle the questions raised by Alan Blyth in a *Daily Telegraph* article in March 1986. Blyth suggested that 'Music on television continues to be a baffling affair. Back in the inquiring sixties, the BBC attempted, through Pierre Boulez and others, to turn the medium to music's advantage ... there was an attempt to relate the visual with the aural, and bring them into some kind of harmony, in every sense. That brave experiment has long been forgotten ...' But Blyth noted that 'Simon Rattle made several exceptionally rewarding programmes a year or so back, built around the year 1911. I hope plans to bring him back to the screen haven't been shelved indefinitely. He is the kind of presenter who combines an engaging personality with an inquiring mind and an ability to communicate quite complex ideas easily to the general public ...' The point appears to have been taken enthusiastically by the BBC: under its new Head of Music and Arts, Alan Yentob, Rattle is very much in favour, and it looks as if the extensive exposure Rattle was given in the autumn of 1986 will be continued in the future. Both BBC Enterprises and Central TV sell his programmes abroad, adding to the international reputation of conductor and orchestra.

Banging the gong for the CBSO: Rattle's television exposure has brought his orchestra wide publicity. Here he returns briefly to his first love, percussion playing, to promote the BBC series *From East to West*

Rattle may have turned down an appearance on *Wogan* – 'I had a gut feeling that it just wasn't for me: if only I could tell stories the way André Previn can' – but he is happy to use television to advance the cause of the music in which he believes.

Simon's Inspiring Musical Offerings Naturally
Ripple Across Townhall Terraces Loudly Echoing:
a packed Town Hall, Birmingham, for the CBSO Proms
in 1982, complete with added slogans

Interlude

Rattle on Conductors:

I just don't know what most of my colleagues are up to. Orchestra-building is completely out of fashion, and all that seems interesting to them is giving concerts with lots of different orchestras who are never really going to change. Some of these people cannot be in it for the music. How do you change anything? Or is it just a question of listening to some records and finding out what the orchestra can do, and then steering the most comfortable course between them?

Rattle on the Repertory:

The repertory is in a terrible state. Most conductors, with the exception of someone like Esa-Pekka Salonen, aren't really committed to new music. In London the question is usually 'Have we got time to get through it,' and the answer is usually 'No', so unusual things don't get done. But that doesn't excuse the conductors who are a bloody sight more powerful than I am, who travel the world without doing a scrap of music by living composers. That's the most dangerous thing for our musical culture.

Rattle on Musicians:

What most musicians lack is a sense of the cultural background to what they're doing. It's not their fault: none of that is taught at the colleges, and you can go through those places knowing nothing except how to make your reeds and how to play the notes. It's frightening. They didn't even teach foreign languages at the Academy. And not much proper analysis: Schenker I don't remember being mentioned. But without some knowledge of art and literature and so on it's difficult to make sense of music; one of the things we've tried to do in the television programmes is to provide the beginning of that sort of background, to treat music in an organic way as part of the culture it springs from. But it really needs a lot of hard work, and musicians are playing so much and so hard they don't have that time.

Rattle on Orchestras:

You have to concentrate on what orchestras like to do and make the best of it. I spend a lot of time in Los Angeles getting them to play softer and a lot of time in Birmingham getting them to play louder. But at least I am making a difference. Some orchestras it's hard to change in certain pieces: some things the Cleveland Orchestra always play as if George Szell were still conducting, so much so that I tend to look over my shoulder and say, 'Look, mate, lay off!' If the Philharmonia still plays certain works as if Klemperer were conducting that's scarcely a tribute to those of us who have come after him. But I can understand now the CBSO would have difficulty playing Sibelius 5 for anyone except me. I pity the poor bugger who tries to change it!

Rattle on the Future:

Orchestras have got to change the way they play. The early music movement has made such strides and has taught us so much, yet how many music directors can you think of who are remotely interested in what it has to offer? A conductor like Nikolaus Harnoncourt is absolutely exceptional. I don't think symphony orchestras are going to become extinct or confined to a tiny repertory, but they have got to adapt, playing different music in different ways. And our experience in Birmingham with Haydn, and then the orchestra working with Nick Kraemer on Handel, is that they love it and they love the challenge. The work will diversify, there's no doubt about that.

Conducting isn't all a piece of cake...

Rattle on Learning:

You have to make many, many mistakes. Whether you have to make
as many as I did I don't know. I can remember my incomprehension
at not being able to get what I wanted. I can remember the physical
sensation of it not working. And what you have to learn is that 90 per
cent of it is your problem. The problems for other kinds of young musicians are quite different. At least they can play their instruments.
And gradually they come to musical maturity. For conductors it's the
other way round: your musical maturity, such as it is, is all you have
to protect yourself against your complete incompetence technically!

It is very hard for young conductors and you must have to have this
opportunity to make mistakes. That's why British orchestras, who
almost to a man are contemptuous of young British conductors, are
crippling themselves for the future by not allowing themselves to
work with them. Where are they going to learn? They are people with
things to communicate. But of course faced with opposition and an
obviously ironical attitude from the players, it's hard for them to
communicate anything.

Rattle on Rhythm:

Setting a pulse is so different from just beating in time. I think at first I had a very brittle-izing effect on orchestras, because I was very insistent about rhythm. But you need to feel the pulse, and the more you try to impose rhythm on an orchestra, on the whole, the less you get. One of the major problems I've had with some orchestras is that if you don't get back what you want from them, you feel completely crippled. You can't function. So you have to try other things, to do less. Watching Furtwängler, I've seen him on film, now there is absolute economy of motion. And take a quite different conductor, Rudi Schwarz: he really set a pulse for anyone who cared to notice it. It's an incredibly personal thing, a sense of rhythm.

Rattle rehearsing, December, 1986 (*photos*: Jason Chenai)

Rattle on Motivation:

I could give you any number of untrue answers as to why I conduct, but the real answer is quite simple, I think. It's to do with the fact that I was never happy as a solitary musician, just doing my own thing. That very awful business of being alone with a recalcitrant instrument just wasn't for me. So it had to be with other people, and things like my first blinding experience with Mahler 2 just told me 'That's what I want to do, to make all that happen.' And also, let's face it, compared with violinists or pianists or whoever, conductors do have some of the best repertory there is!

CHAPTER FIVE

'I didn't realize how important it would be to be here'

Birmingham: 1980–6

The CBSO in the period before Simon Rattle arrived was not altogether a happy orchestra. In March 1978, very suddenly, both the general manager, Arthur Baker, and the principal conductor, Louis Frémaux, had walked out, leaving the orchestra without direction. The story of the dispute is murky, and it finally blew up over the question of who should play principal viola in a particular session.

Birmingham past: Adrian Boult, conducting the Birmingham orchestra during the 1920s; behind them, the Town Hall organ of which Thomas Beecham asked the CBSO's leader 'Would it be at all possible to have it removed before the concert?'

Frémaux declared briefly: 'The orchestra refused to accept my direction, so I left.' To this day he has not commented further on the matter. It was more than a matter of one viola player, however. A player who was involved says:

> It was a revolution. The players took matters into their own hands because they didn't think that the orchestral manager had things under control. The diary was looking empty, and we were very discontented with the quality of the work we were getting. Essentially we expressed no confidence in the general manager, and he left. He was closely involved with Frémaux, acted as his agent as well as managing the orchestra, and Frémaux walked out in sympathy. Our relationship with Frémaux hadn't been bad until his last couple of years, and he had improved the orchestra a great deal, but it was never ideal.
>
> We could understand his action but it left us in a very difficult position. However, there was also a major opportunity to rebuild things, with the players more involved in the whole process of management. The chairman ran things in the interim. There was player representation on the board which chose the new general manager, Ed Smith, who appeared out of the mist, as it were. Then we got a new constitution together, in which the players were more involved. [There were already two players on the council of management, but they were excluded from certain items of discussion.] The new set-up gave us a real part in the running of the orchestra. And players were on the subcommittee who advised on the choice of the new principal conductor as well. So if things go wrong now it's pretty much our fault.

The man who took charge of the CBSO during that difficult period, and who still heads its council of management, is the chairman, Birmingham lawyer and former councillor George Jonas.

GEORGE JONAS: I came to Birmingham in 1952, strictly for one year. And I've stayed ever since. I remember going to the CBSO in Birmingham for the first time with Schwarz doing the Beethoven *Choral* Symphony in December 1952. I also heard one of their first London concerts, just after the Festival Hall opened. That was in the George Weldon days and a pretty awful sound they made; it was a poor orchestra. Then I came on the management committee some twenty years ago when I was a member of Birmingham City Council. When the electors gave me up I stayed on the orchestra's council as an elected member. The orchestra was always thought of as something good, and there was a feeling that it had to be kept going, but without any of the sort of enthusiasm which followed once Louis Frémaux had been appointed and which, of course, is even greater now. It was my predecessor as chair-

man, who's now Birmingham's Lord Mayor, who supported Frémaux's appointment, and there was a lot of opposition to it. I
remember I came out of a hospital bed to vote at a crucial meeting.
After Frémaux came things improved: it began to record again; it
became more of a national orchestra.

But it was always a bit of a fight to keep the thing going. There was
no sponsorship; we had to make all sorts of economies, keeping down
the number of extras and so on, but the sticking point with me, and I've
fought for this often, was cutting down the number of players. I always
resisted that violently as a way of saving money and I would have resigned if it had been done. It was proposed several times in the early
years but was never actually carried out.

After Frémaux left relations between the players and the management were truly appalling. We had quite a struggle to bring them
together but in the end we persuaded both sides that it wasn't a good
idea to have a them and us feeling, so we got two orchestra representatives on to the board of directors, as it now is. And that has worked extremely well. But the situation was horrendous with both conductor
and manager leaving at the same time. First of all we appointed Ed
Smith. And then we took a conscious decision about a new conductor:
either we could find someone to succeed Frémaux pretty quickly or we
could ask the sort of man whose diary would already be full for the next
two years. We took the view that we'd already reached a reasonable
standard with Frémaux and we had Erich Schmid as guest conductor.
Even though he wasn't with us all that often he did a remarkable job
and kept things together. So we worked on the new constitution, and
then we formed a small sub-committee to look for a new principal conductor.

Simon was not an obvious choice. We had a long list of conductors
which became a shorter list and was then reduced to two. Ed Smith
knew Simon, it quickly emerged, and felt we had a genius in our midst;
the greatest credit for the appointment must be the fact that Ed kept on
pushing and pushing for it. We certainly felt we were taking a gamble. I
had gone to hear two of Simon's concerts in Liverpool and I thought
they were a total disaster: I later found out he had trouble getting that
orchestra to play for him. But what changed my mind was that he came
to Birmingham with Glyndebourne Touring Opera in 1978 and did
Mozart's *Così*, with the Bournemouth Sinfonietta, which if I may so is
not the greatest orchestra in the world, and that was a revelation. That
was the turning-point for me, and I was then prepared to take the risk.
But what a risk!

I remember when I first met Simon and had lunch with him he made
the point: 'Don't expect me to conduct Beethoven symphonies and all
the great works.' He has a great respect for that music, which is part of
his marvellous modesty. But those things didn't worry us: what we

weren't quite aware of was that Ed was right and we actually did have a genius.

The first concerts he did gave off an incredible, electrifying atmosphere. It was so exciting to see music-making of that sort, and very soon we snapped him up for a longer period. Any doubts we had were very quickly dispelled.

Beresford King-Smith became concerts manager of the CBSO in 1964, and deputy general manager in 1978; in 1987 he was re-designated deputy chief executive:

BERESFORD KING-SMITH: Somebody gave me a document called 'Birmingham and its Civic Managers 1928'. The headings at the front start with Schools, Finance, and so on, and it ends, 'Sewers, Mental Defectives, Cemeteries, City of Birmingham Symphony Orchestra'. So we've moved up a notch since then.

The whole set-up is so different now from the days of Weldon and Schwarz and even Frémaux. Then you had your permanent conductor and if you had a good one you were on a growth trip up, and if you didn't it must have been murder. And we were doing things like the Prom season where we gave five concerts a week for three weeks, and in practice some of them were not very good. It's interesting that now we have such a success with the subscription series that the one thing we have trouble selling out are the Proms. Perhaps people assume they're sold out, or perhaps we've gone too far up the river the other way. And the orchestra is so used to rehearsing extensively that they have a real problem getting a concert on with just one three-hour rehearsal.

One thing which has changed radically is the number of choral society dates that we do, for instance. One of the very serious things in British musical life is that choral societies now can't afford symphony orchestras. And it was in fact rather a nonsense because we did *Messiah*s all over the place which meant that thirty or forty people were sitting at home being paid to do nothing. There are plenty of freelance and chamber orchestras who can do that sort of thing better.

We were also doing split dates, half the orchestra in one place, half in another, up to about three years ago, and I don't think that did the orchestra much good. But one doesn't want to deprive the people in those small towns we visited then. It's a difficult situation. Now we have much more important series of concerts in the new halls in Nottingham and Northampton and Warwick which we do with the full orchestra: and that gives us another problem – the strings are having to play too much.

We played in Nottingham for many years, certainly back to the '50s, regularly twice a year or more to deplorable houses in the terrible old Albert Hall, but now since the Royal Hall has opened and we play there you can't get a ticket for love nor money. It's the same in Cardiff: we used to play in the New Theatre, which was awful. Suddenly there's a new hall, St David's – well run, beautiful acoustic, atmosphere … 'meet you there for a meal' … and it's an exciting place to go. People come out of the woodwork and it's packed. There's no doubt that concert life is being revolutionized and we are part of the revolution.

Orchestral music in Birmingham has a long tradition. But it was essentially as accompaniment to the great local tradition of choral singing that orchestras were first used there. Mendelssohn's *Elijah* and Elgar's *The Dream of Gerontius* are only the most famous of the many works which have been first performed in the Town Hall. There was a Birmingham Festival from 1768 onwards, when a little band of twenty-five accompanied music by Handel. It was with a view to making these triennial festivals 'finer and more perfect than any that have taken place in the kingdom' that the Town Hall was built in 1834. 'The New Room and Organ were opened last Friday; there were 3000 persons in the room, it will seat ab't 5000 & is a splendid room for sound – not the least echo – O how it will appear with 200 of a Band & 250 Chorus Singers,' wrote one player enthusiastically (though the present seating capacity of the Town Hall is now only 1750). From that date onwards the Birmingham Festival did indeed become the grandest of its kind in the land: an orchestra of 147 featured in the 1834 festival when Handel's music was complemented by that of Neukomm and Spohr. Mendelssohn first came in 1837 to direct *St Paul* and play Bach on the organ. The first performance of *Elijah* was in 1846, and by that time the orchestra's strength was around 130. Many rare choral works were performed over the succeeding festivals, directed first by Sir Michael Costa and then by Hans Richter. The première of *The Dream of Gerontius* in 1900 was a famous disaster, performed without sufficient rehearsal by an unconvinced choir and conductor, and a tenor soloist who, as Vaughan Williams nicely put it, sang 'in the correct oratorio manner, with one foot slightly withdrawn'. Nevertheless, the occasion sealed Elgar's strong links with Birmingham.

The first purely orchestral concerts in Birmingham seem to have been given by William Stockley's orchestra from 1873 onwards: in Stockley's Popular Concerts, as they were known, Elgar played among the first violins and some of his pieces were performed there, including the Suite in D in 1888. A Birmingham Symphony Orchestra of seventy players gave its first concert in 1906 under Sir Henry

Wood, and Julian Clifford was its conductor until war broke out. During the war that great orchestral entrepreneur Thomas Beecham stepped in with the New Birmingham Orchestra, but it failed to establish itself. It was not until 1920 that the City of Birmingham Orchestra was formed under the conductor Appelby Matthews, who had gathered together the players by adding strings to the police band of which he was the conductor!

From 1920 the City Council gave the orchestra £1250 a year, making it the first orchestra in Britain to be truly supported by a local authority. Elgar was invited back to give the orchestra's first concert in November 1920: it consisted entirely of his own works. Among early visitors to conduct the orchestra were Granville Bantock, Holst, Vaughan Williams and Sibelius (whose Fourth Symphony had first been performed in the Town Hall back in 1912). But Lyndon Jenkins, the Birmingham critic who, with Beresford King-Smith, knows most about the orchestra's history, writes that 'Financial difficulties soon loomed large and Appelby Matthews was quickly at loggerheads with the committee. By 1923 matters had reached a point where legal proceedings were necessary and though Matthews won his case, he and the orchestra parted company.'

It was clear that a new direction was needed, and the orchestra found it in the young Adrian Boult, who had been conducting the Choral Society in Birmingham following Henry Wood's abrupt departure. Boult recalled in his memoirs: 'It was during this winter season in Birmingham that it became clear that all was not well there, and I very soon sensed that the direction of the orchestra might be offered to me. I didn't need to think it over: fifty concerts in the six winter months with nothing to do in the summer except prepare for the next season was a plan which suited me perfectly.' Among the letters which Boult received to encourage him was one from Granville Bantock which has some resonances today: 'It has long been my dream to make this city our English Weimar, and the prospects for the realization of this idea were never brighter than they are today. Your advent will bring new life and culture into the place...'

Boult's stay in Birmingham from 1924 to 1930 was distinguished by performances of important pieces such as Bartók's *Dance Suite* when it was only a year old, Mahler's Fourth Symphony and *Das Lied von der Erde*, which was then very little known in England. His main problem turned out to be that summer break: '... it was not at all good for the orchestra to split up and go off to the four winds during the summer, and I always dreaded the first few weeks of the season, when root principles had to be re-established and seaside habits unlearned.' Boult modestly said that if ever he wanted to hear a good orchestral concert he took the train to Manchester. Nevertheless, he did much to improve the orchestra to give it permanence. (There is fascinating new information on Boult's Birmingham years in Michael Kennedy's new biography, *Adrian Boult*, Hamish Hamilton, 1987.) But when he was offered the directorship of music of the BBC in 1930, and subsequently the conductorship of its brilliant new symphony orchestra, he could not refuse.

Boult was succeeded by Leslie Heward, who seemed young at thirty-five though he was a decade older than Simon Rattle would be in 1980. Economic stability for the orchestra in this period was helped by the BBC's decision to found a Midland region orchestra in 1935 based on City of Birmingham Orchestra personnel. Not until 1944 was the orchestra placed on a full-time basis, however, and by then Heward had died tragically young, having just accepted the conductorship of the Hallé in Manchester. Lyndon Jenkins says that Heward 'was noted for his complete honesty and integrity: it was nothing for him to stop a performance in the middle and re-start it, saying to his startled listeners, "I'm sorry, we can do better than that."' Felix Weingartner and Nikolai Malko came during his period, and the orchestra began to record. Under Heward's successor, George Weldon, the orchestra became the City of Birmingham Symphony Orchestra, and gave its first London concert. But standards proved hard to maintain in this period, and the best people say of Weldon is that he was 'a tremendously hard worker' who did 'frankly popular programmes'.

Rudolf Schwarz became conductor in 1952: he had rebuilt the Bournemouth Orchestra after the war, and was much respected by musicians (including, incidentally, Simon Rattle, who has the highest opinon of his musicianship), but he was less popular with the public, who stayed away from his concerts – all the more disappointing as the repertory he included was more interesting than Weldon's. But it was clear that a new force was needed in Birmingham to restore the slipping attendance figures, and when Schwarz was appointed to the BBC Symphony Orchestra in 1957 the management lighted on the Polish composer and conductor Andrzej Panufnik, who had arrived in the West and needed a stable base for his operations.

In his newly published memoirs, *Composing Myself* (Methuen,

1987), Panufnik has some entertaining things to say about his experiences in Birmingham. 'The committee had suggested that my first task would be to improve playing standards in Birmingham. The string sections especially lacked precision and produced a poor sound quality. Spoilt perhaps by my experiences with great orchestras such as the Berlin Philharmonic, L'Orchestre National in Paris, the LSO, RPO and Philharmonia in London, I was determined to make use of the potential talent in Birmingham and concentrate on bringing the playing up to the international standards of which they were fully capable.' Unfortunately Panufnik fell foul of the leader, who would not cooperate. 'The atmosphere during rehearsals became unbearable and I was often frustrated in my struggle to improve the quality of our performances.' This culminated in a battle which resulted in the leader's removal at the end of Panufnik's first season, and though he had a much happier second season and felt he was achieving something, the burden of the post prevented him having enough time for composition and he decided not to accept a third season. Among the presents the players gave him on departure was a blank sheet of unused manuscript paper, with good wishes for his continuing success as a composer.

Once again Birmingham had problems finding a successor, and Sir Adrian Boult at seventy returned for a year before Hugo Rignold came from the Liverpool Philharmonic. By this time the orchestra's strength was up to eighty-eight and Rignold made some strides in training them. His concerts were apparently not much enjoyed ('It's a shame to have to say it, but in those years we went when there were guest conductors,' said one regular attender); nevertheless, the orchestra certainly improved during Rignold's eight years. It was ripe for real development when in 1968 Louis Frémaux was chosen as the next principal conductor. Under him the orchestra improved vastly, went back to the recording studio and made some splendid recordings of French music. Simon Rattle is the first to agree that Frémaux was the decisive force in improving the orchestra, and that it was only the level to which he had brought it that made possible Rattle's job of improving it still further.

One of the most discerning local observers of the orchestra for many years has been the critic Lyndon Jenkins:

LYNDON JENKINS: The orchestra played very well for Frémaux and he worked tremendously hard for them. He did sixty concerts a year

and was at all the auditions: he auditioned all the chorus members too
for the new CBSO chorus. It wasn't just French music he was good at:
Romantic symphonies by Dvořák, Schumann and Tchaikovsky were
excellent and he had an affinity for Shostakovich, Walton and Britten.
It's perhaps not generally known that he was to have recorded the Britten *War Requiem* in 1978, but left before that happened. Among the
recordings the Saint-Saëns Organ Symphony, of course, and the Berlioz
Requiem were outstanding. He was one of the old-style permanent conductors, and as I wrote when he left, 'whatever the circumstances of his
going he was the man who raised the CBSO to the highest point of
prestige in its history to date'.

Simon Rattle's relationship with the City of Birmingham Symphony
Orchestra began in May 1976 in the unlikely surroundings of Oxford
Town Hall, with an unlikely programme consisting entirely of Beethoven, in the unlikely context of the English Bach Festival. The director of the festival, Lina Lalandi, had a young pianist she wanted to
present, Cyprien Katsaris, and with an infallible nose for new talent
which has marked her festival for more than twenty years, she
thought she would present Simon Rattle as conductor 'and together
the conductor and soloist would be younger than I was!' The concert
went well, and Rattle now remembers it as a surprisingly positive experience in view of its being a programme he should never have
agreed to conduct. Others recall that at the time he was worried by
the orchestra and found them a little stand-offish, but that the actual
performance was a success.

He was asked back by them the following year to do two more
dates away from their home base, in Cheltenham and Newcastle, but
it was not until December 1978 that he conducted them in Birmingham in a concert that included Nielsen's Fourth Symphony, and by
then the crisis of Frémaux's departure had overtaken the orchestra. It
was, as Rattle recalls, 'my audition concert':

SIMON RATTLE: I remember the moment when Ed Smith was going
to Birmingham from Liverpool and I knew they were without a conductor, and I said to him, 'I really want to do that job.' I can't believe I did
that. But I told him that if he wanted to work with me I would like to do
it. For some reason I had a very good feeling about it and thought it
would be possible. I'd done Shostakovich 10 with them and that had
been a lovely experience. It all just felt right. I didn't think I would get
the job, but I knew that with Ed there we would be on the same wave-
length. We were very inexperienced, but we could get it to work. I'm

sure I didn't think at the time it would become what it has: I didn't realize how important it would be to be here until I got here.

Rattle's appointment was due to be announced in Birmingham on 2 July 1979. But on 22 June the *Birmingham Post* published the story in advance under the front-page banner headline 'NEW CONDUCTOR HERALDS CBSO HARMONY'. 'After months of debate, the committee

CBSO — change of emphasis

B POST 20·11·79

From Mr. Edward Smith, General Manager, City of Birmingham Symphony Orchestra.

Sir, — I feel I must allay the fears which seem to be growing in people's minds about Simon Rattle's musical likes and dislikes. Please don't imagine that Mozart, Beethoven, Brahms and Tchaikovsky disappear from programmes to happen very audience. To dismiss as worthless stupid and I am sure Mr Anyone

formances of Mozart's *Cosi fan Tutte* at the Hippodrome last year or his recent performances of Haydn's *La Fedelta Premiata* with Glyndebourne Touring Opera will realise that he has a deep love and great respect for this music.

What, I am afraid, we tend to forget is that the twentieth century is now 80 years old

From the work of Pierre Boulez (left) to the genius of Mozart (right) . . . the range that the new principal conductor hopes the CBSO will span

'I do consider it important that an orchestra should have a repertoire of pieces from all over the place'

HE IS 24 years old, sports a shock of black curly hair, wears a striped rugby jersey and admits to t

In January Simon Rattle will come to Birmingham to conduct a Mahler . . .

conductor heralds CBSO harmony

Birmingham Post Exclusive

Simon Rattle — one of Britain's most successful young musicians — is to take over as principal conductor of the troubled City of Birmingham Symphony Orchestra.

After months of debate, a special committee of the orchestra has chosen Mr. Rattle, aged 24, for the prized post abruptly vacated by M. Louis Fremaux last year. The orchestra's full council of management is to ratify the appointment on Monday afternoon.

Meteoric rise

The decision was not due to be announced until July 2 and last night officers of the CBSO declined to comment.

Mr. Rattle has had a meteoric rise to fame since he left school in Liverpool seven years ago. While still a student he studied under the top international conductor Pierre Boulez and was already conducting major works.

 . . .erse headlines about him which say "Whizzkid to call the tune." His career is invariably described as "meteoric" and his future is "filled with potential."

When he was appointed to be principal conductor of the City of Birmingham Symphony Orchestra, the choice was described as "exciting" and "challenging."

His progress to date tends to be littered with claims to being "the youngest" — the youngest conductor at . . .

What BARRIE GRAYSON, the Post's Music Critic, had to say on October 31, last year . . . Simon Rattle is one of the most exciting conducting talents to emerge in recent years.

His big break came when he won the Bournemouth John Player International Conductors' Competition at the age of 19. The prize was helping to conduct the Bournemouth Symphony Orchestra.

In November 1976 he became the BBC's youngest assistant conductor when he was appointed assistant conductor with the BBC Scottish Symphony Orchestra at the age of 21.

He is well known for his interest in contemporary music and Birmingham audiences should expect to hear some unconventional pieces.

Mr. Rattle, who has conducted at Birmingham before, is expected to take up his post for the start of the 1980/81 season in September next year. Last night he was not available for comment.

His appointment follows months of speculation after the sudden departure

of M. Fremaux. He resigned in March last year after a dispute between members of the orchestra and Mr. Arthur Baker, who was the orchestra's general manager and also M. Fremaux's agent, which led to Mr. Baker's contract being ended.

M. Fremaux asked to be released from his contract which was not due to expire until August this year. He said at the time: "The orchestra determined they could not accept my direction." This referred to who should be principal viola at a concert.

The search then began for a new conductor and Mr. Erich Schmid, a Swiss conductor, aged 71, agreed to step in at the last minute to conduct the CBSO Beethoven Festival in May. He was later appointed associate conductor.

The Incorporated Society of Musicians has been pressing for an Englishman to be appointed.

Last night the secretary of the Birmingham centre, Mrs. Margaret Handford, said on being told of the appointment: "Mr Rattle is a very lucky man to get control of the orchestra at such a young age. But he is extremely good, very outstanding and promising and I am very glad it is an Englishman who has got the post. It will be a shot in the arm for the CBSO."

First rank

BARRIE GRAYSON, Birmingham Post Music Critic, writes: Mr. Rattle has a talent and flair which has led to a meteoric rise as a conductor of the first rank and has the musical world at his feet. That this young conductor, one of the most exciting to emerge in recent years, should take this position, is a compliment to the CBSO's stature.

In October last year I advocated the policy of appointing a British conductor, not with any great expectations. Now there is the chance to see whether our faith in our native product is justified.

 . . . . "I know of a couple of organisations which are facing bankruptcy and extinction because of the burden of V.A.T. Mrs Thatcher promised it would be compensated by generous tax concessions for people who put their money into the arts but that has not happened."

Clearly, it's a subject that arouses a certain heated passion in him though he is not what you would describe as an aggressively political person.

But, somehow, conversations with Simon Rattle seem to lead back to the question of age — or, in his case, the lack of it.

Born in Liverpool, he studied piano and percussion as a child. At 16 he was awarded a scholarship at the Royal Academy of Music. He studied conducting under Pierre Boulez and won a . . .

Mr. Simon Rattle . . . a meteoric rise to fame and now the task of principal conductor of the CBSO.

What makes Rattle tick

Baby Rattle comes to Birmingham: the press announces his arrival

of the orchestra has chosen Mr Rattle, 24, for the prized post abruptly vacated by M. Louis Frémaux last year. The orchestra's full council of management is expected to ratify the appointment on Monday afternoon.' Barrie Grayson, the *Post* music critic, who had previously hailed Rattle as 'one of the most exciting conducting talents to emerge in recent years', commented: 'That this young conductor should take this position is a compliment to the CBSO's stature.'

Rattle was introduced to the press on 2 July as planned, and said, 'It is my intention to promote mixed programmes. We have eighty years of music which still needs exploring. I want to establish a sense of musical adventure. Even London concerts, returning time and again to the established classical war-horses, do not attract new audiences.' Predictably these remarks caused some alarm among those who imagined that Rattle was going to throw out the classics altogether, and there was anxious comment in the local press. Ed Smith found it necessary to write to the *Birmingham Post* with a cooling letter: 'I feel I must allay the fears which seem to be growing in people's minds about Simon Rattle's musical likes and dislikes. Please don't imagine that Mozart, Beethoven, Brahms and Tchaikovsky are going to disappear from CBSO programmes. If we allowed that to happen we would naturally very quickly see our audiences diminishing. To dismiss these composers as worthless would be both stupid and arrogant and I am sure Mr Rattle is neither ... What I am afraid we tend to forget is that the twentieth century is now eighty years old and its composers include Mahler, Sibelius, Elgar, Ravel, Rachmaninov and Stravinsky, all of which will feature in Mr Rattle's programmes for his first season...'

For his part, Rattle defused the row in a subsequent interview in the *Sunday Mercury*: 'It's strange what people think they hear. Perhaps I should have said more clearly that at the age of ten I found it difficult to appreciate Mozart, just as a child finds it difficult to grasp Shakespeare. I did my O levels when I was fourteen but how are you supposed to understand plays like *King Lear* at that age? These things come later and so it was with music. Now I revere Mozart above all the others.' He took the opportunity to praise the orchestra as 'one of the finest in the country', and added 'both the orchestra and the management are democratic in their outlook and the set-up is perfect. Louis Frémaux brought the orchestra up to a great height and if it does not go on getting better the only person to blame is me!'

Rattle's relationship with the orchestra was sealed in a notably successful series of performances of Mahler's Tenth Symphony in early 1980, prior to his recording the work with the Bournemouth Symphony Orchestra. He began his tenure as principal conductor in September 1980 with everything to gain but, arguably, quite a bit to lose if it all went wrong.

* * *

Before taking up the new post there was an equally major landmark in Rattle's life: in September 1980 he was married at Finsbury Town Hall to Elise Ross, the singer, composer and expert in the music of the Italian avant-garde, whom he had met when she was singing in an opera by John Tavener at the Bath Festival some years earlier. She had already had a major influence on his musical thinking and was often to appear with him on the concert and operatic stage. Rattle moved from the friendly chaos of a flat in Manor House, on the Marylebone Road, to a small Georgian terraced house in Islington, appropriately enough just off Liverpool Road.

Rattle had also committed himself, before the CBSO post was finalized, to taking a long-promised break from conducting in 1980–81 to study literature at Oxford for a year ('It's hard concentrating on Joyce on the train to Scotland with beer cans flying around me,' as he put it). The CBSO situation rather compromised that: he kept the terms free for study, making only exceptional appearances during them (for instance, a Royal Concert in the autumn of 1980 with the CBSO, and a last-minute engagement in Los Angeles to replace Giulini in Shostakovich's Fourteenth Symphony the following April), but the holidays were packed with activity as a result, and he often travelled up to Birmingham to see how the orchestra was progressing in his absence. In all, though Rattle enjoyed the study, it wasn't quite the year away from it all that he was envisaging, and he says that another sabbatical is needed soon (one is planned for the middle of 1988).

* * *

In the seven seasons during which Rattle has been guiding the CBSO the principle in planning concerts with Ed Smith has always been to create outstanding musical events, and to programme works which would advance the orchestra's learning process. Looking back on the seasons in Birmingham provides an indication of how far the plan has succeeded (the following lists do not include CBSO concerts with

guest conductors, or Rattle's out-of-town and festival dates, when the
programmes were normally based around those for Birmingham):

1980–1

Janáček	*Sinfonietta*
Rachmaninov	Piano Concerto No. 3 (Philip Fowke)
Sibelius	Symphony No. 5
Boulez	*Rituel in memoriam Bruno Maderna*
Mahler	Symphony No. 2 (Alison Hargan, Alfreda Hodgson)
Dvořák	Cello Concerto (Lynn Harrell)
Stravinsky	*Symphonies of Wind Instruments*
Elgar	*Enigma Variations*
Beethoven	Overture, *Leonora* No. 3
Mendelssohn	Violin Concerto (Mayumi Fujikawa)
Britten	*Variations on a Theme of Frank Bridge*
Ravel	Suite, *Daphnis and Chloë*, No. 2
Haydn	Symphony No. 60
Mussorgsky	*Night on the Bare Mountain*
Janáček	*Glagolitic Mass* (Felicity Palmer, Ameral Gunson, John Mitchinson, Malcolm King)
Beethoven	Violin Concerto (Stoika Milanova)
Rachmaninov	Symphony No. 2
Weill	*The Seven Deadly Sins* (Elise Ross)
Sibelius	Symphony No. 2
Delius	*Brigg Fair*
Beethoven	Piano Concerto No. 4 (Paul Crossley)
Stravinsky	*Petrushka*
Fauré	Suite, *Pelléas et Mélisande*
Mozart	Piano Concerto in C minor K491 (Stephen Bishop-Kovacevich)
Schumann	Symphony No. 2

SIMON RATTLE: Ed and I knew absolutely nothing about training
orchestras and what they needed. What we planned at first was affected
by what we had learnt in Liverpool, though you could scarcely find a
more different orchestra from Liverpool than Birmingham. It was only
when I got there that I realized how desperate they were to work. The
whole business of re-establishing a style was vital because that had all
slipped. They wanted to be told how to do things and work at things. I

'The whole business of re-establishing a style was vital': Rattle in rehearsal at Birmingham

remember Felix [Kok, the leader] saying that if he asked them to play things in the same part of the bow they would laugh and ask why. This was all a long struggle, but the attitude is transformed now.

Ed allowed me to have a week of rehearsals before the first concert, and I think they reached every downbeat before I did! We got a lot out of our systems in that period, and there was immediately a feeling of achieving something. For the Boulez *Rituel* we had to do a lot of sectional rehearsal, and that helped such a lot; you met people face to face and assembled a piece from the beginning. You built up trust in that way.

What I wanted to do was to conduct the pieces I knew very well, and which could develop the orchestra and me together. *Rituel* was an exception because that was a recent piece and a dramatic gesture for the start of the season. All the other works were my showpieces: Sibelius 5 and Rachmaninov with Philip Fowke – that had been my first Liverpool concert; Janáček and Elgar I'd done in Los Angeles; Mahler 2 I had done a lot already; and so on. These were things with which I could really work the orchestra and would show us in the best possible light. The Sibelius was terribly important because I think Ed and I had already planned that we would do all the symphonies and would be living with this music. The *Frank Bridge Variations* – they made the strings work and work – and the Dvořák Cello Concerto too were such a help in just working out how to play.

One of the things we instigated in the first year was that we would have rehearsals with just the principal string players, and work on bowings and marking the parts: that hadn't been thought of as something that was important. And in spite of all the problems it worked: I remember doing the Britten on no rehearsal at all a few weeks after we'd learnt it in a church somewhere when the instrument van had broken down. And they pulled it off. Mahler 2 was the highlight. We took it down to London as well but the one I remember was when we did it first in Leeds: players came up and said that was the best concert they'd done for years and years, and it certainly felt like it.

ED SMITH: We will never know what would have happened if we hadn't changed a lot of things all in the very first year. We had our new conductor, but we also changed our publicity from the rather beautifully produced syllabus one had to buy to the sort of free broadsheet which everyone does now. And we much increased our subscription marketing: we used to have about 300 subscribers to our Thursday series and it was received opinion that there were only 300 people in Birmingham who would be prepared to commit themselves to a weekly concert. So the marketing manager, Julianna Szekely, and I were determined to turn that on its head and really go out aggressively to get the committed regular subscriber. We changed the pattern of the concerts from a weekly Thursday series to a fortnightly Tuesday and Thursday series, so for all the people who for decades had not been able to come on a Thursday there was a chance to attend. Those things all happened in 1980, and it's difficult to disentangle them, but together they worked. The rise in attendances was startling:

Series	1978–9	1979–80	1980–81	1981–2	1982–3	1983–4	1984–5	1985–6
Tuesday	–	–	81%	88%	78%	95%	97%	96%
Wednesday	–	–	–	–	–	–	–	97%
Thursday	62%	75%	96%	94%	95%	96%	98%	98%
Saturday	60%	83%	90%	80%	85%	95%	93%	98%
CBSO Proms	70%	77%	91%	78%	85%	85%	86%	77%

Looking back on it now, it is clear that the success of Rattle's first few concerts with the orchestra was crucial to the whole relationship. Morale soared, and the concerts were events of a kind that fully justified the risks inherent in the appointment. They were not, perhaps, fully finished events, but they had a raw energy and commitment which created great excitement in Birmingham. The reviews were uniformly esctatic: under the headline 'GAMBLE PAYS OFF', Lyndon Jenkins reported for *Classical Music* that the concerts 'have provoked an extraordinarily favourable reaction both in the city and elsewhere, and while this was in one way tinged with relief that an exciting gamble was paying off so quickly, there is no doubt that enthusiasm was extensively justified on musical grounds. In four wide-ranging programmes [Rattle's] rapport with orchestra and chorus seemed complete, and while not everything he did reached the same level the performances of Sibelius's Fifth Symphony and in particular Mahler's Second displayed an astonishing maturity that held the promise of stimulating days ahead.' Jenkins was also impressed by Rattle's concerts in the second half of the season, though never uncritically so: 'his grasp of the scale and idiom of Rachmaninov's Second Symphony was so satisfying it was easy to forgive him a cheap trick or two, and he illuminated many points of interest in Beethoven's Violin Concerto...'

Kenneth Loveland wrote in the *South Wales Argus*: 'When someone makes the impact on a nation's music that Simon Rattle has in so short a time, there exists a danger that he will be dismissed as a whizz-kid. The depths his interpretations already plumb, the sincerity of his approach and his evidently ingrained musicality should be the answer. Neither whizz nor kid ... Birmingham is in for exciting times.' Just a month later Rattle and the CBSO took Mahler's Second Symphony to London, pairing it this time with Szymanowski's *Stabat Mater*. In the *Financial Times*, David Murray felt that Rattle's interpretation of the Mahler was 'as yet too quick, too impatient to pounce, for the visionary scope of the work to be fully rendered. But it gripped the attention brilliantly.' And Christopher Grier in the London *Standard*, observing how the 'playing, the singing, the conducting and the choice of programme were alike of the first order', added 'I don't mean that the Berlin Philharmonic should immediately make way for the CBSO, but these Birmingham instrumentalists had not only been impeccably rehearsed but sounded excitingly alert and responsive.' This was just the sort of comment the orchestra needed at that time.

By the summer of 1981, when Rattle brought the CBSO to the Proms for the first time, their relationship was already fixed in the minds of the critics as something potentially fruitful. In *The Times*, Paul Griffiths wrote: 'Simon Rattle has made no secret of his intention to bring the CBSO up into the first division. Already his programming puts many of the London orchestras to shame with its daring abundance of twentieth-century works, and last night, at the end of his first year with the orchestra, he brought them to the Proms to show what wholly magnificent standards they are achieving together.'

The summer also saw the first year of Rattle's tenure as artistic director of South Bank Summer Music season in London, the Greater London Council's answer to the Proms, which brought small-scale music to the halls on the South Bank. Andrew Clements wrote in the *New Statesman* that 'At the moment Simon Rattle seems to be the answer to every jaded orchestral manager's prayers, revitalizing anything he turns his baton to. But his appointment as artistic director of the GLC's South Bank Summer Music was nevertheless unexpected; what had settled into a comfortable and middle-of-the-road fortnight of chamber music promises to have many of its conventions shattered' – as indeed it did, for Rattle introduced a larger proportion of contemporary and twentieth-century works and more orchestral concerts, featuring the CBSO, than in previous years. Among the highlights of this first season with the CBSO was a concert performance of Gershwin's *Porgy and Bess*, subsequently brought to Birmingham.

From Rattle's first seasons in Birmingham, the CBSO Chorus has played a major
part in the concert and recording work, taking part in such highlights as
Janáček's *Glagolitic Mass*, Britten's *War Requiem* and most recently Mahler's
Second Symphony and Elgar's *The Dream of Gerontius*. The chorus master next
to Rattle is Simon Halsey.

Everything had gone sensationally well with the CBSO in that first
season, and before the new season opened in the autumn there was an
announcement that Rattle had signed a new contract as principal conductor for at least another five years. 'We had a marvellous season
last year and the spirit of Simon Rattle was responsible for it. We are
absolutely delighted that he will be staying with us,' commented
George Jonas. But probably even he did not realize for how long
Rattle would actually stay.

The second season's programmes were still more wide-ranging:

1981–2

Haydn	Symphony No. 95
Enescu	*Romanian Rhapsody* No. 1
Elgar	Symphony No. 1
Gershwin	*Porgy and Bess* (Willard White, Laverne Williams, etc.)

Ravel	*Mother Goose*
Mozart	Piano Concerto in B flat K 450 (Imogen Cooper)
Brahms	Symphony No. 2
Mozart	Symphony No. 38
Messiaen	*Turangalîla Symphony* (Peter Donohoe, Jeanne Loriod)
Mussorgsky	Prelude, *Khovanshchina*
Shostakovich	Violin Concerto No. 1 (Ida Haendel)
Stravinsky	*The Rite of Spring*
Berlioz	Overture, *Roman Carnival*
Debussy	*Danse sacrée et danse profane* (Robert Johnston)
Beethoven	Piano Concerto No. 2 (Alfred Brendel)
Sibelius	Symphony No. 4
Britten	*War Requiem* (Ameral Gunson, Ian Caley, Thomas Hemsley)
Haydn	Symphony No. 22
Strauss	Oboe Concerto (Heinz Holliger)
Lutoslawski	Concerto for oboe and harp (Heinz and Ursula Holliger)
Beethoven	Symphony No. 4
Britten	*Sea Interludes* and *Passacaglia* from *Peter Grimes*
Mahler	*Das Lied von der Erde* (Alfreda Hodgson, John Mitchinson)
Dvořák	Overture, *Carnaval*
Mozart	Piano Concerto in B flat K 595 (Tamás Vásáry)
Sibelius	Symphony No. 6
Strauss	Suite, *Der Rosenkavalier*
Wagner	Prelude and *Liebestod* from *Tristan und Isolde*
Berg	Three fragments from *Wozzeck* (Elise Ross)
Mahler	Symphony No. 1
Britten	*Canadian Carnival*
Bartók	Violin Concerto (Iona Brown)
Rachmaninov	*Three Symphonic Dances*

SIMON RATTLE: Ed and I had so many ideas. Many of the things we wanted to do from the very beginning we've not got round to yet: the Liszt *Faust Symphony* still hasn't happened. One would think that during a season we could fit in everything, but it just wasn't true. And especially as we went on, we found the orchestra really needed more rehearsals and I needed to work more with them. They seemed happy enough rehearsing more, though I'm sure some of them were absolutely miserable. But the problem was also to find guest conductors who are actually willing to rehearse the orchestra and make good use of the time. And who are good enough to change the orchestra. I soon found out the difference between coming back to the orchestra after I'd been away for a time, and coming back to them when in a space of three weeks they'd had Jimmy Conlon, Paavo Berglund and Kurt Sanderling.

What Ed and I did was to aim for one or two major contemporary pieces each season; that was a long-term plan, and we had to grapple with what was important. It was very clear that we could choose only what we believed was the very greatest of this music. So that was *Turangalîla* in this season: the work we did on that piece ... and the response! We tended to do these big pieces near the start of the season, because we had extra rehearsal time. Ed found it very difficult to accept at first how much rehearsal I needed, but for the orchestra to put standard repertory together was very difficult. We had a difficult time with *The Rite of Spring* this season, because we missed one rehearsal with a problem over the Town Hall and I thought they knew it well and I knew it well. But we didn't have time to get it right as I felt I had in Scotland by building up each chord from the bottom and then really putting the punch on top; I know we will get it right next time.

One thing I had to guard against in all these designs to get the orchestra to play well, and this is something I discussed a lot with Mark Elder [music director of the English National Opera], is that you so want the orchestra to be well thought of that sometimes you adapt the way you conduct towards making that happen, making things easier for them. The trouble is that it might be temporarily easier for them, but you don't build up, you don't take the risks.

The Rachmaninov *Symphonic Dances* at the end of the season were very important. If I had to specify a work which created the orchestra's sound as it is now then it would be those pieces. All round this time was very fruitful, and really cemented us together: I think they had almost unrealistic expectations of what we could achieve. We were doing such hard pieces: I remember very clearly rehearsing Berlioz's *Beatrice and Benedict* for that year's South Bank Summer Music and thinking that sooner or later there was going to come a crunch and we would have to talk about standards and it would be a problem. But that didn't arise until after the climax of this first period, which was the European Tour in October '82; that was marvellous and we hit new peaks in spite of being very tired.

An impression of Rattle's success with the orchestra this season can be found in some remarks by the players quoted by the press in 1981. 'Simon Rattle is 100 per cent honest. He is a complete professional,' said one player. 'He is simply a brilliant young man. He is completely committed and lets nothing stand in the way of the music...' 'His ability to hold complete scores in his head is absolutely phenomenal.'

Lyndon Jenkins's summary of the early part of the season for *Classical Music* praised the Sibelius 4: '...not only did he assess its size and scale very accurately but he also managed to reveal the toughness of the argument and the passion behind the spareness. This outshone the success that he had with Stravinsky's *Rite* and Messiaen's *Turangalîla*, both of which predictably found him in his element, and certainly eclipsed other symphonic scores by Elgar and Brahms which were nowhere near in the same exalted class.' Jenkins regularly criticized what he saw as weaker performances of the classical and some of the Romantic repertory, and felt that the Britten *War Requiem* was under-prepared: it preceded the recording by a couple of months and was performed with a different team of soloists. Later, Jenkins felt, Rattle 'still seemed a little unsure as to how he wanted Beethoven's Fourth to go', but thought Sibelius's Sixth 'admirably authentic-sounding'.

For the Henry Wood Proms in London in 1982, Rattle revived *Turangalîla*, to which, the *Financial Times* reported, 'the Birmingham orchestra responded with great enthusiasm and no little virtuosity'. Then there was Berlioz's *Beatrice and Benedict* for South Bank Summer Music, which the *Daily Telegraph* praised for its 'refreshingly alert, supple and graphically etched playing', and the *Financial Times* for its 'verve and buoyancy'. Then they worked hard towards the coming climax – the European tour – and the beginning of their third season.

1982–3

Mozart	Serenade for thirteen wind instruments
Sibelius	Symphony No. 1
Stravinsky	*Symphonies of Wind Instruments*
Stravinsky	*Apollo Musagetes*
Stravinsky	*Petrushka*
Knussen	Symphony No. 3
Mozart	*Sinfonia concertante* for violin and viola (Mayumi Fujikawa, Nobuko Imai)
Brahms	Symphony No. 2
Haydn	*The Creation* (Margaret Marshall, Philip Langridge, Stafford Dean)

'We were really getting somewhere': CBSO seasons in the 1980s

Sibelius	Symphony No. 7
Walton	Cello Concerto (Yo-Yo Ma)
Donizetti	Concertino for cor anglais (Peter Walden)
Mozart	Symphony No. 41
Holloway	*Clarissa* Symphony (première; Eilene Hannan, John Mitchinson)
Beethoven	Symphony No. 3
Debussy	*L'Après-midi d'un faune*
Sibelius	Symphony No. 3
Dvořák	Cello Concerto (Lynn Harrell)
Britten	*Sinfonia da Requiem*
Mahler	Symphony No. 10
Weill	Suite, *The Threepenny Opera*
Strauss	*Four Last Songs* (Helena Döse)
Sibelius	*Luonnotar*
Debussy	*La Mer*
Beethoven	Piano Concerto No. 4 (Emanuel Ax)
Ravel	*Daphnis and Chloë* (complete)
Stravinsky	*Scherzo à la russe*
Prokofiev	Piano Concerto No. 3 (Janis Vakarelis)

The European tour in October took the orchestra to Holland for three concerts, then to Bratislava, then to Vienna for one concert, and then for three in Frankfurt. All the programmes were demanding, and the repertory included Oliver Knussen's Third Symphony, Brahms's Second, Rachmaninov's *Symphonic Dances* and several Stravinsky works. Rattle was already well known in Holland because of his connections with the Rotterdam Philharmonic, and the concerts were full. The new hall in The Hague proved exceptionally difficult for the musicians (offering some lessons to be learned in the design of Birmingham's new hall), but in Amsterdam's Concertgebouw everything sounded much better. The final concert in Rotterdam was very well received, and the Dutch critics commented that they could see why Rattle had turned down the offer of the post of principal conductor in Rotterdam when 'the Birmingham ensemble is an excellent orchestra which gives the young conductor a permanent chance of demonstrating his ability on the British music scene'. Another wrote: 'It is difficult to see how Rattle can produce such exquisite clarity in every composition. Nothing is left to chance, everything is given great consideration and is expertly carried out by the English orchestra.'

There were problems getting to and from Bratislava because of border troubles, and the concert there started late, but it was rapturously received. In Vienna an all-Stravinsky programme was part of the Stravinsky Festival in the Konzerthaus, and the warmth of the reception led to an unexpected encore: as someone noted, it was probably the first time that Delius had been heard in a Stravinsky Festival. The concert in Frankfurt took place in the studios of Hesse Radio, consisting of Knussen, Rachmaninov and Stravinsky, and that was attended by a large contingent of City Council representatives from Birmingham. The Frankfurt concert provoked a fine review in the *Frankfurter Allgemeine Zeitung*:

> The generally accepted notion that outside London is musically provincial is fostered consciously or otherwise by the media and on occasion by the record industry ... A minor flutter was caused some time ago by the news that EMI had entrusted Mahler's Tenth to the Bournemouth Orchestra. The outcome was a pleasant surprise. Many people who experienced the CBSO the other day may well have come to a similar conclusion. A well-tuned body of musicians, lacking in nothing except perhaps a reputation. The orchestra has throughout its sections musicians of the highest calibre and ability, who are capable of transforming these qualities into an unmistakable sound of their own. The same could certainly be said of the conductor, a highly talented orchestral trainer with the gift of formulating his very complicated interpretational intentions clearly, and transforming them convincingly into sound...

No one could doubt the boost in morale which the tour had provided: as Lyndon Jenkins, who accompanied the orchestra for the *Birmingham Post*, noted: 'The overriding impression is that we have been listening to a different CBSO from the one we hear at home: this has nothing to do with playing standards, but everything to do with locations. Put straightforwardly, the orchestra sounds good at home; this weekend, in halls with good acoustics, it has sounded superb.'

The return to Birmingham for the rest of the 1982-3 season was bound to come as an anticlimax but it proved more painful than had been expected; several matters came to a head.

SIMON RATTLE: This was one of the great hard times. It was the point where after the euphoria of the tour we came back to earth with a bump. We made the first changes, seemingly simple things like re-seating the first violins. Until then the relationship had been ludicrously sunny, but now things came out in the open. It was the day after the performance of *The Creation* that it all blew up. We insisted that things had to be done because of the standard of the orchestra, and suddenly everyone was churned up and asking why standards should really come into it. That's the big difference between the orchestra then and now: then there was still the feeling of 'we're willing to do anything as long as you don't compromise the comfort of our work. We're still a provincial orchestra and we came here to avoid this sort of problem. How good do you want us to be? How good do we want to be?'

This was the start of our growing up, the fact that these questions came out. There was still really a taboo about talking about the actual abilities of any player, and admitting that there might be a problem. We had begun to reach the first ceiling by this point, and without raising these things we would not have got any further. It caused chaos and difficulties, but by the time I came back in March the next year it was already much improved. The end of that season was difficult again: we had the first sacking of a player, the first time the problem arose of a player having to leave the orchestra because of his lack of capability. It hadn't happened quite like this before in a regional orchestra, I don't think, and the orchestra having to face that sort of difficulty and realize that playing standards had to be talked about was a big step. Perhaps some of them never really recovered, but now there's such a different feeling. I'm glad we waited a couple of years and made the changes when we did.

The première of Robin Holloway's *Clarissa* Symphony, drawn from an opera which had not been performed, had a good deal of attention from the London critics, and for the first time the developments in Birmingham demanded their attention. Among many comments, Andrew Clements in the *Financial Times* reported that 'Mr Rattle, his singers and orchestra, coped with the manifold difficulties of the score with great enthusiasm and assurance.' Peter Heyworth in the *Observer*, while reserved about the piece, praised the 'stirring account' of the work, while Bayan Northcott in the *Sunday Telegraph* noted that the performance 'was not without occasional roughnesses of detail, but glowing with the conviction of all involved'. Desmond Shawe-Taylor in *The Sunday Times* noted the 'impassioned playing of the orchestra under Simon Rattle's inspired guidance'. This sort of attention to Birmingham's regular subscription series concerts, rather than to just their occasional visits to London, was valuable and welcome as well as being encouraging.

1983–4

Brahms	Symphony No. 4
Stravinsky	*The Firebird*
Berlioz	Overture, *Le Corsaire*
Debussy	*L'Après-midi d'un faune*
Henze	Symphony No. 4
Beethoven	Violin Concerto (Kyung-Wha Chung)
Britten	*An American Overture* (première)
Mozart	Violin Concerto in A K 219 (Iona Brown)
Rachmaninov	Symphony No. 2
Elgar	*The Dream of Gerontius* (Janet Baker, Dennis Bailey, Willard White)
Webern	*Passacaglia*
Beethoven	Triple Concerto (Young Uck Kim, Yo-Yo Ma, Emanuel Ax)
Nielsen	Symphony No. 4
Ravel	*Valses nobles et sentimentales*
Mozart	Horn Concerto No. 3 (Hermann Baumann)
Strauss	Horn Concerto No. 1
Brahms – Schoenberg	Piano Quartet in G minor
Delius	*Walk to the Paradise Garden*
Elgar	Violin Concerto
Grainger	*A Lincolnshire Posy*
Ravel – Grainger	*La Vallée des cloches*
Grainger	Suite, *In a Nutshell*
Mahler	Symphony No. 6
Berg	Suite, *Lulu*
Beethoven	Piano Concerto No. 3 (Radu Lupu)
Sibelius	Symphony No. 5

SIMON RATTLE: We were really getting somewhere at this time. We had put together the Sibelius cycle and we did it in Warwick over a weekend, and in London during South Bank Summer Music. The last concert of that festival was a landmark: three Sibelius symphonies, and a superb response from the press, public, everyone. That was when John Willan decided to do the Sibelius cycle for EMI with the CBSO rather than the Philharmonia, which was the original plan. We had a big, big summer and it helped with the season. We realized that there were areas of the repertory where the band had special expertise and that those should be toured, and others where we just experiment at home. I wouldn't have dared to take the Brahms 4 to London because so many orchestras play it well. Now I *have* taken it to London because I think we've got a real contribution to make to that piece. If we had a healthier musical climate in London I wouldn't be searching so hard, but you have to make something that's different.

An example of that was the Brahms–Schoenberg Piano Quartet. I think I was very much looking for unusual works which would make an event, and also looking for recording opportunities for the orchestra. It was a matter of finding works that this orchestra would play well but others didn't. There were big landmarks this season, Mahler 6 in particular. You can measure them by what the orchestra is likely to achieve and how much it improves in the process.

The Warwick Sibelius weekend was a major undertaking which brought to fruition one of Ed Smith's and Simon Rattle's first major plans: to perform all the Sibelius symphonies as a cycle. In three concerts on successive days they were all played, though not in chronological order. In an interview at the time, Rattle spoke about the importance of the cycle to him:

> For a long time now I've had strong views on how Sibelius should be performed. I've felt that generally he's not taken as seriously as he deserves. I'd go along to performances and then look at the scores, and I'd find a great discrepancy: details would be smudged, or else considered just to be background noise, instead of it being shown how everything grows out of the very tiniest cells. I learnt a lot from Paavo Berglund in Bournemouth. He taught me, for instance, how a great many of Sibelius's melodies have to do with Finnish speech rhythms. And that's important in the woodwind chorale in the finale of the Second, where you have to take account of the fact that there's no anacrusis in Finnish. The music has had a Romantic tradition foisted on to it, and orchestras have developed traditions you have to try to get rid of.

Lyndon Jenkins reported: 'What intrigues me about Rattle's Sibelius is that he is more successful with the greater challenge of the Fourth, Sixth and Seventh than with the others ... the revelation was the Seventh, which had evidently been rethought after disagreeably sleek and Latinized accounts. If he can do that with the Fourth and, yes – *pace* the rest of the world – the Fifth, and sort out some more convincing tempi in parts of the Sixth, this would be an immensely distinguished cycle.'

What reservations were expressed about the Warwick cycle were quite swept away by the acclaim which greeted the London cycle, given this time in chronological order during the South Bank Summer Music, and culminating in the Fifth, Sixth and Seventh Symphonies in one concert to end the festival. This single event surely marked the maturing of the partnership between Rattle and the CBSO, and turned his work in Birmingham from an interesting provincial experiment to an event of national significance:

> For a London listener the first thing to say is how much the success of the Sibelius series owed to the orchestra. On this showing ... the Birmingham orchestra under Rattle can match almost anything we hear from our regular orchestras. The refinement of the strings in particular – so vital in Sibelius whose poised paragraphs so often hang by the thread of a pianissimo tremolo on high violins – was a consistent delight. [Edward Greenfield, *Guardian*]

> Simon Rattle was equal to every interpretative challenge. Crucial questions of balance and pacing were expertly settled; the musical flow was ordered with passion and precision; and the tonal quality of wind and specially strings was full, fresh, and enthusiastic ... In building up this cycle, Rattle has also built up his orchestra into a major rival for the London bands. [Paul Driver, *Daily Telegraph*]

> One of the many odd things about Sibelius is that the better his music is performed, the more difficult it is to understand. Any number of conductors can show his Fifth Symphony as a triumph of heroism, his Sixth as Olympic games in fairyland, his Seventh as a long labouring colossally gratified. But these perhaps are the symphonies Sibelius wished to write: the ones he actually composed are a great deal more enigmatic, as indeed they appeared in the magnificent and important concert with which Simon Rattle brought his directorship of South Bank Summer Music to an end ... Simply to play these last three symphonies together is a feat in itself, but the CBSO have proved before that they thrive on such a challenge when Mr Rattle is conducting, and the audience on this occasion responded with mounting concentration. [Paul Griffiths, *The Times*]

The acclaim was international too:

> Rattle ... must be the best thing that has happened in English conducting since Beecham. He inspires players and elates audiences, holding them intent on every line, every colour, every turn of the argument. [Andrew Porter, *The New Yorker*]

Then the orchestra went up to the Edinburgh Festival for the first time, taking programmes which included Mahler's Tenth, Britten's *Sinfonia da Requiem* and Sibelius's Fifth. These too received high praise in the press: morale could scarcely have been higher as the following season began.

1984–5

Schubert	Symphony No. 5
Takemitsu	Concerto for guitar and oboe d'amore (John Williams, Peter Walden)
Rodrigo	*Concierto de Aranjuez*
Debussy	*Ibéria*
Webern	Six Pieces Op. 6
Brahms	Violin Concerto (Henryk Szeryng)
Walton	Symphony No. 1
Mozart	Overture, *Idomeneo*
Haydn	*Sinfonia concertante* for violin, cello, oboe and bassoon
Sibelius	Symphony No. 1
Sibelius	*The Oceanides*
Mussorgsky	Prelude, *Khovanshchina*
Rachmaninov	Piano Concerto No. 3 (Peter Donohoe)
Stravinsky	*The Soldier's Tale*
Scriabin	*Nocturne*
Shostakovich	Violin Concerto No. 1 (Victor Lieberman)
Haydn	Symphony No. 89
Ives	*The Unanswered Question*
Bernstein	*Prelude, Fugue and Riffs*
Mahler	Symphony No. 7
Copland	*Appalachian Spring*
Stravinsky	Concerto for piano and wind instruments
Beethoven	Symphony No. 3
Berlioz	Overture, *Le Corsaire*
Martin	Three Dances for oboe, harp and strings
Mozart	Oboe Concerto (Heinz Holliger)
Ravel	*Daphnis and Chloë* (complete)
Mozart	*Requiem* (Elise Ross, Mary King, Alexander Oliver, Henry Herford)
Ravel	*L'Enfant et les sortilèges*
Walton	Viola Concerto (Nobuko Imai)
Strauss	*Don Quixote* (Robert Cohen)

ZAP! Simon Rattle receives an award for the most popular concert in the 1986 Brighton Festival

SIMON RATTLE: It was at this time that we began to think seriously about the future, about how things could improve radically for the orchestra so that the learning process could continue. It was clear that we would hit the ceiling again quite soon and this time it needed a plan. So that was the beginning of the famous development plan – really just a scheme for keeping growth going. We needed to pay people more: an orchestra isn't a charity, and our rank-and-file strings were earning less than Birmingham bus-drivers. That side of things is outrageous. And it was clear to me what a difference just having one or two really good people in important positions in the orchestra made: perhaps a system of co-principals could help to lift the thing on to a new plane. The players needed to work less hard, not to do absolutely every date.

An interesting piece in this season was the *Eroica*. I'd hacked it a few times as a student, and then it was the only piece I seriously learnt during my time in Oxford. I did it with the Scottish Chamber Orchestra, as I did the Ninth this year, and I think it started all right, got worse when we first did it in Birmingham in 1982 and then gradually got better again. I rethought a lot of it. I was hearing a lot of Reggie Goodall's performances around then, and I think I got terribly influenced by the steadiness and the measuredness and the thing of giving every note time to speak. As a result I must have done some colossally boring and

CBSO abroad: Rattle at the Philharmonie, Berlin, 1984

CSBO abroad: Rattle and the players take the plane

soporific performances of Beethoven and Brahms during that time! We did a *South Bank Show* partly on the *Eroica* and it was all very broad and I was showing that the metronome mark for the first movement couldn't possibly work. But I've changed my thinking a lot since then and it came out in this second Birmingham performance and in the one with which we opened the next season.

The thing now is that this orchestra will work endlessly at something which is going to be horrendously difficult, they will even work against easy virtuosity in a piece, for example in the first movement of Mahler 7 which is ludicrously difficult, and come out with something that sounds absolutely marvellous. On the other hand, one of the hardest things we did was the Strauss *Don Quixote* with Yo-Yo Ma, who has a technical ease which we couldn't match; it was very difficult to cope. The only times you can't ask for the whole lot from them are the rare occasions when there's simply not the technique to carry it off.

Other highlights of that season included a pair of important foreign visits in the autumn of 1984. The CBSO was invited both to the Paris Autumn Festival and to the Berlin Festival, appearing for the first time in Berlin's famous Philharmonie. The Paris concert included a work by Iannis Xenakis as part of the continuing exposure of his work in Paris: Rattle's handling of the horrendously complex *Synaphai* (a work even he has not dared to import back to Birmingham) was praised as revealing his 'qualities as an analytical technician'. 'SIMON LE MAGICIEN' was one headline; 'UN JEUNE PREMIER BRITANNIQUE...' another. 'I really believe that the musicians of the CBSO are the kings of the legato. I have rarely heard such a sonorous texture so lovingly blended, in the manner of those sauces which mysteriously reach their optimum consistency. That the strings should achieve this supreme flow fairly easily one can accept, but that one could obtain from the woodwind and brass the same lines, tenderly and subtly intertwined, was much more surprising,' wrote the critic of *L'Aurore*. *Le Monde*, noting that Rattle's reputation in France was built entirely on his records, was impressed by his technique: 'his supple and economic gestures seem to synthesize and encompass the entire music whilst rising above it ... [he has] a delicacy of articulation, but also a sharp precision in his accents, which are the salt of his interpretations.'

No less remarkable was the orchestra's reception in Berlin, where Sibelius's Fifth and the Brahms–Schoenberg Piano Quartet were coupled not with Xenakis as in Paris but with the Britten *American Overture*, a local novelty. 'Triumphant success,' wrote the *Morgen-*

post, while in a long review *Der Tagespiegel* praised both orchestra and conductor: 'The phenomenal Simon Rattle, his baton held like a sceptre in his hand, was called out again and again; with amiable modesty he directed the applause to the orchestra, which was then able to show off again in two encores'; the paper concluded that 'this concert, in which right up to the last note orchestra, conductor and audience were involved with the greatest concentration, must surely rank amongst the musical climaxes of the festival, and will surely be remembered for a long time'. Slowly but surely the CBSO was making a major reputation abroad.

1985–6

Beethoven	Symphony No. 3
Rachmaninov	*The Bells* (Elise Ross, John Mitchinson, John Shirley-Quirk)
Beethoven	Overture, *Leonora* No. 1
Sibelius	Symphony No. 3
Beethoven	Overture, *Leonora* No. 2
Sibelius	Symphony No. 7
Beethoven	Overture, *Leonora* No. 3
Berlioz	Overture, *Beatrice and Benedict*
Ravel	*Pavane pour une infante défunte*
Dutilleux	*Métaboles*
Bartók	*Bluebeard's Castle* (Maria Ewing, Willard White)
Mozart	Symphony No. 40 in G minor
Debussy	*Jeux*
Brahms	Piano Concerto No. 1 (Alfred Brendel)
Haydn	Symphony No. 70
Brahms	Violin Concerto (Kyung-Wha Chung)
Bartók	*Concerto for Orchestra*
Murail	*Time and Again* (première)
Messiaen	*Turangalîla Symphony* (Peter Donohoe, Tristan Murail)
Webern	*Passacaglia*
Beethoven	Piano Concerto No. 4 (Alfred Brendel)
Debussy	*Images*
Mahler	Symphony No. 2 (Arleen Auger, Felicity Palmer)
Ravel	*Alborado del gracioso*
Holloway	*Seascape and Harvest* (première)
Brahms	Piano Concerto No. 2 (John Lill)

Mozart	Serenade for thirteen wind instruments
Mozart	Piano Concerto in C minor K 491 (Radu Lupu)
Mozart	Symphony No. 38

For this season, because the Tuesday and Thursday series had regularly been sold out in previous years, the orchestra decided to add a Wednesday series. A small grant was received from the Arts Council to help with the marketing of the new series. Much to the orchestra's surprise, this too was almost immediately sold out.

SIMON RATTLE: This was a tremendous season: so many mountains to climb. Those very big things, like Mahler 2, are vastly important things for us. Our re-establishment of *Turangalîla* was also very important, particularly because I really cannot imagine anywhere that piece could be better played. One small thing was working on Haydn 70, and finally establishing that a symphony orchestra could really play like a good authentic ensemble, and that has been absolutely seconded by the orchestra's experience just now, working with Nicholas Kraemer, whom they adored. This could be a terribly important step forward, because it shows that it can be done and that the symphony orchestra doesn't just have to go into its post-Brahms shell.

'I would be happy to conduct Beethoven symphonies like he plays the sonatas': Rattle with Alfred Brendel, soloist with the CBSO on its Paris visit in 1986

The other highlight was to be able to work with Brendel – we took that programme with the Brahms concerto to Paris – and to be able to do what he asked instead of *nearly* being able to do it which was always our experience before! I would be very happy to conduct Beethoven symphonies like he plays the sonatas. That would be my ideal: to have that sort of flexibility, and that type of joy and life and daring.

By the end of this season the CBSO were receiving notices in the press that were remarkable by any standards: when they visited the Proms in September 1986 Robert Henderson in the *Daily Telegraph*, under the headline 'BIRMINGHAM BIG GUNS' wrote: 'That the CBSO is at present in peak form, equal to every challenge offered by any other British orchestra, was again instantly confirmed at the start of their Prom ... a performance [Debussy's *Images*] of an imaginative precision of detail, of a magic realism in the phrasing and texture, that meticulously reflected the composer's own description of the music, that here he was attempting something quite new.' And *The Times* agreed: 'They really are in the top league.' The stage was well set for the orchestra's leap into the national limelight.

CHAPTER SIX

'London has some absolutely great players and that's about it'

Around London:
May–October 1986

Simon Rattle's closest musical ties in England, apart from those with the City of Birmingham Symphony Orchestra, have been with three organizations: the London Sinfonietta, the Philharmonia Orchestra and Glyndebourne Festival Opera. Each dates back to the very beginning of his professional career, before Birmingham had come on the scene; each has proved, in spite of some ups and downs, continually fruitful; and during 1986 each provided some unquestioned highlights of Britain's musical year.

He has only rarely accepted posts with other musical organizations. From 1978–1983 he was principal conductor of the London Choral Society, which enabled him to try out for the first time in London some of the major choral works he had prepared at the Dartington Summer School and was to perform in Birmingham, including the Janáček *Glagolitic Mass* and the Britten *War Requiem*. In 1982 he became one of the many artistic directors of the Aldeburgh Foundation, and some hoped both that he would have a major influence on the planning of the Aldeburgh Festival, and that the CBSO would be regular visitors to Snape Maltings. Neither materialized to the degree Rattle could have wished, and there has been considerable friction over programming for the festival. Rattle's friend Oliver Knussen, who has been much more involved at Aldeburgh in recent years, suggests one explanation:

OLIVER KNUSSEN: The basic thing about Aldeburgh since Britten died is that, whatever the appearances, Peter Pears held the reins very tightly indeed until his death, and didn't allow anyone to get too close to the flame. The advent of Simon gave cause for much excitement at Aldeburgh in that period, but he was frankly kept at a distance. I know

he became exasperated by committee meetings, and can't work in that
way. He has very strong ideas about what he wants to do in general,
and Aldeburgh has very strong views collectively about what it wants,
and sometimes the two don't gel at all. To adopt his ideas wholesale
would, some say, amount to virtually abandoning any connection with
the character of the festival as it has been. But as a component, as a con-
tributory element in the gradual development of that character, then
Simon is a very positive force at Aldeburgh indeed. As a supporter of
new music he is invaluable, and he's one of the best living interpreters
of Britten's music, so therefore has to be involved there.

Rattle's involvement at Aldeburgh over the last few festivals has
generally been limited to one major concert with the CBSO – memorable occasions have included Mahler's *Das Lied von der Erde* and
performances of contemporary works by Takemitsu and Henze as
part of the composer-in-residence scheme. But the extent to which
Rattle's ideas do not necessarily chime in with Aldeburgh's could be
seen in 1987, when his Beethoven Choral Symphony was the first occasion on which any Beethoven symphony had been performed in the
festival. Moreover for the first half of the concert he had suggested
extracts from Gershwin's *Porgy and Bess*, which was rejected in
favour of Britten's *Sinfonia da Requiem* but had the nice result that
all the soloists in the Beethoven were from Rattle's Glyndebourne
Porgy cast.

    Rattle has also resisted for a long time extensive involvement with
the London opera houses. Considering his close friendship with Mark
Elder, music director of English National Opera, it is perhaps surprising that he did not make his début there until 1985, in a highly-
praised staging of Janáček's *Katya Kabanova*. At Covent Garden the
début is yet to happen, in spite of many approaches:

> SIMON RATTLE: Colin Davis took me to lunch a few years ago and
> asked me to work on the Mozart cycle with him, but I just didn't think it
> was going to be a particularly good idea. They were never very serious:
> they said you could do whatever you liked and so on but then they
> would come up with the *n*th revival of *Salome*. But now things are much
> more sensible and much more serious, and I'll go to do *The Cunning
> Little Vixen* probably in 1990.

Though Simon Rattle enjoys short, coherent, concentrated bursts of
work outside Birmingham, he has for years now been extremely critical of the orchestral set-up, or lack of it, in London. 'The problem is that

the London orchestras have some absolutely great players and that's about it. They don't have the halls to rehearse in, and they don't have time to rehearse, so they don't have the repertory. It's just not good enough. I work with the musicians themselves with enormous pleasure, but in terms of actually building something up as we're trying to do in Birmingham, forget it. They should have some diktat: no more all-Tchaikovsky programmes for ten years. No Beethoven 5 without an unusual work in the programme. I can't see any way that things will improve just as long as they're all trying just to do great works with stars.'

There is one London organization outside the main symphony orchestras, however, with which Rattle has been able to build up a consistent and fruitful relationship over the last decade, and that is the London Sinfonietta.

Visiting the metropolis: Rattle in the Royal Albert Hall,
preparing for his début at the Proms

OCTOBER 1986:   Queen Elizabeth Hall, London. The London Sinfonietta's Britten–Tippett Festival has been, until now, a little patchy
– some low-voltage concerts, and some low attendances. But the final
concert, like the previous week's, is packed to the doors and provides
some quite exceptional music-making. The tension in the hall is electric, and the atmosphere in the green room afterwards is ecstatic. The
pianist Paul Crossley sums it up when he says to Rattle 'Congratulations! We were hearing world premières. They really sounded like
first performances!' In the typically long and generous second half of
the concert Tippett's *Ritual Dances* from *The Midsummer Marriage*,
Britten's early *Four French Songs* sung by Jill Gomez, and then the
famous *Young Person's Guide to the Orchestra*, can scarcely ever
have sounded so fresh. There is a vast throng of people waiting to see
Rattle – including, it's chastening for a hard-bitten critic to note,
several members of the Sinfonietta who haven't just packed their bags
and fled at the final chord but have waited to thank the conductor for
an exhilarating evening.

   'Phew!' exlaims Rattle. 'I was very depressed this morning thinking
oh, there's far too much to get through today. Tippett's so annoying:
you rehearse and rehearse the difficult bits and in the concert they still
sound awful, and the simple bits take no trouble and they sound just
wonderful. There's still one bit in between two of the *Ritual Dances*
where I really haven't a clue what's going on.' But it's the Britten
Guide that has got people worked up: 'One of the most exciting concerts I've ever been to,' says the composer David Matthews. Certainly
the fugue in the Britten raced away as never before, and as usual it's
John Carewe who has observed the occasion most precisely. Over a
crowd of well-wishers, he shouts to Simon, 'I heard you speed up in
the fugato and you should have seen the look on the faces of the string
players when they realized how fast it was going!' Rattle ripostes:
'*They* went that fast so I thought sod it, it's your fault, I'm not going
to slow it down!'

   It is this sort of electrifying, unpredictable partnership which
makes Rattle and the Sinfonietta such an exciting combination. He
has always felt able to tackle almost anything with them, and the only
reservation he will come near to expressing about their playing is that
'they don't yet play Mozart as well as they play Stravinsky'. Rattle
has become a close friend and collaborator of the Sinfonietta's artistic
director, Michael Vyner, and together they have cooked up some of
the most stimulating brews in London's music-making over the last

few years. There has been a whole sequence of annual Proms, there have been Rattle's contributions to regular Sinfonietta series and the Sinfonietta's contribution to Rattle's three South Bank Summer Music series, as well as a week-long series of concerts in April 1985 they called the Bean Feast.

Like some of the more adventurous Proms of the 1960s, Rattle's Sinfonietta Proms were conceived as three-part evenings with two intervals. In 1979 they had shared a three-part concert with a gamelan orchestra, surrounding it with Messiaen's *Trois petites liturgies* and Maxwell Davies's *A Mirror of Whitening Light*. In 1981 it was Boulez's *Rituel*, Berg's Chamber Concerto and Messiaen's *Et exspecto resurrectionem mortuorum*. One of the highlights of 1985's music-making in London was an all-American Bank Holiday Monday Prom, televised live, in which Rattle conducted the Sinfonietta in Charles Ives, Aaron Copland and George Gershwin's *Rhapsody in Blue*.

But perhaps the most characeristic Rattle–Sinfonietta collaboration was the Bean Feast of April 1985, 'knocking around favourite things without any attempt to make a theme', as Rattle put it at the time. 'We have pieces I wanted to hear the Sinfonietta play or works that have proved popular in the past. Most of the programming in London is so conservative that it's deeply depressing ...' In *The Times*, Stephen Pettitt was rather dubious: 'First they lure crowds by creating a festival atmosphere, with the help of good publicity and puppetry and folk-music in the foyer. Then they play easily palatable music by composers like Britten, Ravel, Weill and Gershwin, making sure that the programme tells everyone that this really is twentieth-century music in the hope that people will thus be encouraged to return to try things more adventurous another time.' Put that way it seemed a rather good idea. The main events included a wild staging of Weill's *Mahagonny Songspiel* by David Alden, and a more restrained one of Falla's *Master Peter's Puppet Show*. The final concert brought together jazz-inspired pieces: Milhaud's *La Création du monde*, Stravinsky's *Ebony Concerto*, Gershwin's *Rhapsody in Blue* in its original arrangement for the Paul Whiteman Band, and song arrangements by Whiteman himself. Almost two years later, in the first week of 1987, this programme formed the basis of the long-delayed first recording for EMI by Rattle and the Sinfonietta. It's a partnership that shows no signs at all of weakening.

MICHAEL VYNER: In 1974 I was rung up by Martin Campbell-White, who's on our board, to say that he'd come across this very talented boy, and Tony Pay also mentioned him to me about the same time as someone who was amazingly bright. I went along to hear him do the Ravel and Stravinsky double-bill at the Royal Academy and all the drawbacks were those of a young person – lack of experience, lack of technique – but it was clear he knew exactly what he wanted, and he didn't want what everyone else wanted. Simon's *Pulcinella* was quite unusual: most people start with a sharp, pointed, neo-classical sound, but Simon's was smooth and elegant and legato; very original. He had a long way to go but it was obvious he would get there. He had a wonderful manner, a lovely smile, and if I'd had my violin under my arm I would have wanted to play for him.

Initially did you suggest programmes to him?

In the early days there were things I wanted to interest him in, but it soon became clear that he had a very definite mind of his own. What actually happened was that I would say to him, 'Could we have the Schoenberg *Chamber Symphony* in this programme?' and there would be a long pause – you know how difficult it is sometimes to work out what he's thinking – and either he would dismiss it out of hand and you'd start again or there would be another pause and then he'd produce some complete programme scheme which worked perfectly. He was very astute and planned very carefully: he would do pieces in Scotland or Liverpool and then bring them to us in the Elizabeth Hall knowing them extremely well. It gave him great pleasure to plan to do things that were unusual or ought to be heard more often – like taking up Henze 7 this year – and his tastes are very strong. He has tastes as catholic as any conductor I know, but his dislikes are very strong too. If he believes in a work then he will insist: it was Simon who said to Claudio Abbado when we did a concert in the 'Mahler, Vienna . . .' series that he wanted to do Alexander Goehr's *Little Symphony*: most people might be slightly scared of forcing something on Abbado and would give up the idea because they wanted to keep in with him, but Simon just doesn't have to worry about that sort of thing; and in the end it was accepted.

So how do you plan programmes now?

Simon isn't the sort of chap who will take fifteen lunches off you while ideas gradually work their way through. One cup of tea and perhaps a serious dinner and he'll have produced a week of programmes. Some of the things we've done together have been very much his idea: the Busotti *Rara Requiem*, which Ellie, who knows the repertory from at least 1400 to the present, was keen on, they talked me into doing. But he is such a wonderful suggester of programmes and builder of programmes that we could work together happily doing that for ever. The

Bean Feast just evolved like that – projects we wanted to do, pieces we liked – and with Simon it doesn't come out as miscellaneous but hangs together.

Have you seen his skills change and improve?

Oh yes. In the beginning the performances were always good; whatever the drawbacks from his lack of experience, they were still wonderful. But now he has become so much better a trainer of musicians, and Birmingham is the result. He knows what he wants, very clearly, but I think he's more willing to take what comes from a player and use that too. It takes two to tango: if Simon likes something he hears from a player he'll keep it and use it. He likes music a lot and he likes people a lot, and that is what gives his music-making such amazing communicativeness. When he steps on that stage and smiles he's got the audience there where he wants them, and he can use that in a completely musical way. He's a popularizer in the best sense of the word: he really wants to get through his enthusiasm about twentieth-century music.

Any particular pieces which you remember him conducting?

Lots and lots; but there was one in particular, Messiaen's *Des Canyons aux étoiles*. This piece had one performance in England by Pierre Boulez and everyone said it was substandard Messiaen so it was neglected. But then Ollie Knussen persuaded me to have another look at it because he was sure it was a great work; it's for forty-odd players, just about possible for us, Paul Crossley was keen to do the piano solo part and Simon agreed to take it on. Now he accepted that there was a lot at stake here: the first performance since the original one of a piece which many people hate. He really went at it incredibly hard: three extra rehearsals, an extra hour on the day, and the result – well, it was one of the great highlights of my musical life, and of the Sinfonietta's, too. That performance re-established the piece in the repertory, and we've now done it with other conductors and taken it abroad and repeated it often, and all because Simon realized how hard it was to pull off and made it work.

Do you wonder what he'll do in the future?

The things I wonder about him are: Why does he never lose his temper? Why is he always so thorough? Why does he never let anything go? Why does he always buy his own cup of coffee at rehearsals and probably one for the players as well? Why does he go on working so hard? Those are the sort of questions about him. As for the future, I'm sure he will go on and make the Birmingham orchestra the best in the country. He'll go on helping composers and interesting audiences in Henze and Haydn. I do think he's got to do less, otherwise he'll work himself to death. But the thing is that I don't think the future for him will necessarily be drastically different: it'll just be a slow process of expansion.

Rattle in London, conducting the Philharmonia at the 1983 Proms (*photo* G. Macdomnic)

The Philharmonia, in the days when it was still the New Philharmonia, was the first London symphony orchestra to engage Simon Rattle and present him in the Festival Hall. That was thanks to the enthusiasm of the then chairman, Basil Tschaikov, and after the success of his début concert with them in 1976 there were immediately plans for more concerts, and particularly recordings for EMI. Holst's *Planets* followed in 1977, but this was neither a piece nor a performance on which Rattle was very keen. There were reservations from the critics about some performances at this time: of Ravel's *Daphnis and Chloë* in the same Festival Hall concert Paul Griffiths wrote in *The Times* that 'the score is a long way from the Straussian opulence which Mr Rattle pressed on it'. One early Philharmonia project, undertaken when Gavin Henderson arrived as general manager in 1975, was the forging of a link with one of London's commercial radio stations, Capital Radio, which had an obligation to provide some live orchestral music and were keen to use the Philharmonia with Rattle for this purpose. Among other concerts, they celebrated Capital's third birthday in 1976 and also gave a live relay from Henry Wood Hall of an all-American programme on 4 July.

The event which drew most attention to Rattle's continuing work with the orchestra was, however, the long-awaited première of Peter Maxwell Davies's First Symphony in February 1978 (it had been commissioned some five years earlier). Rattle was surprised to be asked to undertake the piece and described it as 'just about playable' but 'quite horrifically, quite cosmically difficult ... It's not all pleasant music – part of the last movement is unbelievably violent ... It's one of those works which scream from the page that it will still be played fifty years from now.' He gave a remarkably assured première which received good notices everywhere: 'Simon Rattle did a masterly job conducting the Philharmonia Orchestra, taxed to the limit in each movement' (Edward Greenfield, *Guardian*); 'Simon Rattle conducted with evident skill and enthusiasm, and, far from exhausted by the experience, he and the orchestra returned refreshed to give us another hour-long symphony, Mahler's *Song of the Earth*, in a performance of considerable authority and touching delicacy' (David Cairns, *Sunday Times*). It was impossible to tour the performance, and Henderson estimated that the subsidy per seat required to prepare the single Festival Hall performance was £150! However, it was subsequently recorded, and there was a Prom performance as well as a foreign hearing at the Flanders Festival. Rattle took the orchestra to the Edinburgh Festival in 1979, conducting alongside Muti and accompanying Sir Clifford Curzon; all this season's concerts went well, and they culminated in a riveting Janáček *Glagolitic Mass* the following June.

While Gavin Henderson was manager of the Philharmonia he considered asking Rattle to become an associate conductor of the orchestra, as Andrew Davis had been. But the plan ran into problems with the principal conductor, Riccardo Muti, who was not in favour of extra appointments when Lorin Maazel, whom he regarded coolly, was principal guest conductor; the plan was quietly shelved. Gavin Henderson moved on and subsequently became artistic director of the Brighton Festival, where he regularly collaborated with Rattle and put on two of the CBSO's finest concerts in 1986. Rattle was eventually offered an arrangement with the Philharmonia when in 1979 the new general manager, Christopher Bishop – already a fan of Rattle's through his previous work for EMI – took over and negotiated an arrangement. The following year they signed an agreement, with no title attached, under which Rattle would work with the Philharmonia exclusively of the other London symphony orchestras for the following five years. It fitted in well with Birmingham and was welcome to Rattle, but any hope that it would produce extra EMI recordings for the orchestra soon dried up as Rattle did more and more of his recording work with the CBSO alone.

At this time, too, the Philharmonia decided to respond to the Arts Council's frequent accusation that the London orchestras did too little for contemporary music. It established a *Music of Today* series which featured open rehearsals and discussions; Rattle was an obvious choice as conductor. Along with Oliver Knussen (who has the largely honorary title of the Philharmonia's Composer-in-Residence) and the critic and composer Bayan Northcott, Rattle formed part of the think-tank which chose the projects, and he conducted a couple of the concerts in the next two seasons: David Matthews's Second Symphony was rehearsed and performed in one such concert. Rattle also was in charge of the Philharmonia's contribution to the Arts Council's own series, *Music of Eight Decades*, giving the première of Maxwell Davies's *Black Pentecost*, a less successful offshoot of the First Symphony.

All these one-off concerts were enjoyable up to a point, but Rattle felt frustrated by the lack of continuity and connection between the various parts of his Philharmonia work. The chance to create something more coherent – and to set a whole new fashion for London concert planning which was to be of immense significance – came almost by accident in 1984.

SIMON RATTLE: The Philharmonia had a tour of Spain planned, and it fell through. So one day when I was rehearsing, Chris Bishop came up to me and said, 'We've got this time and some dates free. Why don't we do a series of concerts at the Festival Hall, and add in a couple at the Elizabeth Hall, with a theme? You think about it.' So in my bath that afternoon I dreamed up this collection of Mahler and Strauss and the Second Viennese School with all my favourite pieces in it, and I thought they would soon shoot it down. It was a marvellous opportunity, which you don't often get in London, to put together concerts which really make sense. Surprisingly they liked it, and some of the players like the trumpeter John Wallace said, 'We just must do this.'

CHRISTOPHER BISHOP: It is typical of Simon that when I said, 'Can you let me have a few ideas for a possible series?' (and usually with a conductor you're lucky if the ideas turn up ever) virtually by return of post, on a filthy piece of paper which I've kept – this one was really historic – there came a scheme which was absolutely perfect and we did it virtually without a change. (In the end Simon couldn't face doing the Clinton Carpenter completion of Mahler 10, so we did *Das Lied* instead, but that was the only alteration.) He really is a superb concert planner.

We had one horrific experience in that series, which shows how difficult the situation is in London with repertory and contemporary music. We had a Mahler 2 with Simon which was sold out, and before the interval we'd put the Webern *Passacaglia* and the Schoenberg *Five Pieces*. And at the start of the concert the place looked half full and I wondered what on earth was going on because I knew it was a sell-out. After the interval they all turned up for the Mahler. So these people couldn't even be bothered to come and hear some pretty early Webern and Schoenberg when they had already paid for their tickets. That is a ghastly story which reflects very badly on the London situation.

The Mahler–Strauss series in April 1985 received excellent reviews, good attendances, and alerted London's orchestral managers to the virtues of a concentrated, thematic set of concerts over a short period of time. The Philharmonia immediately began to plan a new series, and that turned into one of the highlights of London's music-making in 1986: *Après L'Après-midi*, a survey of French music since Debussy. This changed slightly more than the Mahler–Strauss series between conception and realization. Rattle's original plan, sent this time in a telegram to Martin Campbell-White just a month after the success of the first season, included Messiaen's *Poèmes pour Mi* for which Rattle indicated his preference for soloist with the line 'Jessye Norman or bust ...' She was also the desired soloist for two other concerts, but she could not take part (though she did sing Mahler with him at the 1985 Proms). This series was an exceptionally expensive undertaking: as Rattle put it at the time, 'They'll lose a colossal amount with this enormous rehearsal time. But without a real tradition of exploring and experimenting, great masterpieces go down the same hole of over-familiarity.' Of the Philharmonia's risk in undertaking the series, he said, 'If I was their accountant I'd have stopped them doing it' – a reasonable sentiment, especially in view of the fact that French music has always been of uncertain popularity with the London audience, and Rattle's series mixed the familiar with the unfamiliar in even measure:

Debussy	*Prélude à l'après-midi d'un faune*
Ravel	*Shéhérazade* (Maria Ewing)
Boulez	*Rituel in memoriam Bruno Maderna*
Ravel	*Trois poèmes de Mallarmé*
Debussy	*Iberia*
Ravel	Fanfare, *L'Éventail de Jeanne*
Satie	*Parade*
Duparc	Songs (with orchestra; Ann Murray)
Debussy	*Le Martyre de Saint-Sébastien* (symphonic fragments)
Koechlin	*Les Bandar-log*
Ravel	*La Valse*
Ravel	*Alborada del gracioso*
Poulenc	Concerto for two pianos (Katia and Marielle Labèque)
Debussy	*Jeux*
Ravel	*L'Enfant et les sortilèges* (Elise Ross, Dinah Harris, Mary King, Ameral Gunson, Peter Hall, Henry Herford, Raimond Herincx)
Debussy	*La Boîte à joujoux*
Messiaen	*Oiseaux exotiques* (Peter Donohoe)
Boulez	*Éclat*
Ravel	*Ma Mère l'oye*
Poulenc	*La Voix humaine* (Elisabeth Söderström)
Messiaen	*Et exspecto resurrectionem mortuorum*
Ravel	*Daphnis and Chloë* (complete)

French flavour: one of Rattle's greatest successes in 1986 was the Philharmonia's series *Après L'Après-midi*

CHRISTOPHER BISHOP: I was petrified, because we planned it and were intending to go ahead but we had no extra money, no sponsorship and nothing extra from the Arts Council. Suddenly we got £40,000 from Chanel [the French perfumiers] just like that, and we got something extra from the Arts Council – difficult to say exactly how much, because it was put into the whole grant, perhaps £30,000 – so that we had the largest grant for that period of all the London orchestras. In the event the series did extremely well, had a great deal of attention, Simon conducted quite superbly, and there was an average 75 per cent attendance, which for those programmes was remarkable. Simon is very aware of the financial problems of the London orchestras, and he is very clever at arranging rehearsals so that not a minute is wasted, so it was all done as economically as possible.

The reviews of *Après L'Après-midi* were outstanding, reflecting something of the almost total enthusiasm with which the London critics now regarded Rattle: 'Conducting his first two concerts ... Simon Rattle proved that he knows how to secure playing of French music with a perfect accent' (*Guardian*). 'Rattle has a special gift for making the simplest orchestral statement or instrumental combination resonate in a subtle and telling manner – and a special gift too for gauging exactly the right pacing for related gestures' (*Financial Times*). 'Simon Rattle's series has been marvellously enriching, with the standards of the Philharmonia Orchestra's performances over the fortnight remaining amazingly high, and perhaps most warming of all, near capacity audiences greeting music by the likes of Boulez and Messiaen with something like rapture. And it came to a suitably glorious close last night ...' (Stephen Pettitt, *The Times*). Ravel's *Daphnis and Chloë* was 'a fitting conclusion to one of London's major musical events of the decade, and further evidence of Rattle's genius for planning programmes and then performing them with utter conviction' (Robert Henderson, *Daily Telegraph*). A someone wistfully put it, 'Can Simon Rattle do no wrong?'

Much to some people's relief, he could. His relationship with the Philharmonia had not been uniformly sunny between the Mahler–Strauss series and the *Après-midi* series. An awkward tour of Japan in 1985 was one problem. Rattle agrees that it was unhappy, and he puts the cause down to a relatively small matter: programming the Brahms *Haydn Variations* which he had not re-learnt properly and felt incapable of doing well. ('I couldn't even admit to myself that I funked it. It shows you have to be prepared.') However, another cause of tension may have been Rattle's open criticism of some Philharmonia appointments (though not that of his friend Esa-Pekka Salonen as principal guest conductor). Certain conductors, including former principal conductor Riccardo Muti, were drifting away from the Philharmonia at this period towards the London Philharmonic, where former EMI producer John Willan was newly installed as manager. Towards the end of 1986, Rattle unwittingly became a major factor in the talk of a takeover that erupted between these two orchestras (see pp. 196–8).

At the end of 1985 John Willan attracted Rattle to the London Philharmonic with ready agreement to Rattle's requests for extra rehearsal. The two programmes he did, one of Stravinsky and one including Rachmaninov's Second Symphony, fulfilled the highest promise. Many observers thought this was the beginning of an important new relationship:

JOHN CAREWE: He was suddenly conducting an orchestra which was really great, and which had probably seven-tenths of all his ideals already built into it. In the Rachmaninov Second Symphony I have never seen a London orchestra so totally committed, to the last player. They really did for one night forget that they had to earn their living at ten o'clock the next morning, and I would not like to have been the conductor they had the next day! I think it was one of the greatest concerts I have heard him conduct.

It had always been thought that the Philharmonia would provide Rattle's strongest tie to London, but in 1986 the balance was changing. At the end of that year John Willan made the suggestion to the *Sunday Times* – displayed with sensationalist headlines on its front page – that collaboration between the two orchestras, mooted for many years, should be in the form of an LPO 'takeover'. This soured relationships considerably, and there were more than a few who thought that Willan's pre-emptive strike might have something to do with his wanting to create the conditions which might lure Rattle to come and throw in his lot with an LPO-dominated London in the foreseeable future. In fact, for all that Rattle was in sympathy with the ultimate aim of bringing order to London's musical life, he felt the methods used by the LPO, and the involvement of the press in place of negotiation with the Philharmonia, were naïve.

Within the Philharmonia, impressions of Rattle as a conductor were generally enthusiastic but were mixed with some reservations. One player recalls:

There was a period when his rehearsals were a little slack and discipline was not very good. He would want to work laboriously at little details, the sort of thing that most conductors would expect us to put right on our own, and perhaps that irritated some of the players. I felt it was so positive to work with someone who was so open and so good at communicating what he wanted. The best things were the things he really enjoyed: the recording of Janáček's *Taras Bulba* and the *Sinfonietta* was tremendous, and I remember being surprised when the record came out quite how good it was, because from where I was sitting I thought there were a few bits we'd never got together. He makes it his business to make sure that everyone can play everything and so to some he seems demanding. He likes to take things apart but if there are players who think that is all too much trouble then the fault is their arrogance and not his conducting.

There was certainly at one point a coolness in the relationship: I think players who had been in the orchestra since he started conducting felt that the early promise perhaps hadn't been fulfilled quite as quickly as we'd hoped, and there were some concerts which didn't work. They felt that he went through a stage of being rhythmically rather unclear, and simply not quite reliable technically. I remember some rather wearying rehearsals for Mahler 10, one interrupted by a bomb scare, another by a party: we didn't get as much done as we might. But the first highlight was the Mahler–Strauss series: there was plenty of music there we hadn't touched before and he worked hard at it, and I think we learnt a lot. Then this year's French festival was absolutely outstanding, and I think that if there were any people in the orchestra who thought he hadn't matured fast enough, or were disappointed, they were won over by this. He insisted that the whole festival was tied from the point of view of the players: we had to accept all the work or none of it, so that he had absolutely regular personnel for all the concerts, and he could really work on getting this special French sound he wanted for the repertory. Everyone was very enthusiastic about the way he worked on that series.

I think orchestral players generally very much respect his stand on staying in Birmingham, working gradually through the repertory, and especially – because there's so much jealousy of conductors among players – not behaving like a jet-set conductor and demanding huge fees, behaving like a prima donna and having a glamorous lifestyle. We've seen so many of those come and go. He's always among the two or three who are talked of as possible principal conductors, though I'm sure that before Sinopoli came he wouldn't have been interested, and now he would only come on his own terms, and I imagine they would be quite extreme. But I think there's a feeling in the orchestra that as he so obviously is now going to be a great conductor of the future, we ought to get hooked in with him one way or another.

Had the Philharmonia management in the past wanted Rattle as principal conductor?

CHRISTOPHER BISHOP: We had Muti until 1983, and at that point Simon would certainly have been one of the people we thought of, but he was then very heavily into Birmingham and indeed had a contract for two or three more years, so we would have had to wait leaderless for a long time. He really wasn't in the market at that point, nor had he quite taken off in the way that he has in the last two or three years. And I think he's doing such a clever thing in Birmingham, because the orchestra is absolutely associated with him in a way that wouldn't quite be the case in London even if he was a principal conductor.

There was a slight dip in our relationship with him after we went on tour to Japan in 1985. I don't think he enjoyed touring and there were a couple of things that didn't go well. It's a very delicate relationship between an orchestra and a conductor and it only takes tiny things to disturb that. You can either ride rough-shod over the players and tell them to get on with it, or you can adjust. But if there was a cooling-off then, it was totally and completely restored by *Après-midi*. We are extremely happy now with Sinopoli, but if in the future the time came when we needed a principal conductor and Simon was there I'd be on to him like a shot, of course. But somehow I can't see that he'll come to London after Birmingham. His next move will be a very interesting one, but I should think he'll go abroad.

But surely you must want to make the sort of conditions which will make Simon want to come to London, if not permanently then at least regularly?

Not just for him, but for all our major conductors, for Sinopoli and Salonen and so on. Yes, it would be good to think we could find the money for that to happen. Simon is still coming for one-offs: we'll do Mahler with him in November [1987]. For the larger projects, with the new South Bank Board, series will be in favour and we can do more of that sort of thing because I know that's what Nicholas Snowman wants. I have a plan to do a joint series with the London Sinfonietta, with Simon and Esa-Pekka Salonen (who are great friends) conducting both groups. But it's very hard to plan, and to get five days together when the hall's free, the orchestra's free and Simon's free.

Do you then regard the Birmingham development plan as a threat to London?

No, not at all. I don't regard anything which improves the musical situation anywhere in the country as a bad thing. Birmingham is a great city and it deserves a great orchestra. This is Arts Council development money; so it's there for whoever puts up a good case for it. I think it's far better that it should go to anything in music rather than other art-forms because for so many years music has been the Cinderella of Arts Council thinking.

Doesn't the London Philharmonic scheme for running two London orchestras together offer the best chance for an orchestra that would attract Simon here?

I don't think amalgamating the best two orchestras in London is a sensible idea at all. If you put together the best players from the two orchestras you wouldn't necessarily get a super orchestra. There's the whole character of the two orchestras: if you put together the best journalists from the *Financial Times* and the *Observer* you wouldn't necessarily get the best newspaper. The real answer is to fund them properly. The Arts Council have got the right idea now, which is to be selective, to say that they will give more money if they like the programmes and so on. And we get the largest amount of money at present. But you can't just kick players in the teeth. I think the LPO stunt was destructive.

Meeting Bess: after a triumphant performance of *Porgy and Bess* at Glyndebourne,
Rattle meets Anne Brown, who sang Bess in the opera's première, with Cynthia
Haymon (Bess) and Damon Evans (Sportin' Life) (*photo* Guy Gravett)

JULY 1986.   The first night of George Gershwin's *Porgy and Bess*
at the Glyndebourne Festival, conducted by Simon Rattle and directed by Trevor Nunn of the Royal Shakespeare Company, brings the
audience to its feet in the most sustained, emotional reception of an
opera I can remember there. Of all the extraordinary and gripping
evenings for which Simon Rattle has been responsible this year, this is
the most extraordinary and the most gripping. The thing was just
magic. And yet it could have gone wrong at so many points, and initially the whole project seemed deeply suspect. As one press report
put it, 'The arrival of Catfish Row at Glyndebourne must be the most
spectacular geographical move since Birnam Wood came to Dunsin-
ane.' The *New York Times* reported: 'The denizens of George Gershwin's Catfish Row took possession on Saturday night of the English
stately home renowned for its productions of classical operas, and
what might have been seen as a gesture of musical condescension
became instead the triumph of the operatic season. *Porgy and Bess*
and the Glyndebourne Festival are almost the same age, having been
born in 1935 and 1934 respectively, but until recently no one could

have imagined their convergence ... [but] as jointly conceived by Simon Rattle, the young British conductor, and Trevor Nunn of the Royal Shakespeare Company, who shaped *Nicholas Nickleby* and *Cats*, it was meant to demonstrate that *Porgy and Bess* did not have to be patronized either musically or dramatically ...'

My own reaction in the *Observer* was one of complete amazement that the opera could work so faultlessly: 'The element of surprise is crucial. It could have been awful. Gershwin's opera has not met with universal approval: there are question marks over its musical substance, its descents into sentimentality, its condescension towards its subject-matter, and its supposedly patronizing attitude towards blacks ... So we have what Virgil Thomson, in his review of the première, described as "a libretto that should never have been accepted on a subject that should never have been chosen" being performed in the place most likely to make us squirm with embarrassment at the conflicts it throws up. And yet it moves. It moves because, performed with fantastic commitment and accomplishment by a cast who demonstrate not the slightest qualms about its problems and a conductor with not the slightest doubt about its musical stature, it hits you straight in the guts.'

BRIAN DICKIE (the festival administrator): It would be fair to say that we took the idea of *Porgy* from the English National Opera. In the summer of '83 Frank Corsaro and David Pountney were having a picnic at Glyndebourne, and Pountney said that they wanted to do *Porgy* at the Coliseum with Simon. Corsaro came and told me, because I think he would have liked to do it for us himself. But just at that time we were looking for something for Simon and Trevor Nunn to do after they worked on *Idomeneo*, and I thought it would be a thrilling thing for us, though full of problems. (I think if I'd realized how many problems I wouldn't have gone on with it ...) And it seemed to me unlikely that the Coliseum could possibly meet the Gershwin estate's stringent conditions about performing the piece.

At that time we were also thinking of a Janáček *Jenůfa* with Simon and Trevor, so we discussed it and Trevor said that if we offered him either of those pieces with Simon he'd sign the contract tomorrow. So it was quickly fixed with Peter Hall, who was then away doing the Bayreuth *Ring*, that we should pursue *Porgy*. In November I flew out to Los Angeles and met the lawyers and everyone to do with the Gershwin estate. Meanwhile I think George Harewood was still writing letters to them, and I think the fact that I went out there gave us an advantage. And we were prepared to do it with a completely black cast, whereas I think the Coliseum wanted to have a compromise with the chorus. So they agreed, and we'd crossed the first bridge.

Contrary to popular supposition, by the way, there was absolutely no mention of the all-black cast in the contract we signed with the estate. I think they were just satisfied that we would do it in accordance with their wishes, but there would have been no legal comeback if we hadn't. There was no discussion about production style, or faithfulness to the text and so on, no instructions about that. Perhaps if they'd heard we were going to do it with someone called David Alden they might have inquired further. It just stipulated we had to give it a first-class production, which is rather nice. I don't know who would have arbitrated if they had thought it wasn't first class!

Was the casting a headache?

Yes, because it was a completely new cast. Think of getting a complete chorus from scratch. We'd had a couple of black chorus members previously and about half a dozen came in for *Simon Boccanegra*. Apart from Willard White, whom Simon had worked with and immediately said was the Porgy, the rest was pretty well open, with not much to go on. Terrifying! So we planned a couple of days of auditions in New York with Trevor around the time Simon was there with the LA Philharmonic, in December 1984, to get the principals. We found some – Harolyn Blackwell sang there and we got her in at once – but there were plenty of holes. Bess was a real problem, for instance, and in the end I was the only person who heard her and also the Crown, and they were chosen only about a year in advance. And the last half dozen or so of the chorus I found myself last March in New York in some 9 a.m. auditions.

When did you suspect it was going to be such a success?

Oh, from day one of the rehearsals. We had five weeks of ups and downs but the place really buzzed as never before, and we knew we had it made. It was extraordinary, the sheer energy that went into this production. And it wasn't easy, because we're not a commercial operation like *Cats* or *Starlight Express*, the sort of operation Trevor Nunn is used to. There were very serious technical problems with the set which is heavy and elaborate, and things became pretty tense in the last week or so when rehearsals had to be cancelled just to give time to make the set safe. But there's such a different atmosphere in the place when you know a production is going to work – and this one did. The cast were marvellous – total integration – and they livened up Glyndebourne no end. There were a few problems down in the village, I gather; incredible, really.

For Simon Rattle it was the culmination of a ten-year relationship with the opera which went back to a Chelsea Opera Group concert performance in 1976. He'd also done it in Liverpool and Birming-

ham, and had brought it with Birmingham forces to London for his
1981 South Bank Summer Music season. It was a work he knew
thoroughly and loved passionately.

SIMON RATTLE: There are tunes in the opera I've known since I was a
kid. We must have had piano arrangements of it lying around at home,
and my father would play Gershwin songs day in and day out. It was
very much his kind of music. One of my earliest things as a pianist was
to do *Rhapsody in Blue* and my father would bash through it with me
telling me how square I was, so there is some of that in my bones.
   Were the rehearsals lively?
   Amazing in every way. Both Trevor and I at various times hit the tension of being white people telling black people what to do – particularly
difficult in a piece which they know so well. Very near the end was very
tense and a very difficult time for me, and the problems with the stage
and set and cancelling rehearsals didn't help. But the problems certainly
resolved themselves!
   The moment I will never forget was the first meeting of the orchestra
and the chorus. I insisted we had just one rehearsal in the rehearsal
room rather than on stage so that the chorus and the orchestra could see
each other, without the players being hidden in the pit. I had brought in
some singers to work with the orchestra, but it was just seeing the effect
of the whole chorus when they began to sing, the noise that came out of
them. The players were sitting back, mouths wide open: it was one of
those extraordinary atmospheres. I've never felt anything quite like it,
and it makes me quite weepy to think about it now. When the orchestra
did something marvellous the chorus would cheer and so eventually if
the chorus did something marvellous the orchestra would cheer. After
that there was so much contact behind every scene. I've never seen that
orchestra enjoy itself so much: down in the pit during performances it
was incredible – people rolling around, tap-dancing – a real feeling of
something going on and a masterpiece being rediscovered.
   The point about the singers is that they were all great. I may never
again conduct an opera where every member of the cast is a great singer
in their own right. You don't get that in Verdi. And what is astonishing
is that many of these people don't have much work, purely because they
are black, and not for any other reason. There are people there who I'll
be wanting to work with in my next Janáček opera or whatever. That
level of feeling and generosity is very rare, and the emotions were very
close to the surface the whole time.
   Leonora Gershwin said it was the first time the piece had ever been
done properly: the first time there had been an orchestra that could
really play it; the first time there had ever been a proper production;
and of course the cast. It was still very strange to play that music to that
audience, but in every way it was a milestone.

Rattle's triumph with *Porgy and Bess* was one climax of a decade of work at Glyndebourne. He was first there at the age of only twenty, the year after he won the John Player Competition, to work on *Eugene Onegin* with Haitink and conduct *The Rake's Progress* for the tour.

SIMON RATTLE: I very nearly didn't make it in Glyndebourne. I was almost sacked for not turning up to all the rehearsals, and insisting that I was going back to conduct the Liverpool Philharmonic. And I remember Martin [Campbell-White] ringing up: I was given the chance of leaving, or going back and having six weeks of my very little pay docked. The only thing that made me go back was that it seemed dumb not to have the opportunity to work with Bernard Haitink. But almost everyone has some horror story like that about Glyndebourne!

It was Brian Dickie who first brought Rattle to Glyndebourne:

BRIAN DICKIE: I'd gone to see the Offenbach opera he conducted one performance of at the Academy in 1973, and was very impressed. Then there was the Ravel *Enfant* rather later, at the end of 1974, which was superb, but I think it had been fixed by then that he would come in the summer of 1975 to work on *Onegin* and *Rake's Progress* with Bernard and then do the tour of *Rake*. I may say it took a fair bit of persuading my colleagues and I had to be a little bit imprecise about his age ... And I was really pushing the boat out a bit in saying we should have this young chap not only as a repetiteur but also to do the tour. And I wasn't even sure I'd done the right thing when it happened.
I gather there were problems in the first couple of years ...
Initially Simon made a tremendous impression: lots of energy, and for the younger members or the newer members of the company this was great. But the more established people, and some of the more insecure ones, found this young upstart extremely threatening and tiresome, and he soon made a few enemies. The thing about Simon was that his instincts were extraordinary, though, and he soon got a great deal of respect. His learning curve just zoomed upwards.
Then there was a rather tiresome period when he always seemed to be double-booked. This was after he'd won the Bournemouth competition, and he was conducting there and always trying to get back to Glyndebourne by British Rail – he's never driven, which is rather irritating. Oh, and then he would go off to Liverpool for the odd concert, that sort of thing. So I think we did become a bit annoyed by all that, and Bernard certainly found his unreliability annoying.
But he was just so good, and so talented, and so efficient when he did rehearse, that I think this sort of thing was gradually forgotten. He did

Cross-hatched Hockney: *The Rake's Progress* on the 1975 Glyndebourne tour, the first opera Rattle conducted for the company, with Alan Charles (Nick Shadow) and Ian Caley (Tom Rakewell) (*photo* Guy Gravett)

some splendid things with the touring company: I particularly remember the *Così* in '78. There came a time quite early on when we wanted him to become musical director of the touring company in succession to Kenneth Montgomery. But I don't think he felt that committed to it, and he had so much else going on. So we just established the pattern that he would come back regularly to the festival, as often as he wanted, and we would do some special things. So now after being with us every year for the last few, he will do every couple of years, doing a new *Figaro* in 1989 with Peter Hall and then coming back in '91 and '93.

When Bernard Haitink went to Covent Garden, did you want Simon as musical director of the festival?

Certainly, yes. But by then he was fully involved in Birmingham, and I think it had become clear too that while Simon has the most marvellously invigorating effect on Glyndebourne when he comes and does something like *Porgy*, he preferred that the relationship should be regular rather than permanent. I know he has reservations about many aspects of our operation – playing to small audiences, the ticket prices, and so on. There is a set of values which prevail at Glyndebourne which are not necessarily Simon's. We've had this out with him and we know there's no real way we can greatly extend the scope of things or bring down the ticket prices. The way we get out to a larger public is first through the tours, and then through television, video and so on. So I don't think Simon could have been fully enough in agreement with the basis of things at Glyndebourne to want to be musical director of the organization.

Would his control over casting have been a problem too?

Any musical director *could* cast everything if he was around enough. If he was free for all the auditions I go to, and so on. But usually they're not. As we found with *Porgy*, in the end certain decisions have to be made, and we have to take the responsibility. OK, sometimes we get it wrong, but I think our casting is pretty good. No, I don't feel casting would have been a basic problem with Simon, though I do think he has a lot to learn about singers, and that does tend to be the area where we have what I can euphemistically call our discussions.

Whatever the tensions at Glyndebourne, the results of Rattle's work there were universally praised from the very beginning: in 1977, Janáček's *Cunning Little Vixen* drew Max Loppert in the *Financial Times* to say that 'Simon Rattle, young in years, is an excellent choice of conductor. From the lithe, clean, infectiously vibrant manner in which the London Philharmonic attacked Janáček's nuggety little cells and repeated rhythmic patterns, it was immediately and rewardingly apparent that he has an instinctive command of that eternally youthful rhythm. Some of the playing had rough edges, but the spirit behind it, energetic and also lyrical, was just right.' The Janáček was coupled with Poulenc's *La Voix humaine*, which Rattle was to revive in his Philharmonia French series in 1986. And subsequent collaborations have ranged from Haydn's *Le fedeltà premiata* to Strauss's *Der Rosenkavalier* and *Ariadne auf Naxos*. Most recently, in the summer of 1987, he returned to one of his favourite operas, Ravel's *L'Enfant et les sortilèges*, pairing it with *L'Heure espagnole* in a new production designed by Maurice Sendak.

Once again the critics were unanimous in their praise of Rattle's conducting. Paul Griffiths wrote in *The Times*: 'The two works are a gift to Glyndebourne, and with Simon Rattle there to conduct them, the musical pleasures are intense: I knew that [*L'Enfant et les sortilèges*] was a toy box of inventions, but was not so prepared for the fine subtlety, the whisk and ripple of silk, that Mr Rattle finds in *L'Heure espagnole*.'

Perhaps the most striking of all his Glyndebourne performances, Mozart's *Idomeneo* in 1985, revealed that Rattle had an approach to

Mozart that was quite distinct from the Glyndebourne house style, and apparently caused some trouble to push through the rehearsals. 'Simon Rattle ... intensifies the emotional thrust of Mozart's score, not with unwanted Romantic mannerisms but with an extra rhythmic incisiveness established at the very start of the overture. Where Bernard Haitink two years ago took a broad, spacious view, Rattle has you registering with new excitement the close continuity of the piece' (Edward Greenfield, *Guardian*). 'With Rattle in the pit the meticulous orchestration and sense of constant dramatic recharging unique to this score are revealed ... with Simon Rattle conducting the opera for the first time, it achieves the stature for which it has waited so long' (Hilary Finch, *The Times*). Rattle made no secret of his intense admiration for Nikolaus Harnoncourt's recording of this opera, and as a result of his increasing interest in performances on period instruments, he decided to use *Idomeneo* as his first dip into those problematical waters. In the summer of 1987 he appeared for the first time with a period-instrument ensemble, The Age of Enlightenment, doing *Idomeneo* in concert performances in the Queen Elizabeth Hall, London. It was an extraordinary success. In rehearsals, far from being uncertain about the potential of the period instruments, Rattle displayed a detailed knowledge of their possibilities and invigorated the players with his quest for higher and higher standards. He demanded far more flexibility in tempo and expressiveness than old-instrument bands usually expect: as a result there were some problems in actually getting the orchestra to play together. But those were quickly overcome, and the two performances in the Queen Elizabeth Hall were electrifying experiences: disturbing for some who expected a more purist approach to eighteenth-century style; thrilling for others, who heard the range and accomplishment of period-instrument performance suddenly enlarged. 'Unalloyed pleasure', wrote David Murray in the *Financial Times*; 'I have not heard a more exciting *Idomeneo*.' 'Rattle clearly relished the pungency and delicacy of sound available,' commented Jan Smaczny in *The Independent*; Rattle displayed what Paul Griffiths in *The Times* called 'a sure, wonderfully revealing sense of the heroic romantic'. It is difficult to imagine, after such a tumultuous success, that this is an orchestra to which Rattle will refuse to return: as ever, new doors are opening, and this one leads in a particularly interesting direction.

CHAPTER SEVEN

'On the whole I'm in favour of monogamy'

Guest conducting: November 1986

NOVEMBER 1986: Concertgebouw, Amsterdam. Simon Rattle is making his début with the Concertgebouw Orchestra, the first major new orchestra he has conducted since his début with the Boston Symphony Orchestra three years ago. I have flown over for the opening concert of the second programme he is conducting, which consists of Mahler's Tenth Symphony in the performing version by Deryck Cooke. Since discovering the published score of this work in an Oxford music shop shortly after it appeared in 1976, Rattle has made it one of the most powerful and convincing performances in his repertory, and has conducted it many times as well as recording it. The hall of the Concertgebouw is packed and the audience is expecting something special: the orchestra, perhaps the most famous in the world for its Mahler performances, has never played the complete Tenth before.

But from the very beginning of the concert it is clear that something is wrong. Rattle gives a very slight upbeat for the violas' unaccompanied first line, and they don't enter together. The playing is tentative – professional but scarcely committed. Rattle is having to work very hard: his gestures become broader and broader in his effort to draw the sound out of them. There are more fluffs and imperfections than one would expect from such an orchestra, and though some of the greatest moments make their impact, the overall effect is muted. Afterwards, Rattle looks exhausted.

Backstage, while we wait for Rattle to emerge, I ask Martin Campbell-White, his agent, how the first programme, which included Stravinsky's *Petrushka* and Ravel's *Shéhérazade* with Maria Ewing, had gone. 'Later, later,' he whispers, and introduces me to the orchestra's manager who is standing close by. He confirms that the orches-

Rattling noises: among Simon Rattle's lively encounters with the Los Angeles
Philharmonic have been surprise kissograms, a nudie pic slipped into the final page
of his score of Mahler's Tenth Symphony, and this warning notice

tra has never played the Cooke completion of Mahler 10 before. There is to be a conference in Utrecht over the next few days at which all the attempts to complete this torso are to be discussed and some of them played. Then Rattle and the orchestra will give another performance of the work in Utrecht. But I don't gather whether the orchestra has enjoyed the experience or not.

Rattle, tired but ever cheerful, comes to say hello to his friends. His first reaction is that 'it was all such hard work ...', leaving the rest unspoken. We wander Amsterdam looking for a place to have a drink and something to eat. It is noticeable that the crowd of Dutch friends who have come along are all players from the Rotterdam Philharmonic, with whom Rattle has had many happy experiences, rather than from the Concertgebouw. After many attempts to find somewhere with space enough for the whole crowd of us, we end up back near the Concertgebouw in a café where some of the orchestra are having a drink. One of the viola players comes over to Rattle and apologizes for the beginning of the symphony. 'Well, at least you started!' says Rattle, putting a cheerful face on it. The player goes back to his friends. 'Was he the one who played together?' someone quips.

In conversation with the Rotterdam players I gather that while the first programme presented fewer problems, it didn't go especially well either, and that Rattle feels he simply hasn't made contact with the orchestra at all. 'He's had a bad time really,' admits Martin Campbell-White, which given his customary discretion is rather a major admission. It seems that the orchestra were not keen to play Mahler 10, which they didn't know, and thought that in any case it would be rather easy, which it isn't: it is fiendishly difficult, and that shows in performance. Rattle has worked very hard during rehearsals but the orchestra, which likes learning gradually and gently, has not responded to his businesslike approach. All in all, it's been a mismatch.

Back in London a couple of weeks later, Rattle reflects on the experience.

SIMON RATTLE: I think they got the impression that I was very cold, which is very interesting, because that's exactly the impression that I got of them, so we must both have been very mystified by each other. They couldn't understand why I was so no-nonsense all the time. I tried to explain that in England that would be a compliment. But the very fact that I take it for granted that the orchestra wants to use rehearsals to work and make it better was a problem. I really think they work in another way: rehearsals are used for playing a great deal, gradually homing in on things that they think are important. They are allowed to make their own shapes; they think in phrases, which is one of the things I liked about them. But their sense of rhythm I have yet to come to terms with.

They must consider themselves to be the greatest Mahler orchestra in the world; they play the other symphonies very often and sometimes very well. They probably thought that this would be just as easy, but of course it's no more easy than doing the Ninth Symphony for the first time – probably more difficult. One of the orchestra said to me that if I'd come expecting English or American discipline it just doesn't happen there. He said we're used to making a lot of noise, playing on to the ends of phrases, and so on. They're not very disciplined, but Holland is a very liberal society so maybe discipline like that is hard to imagine there.

I was physically so tired. I have not had to move around like that for years.

Was part of the problem that you were handed too much by them, in the sense of a playing style that was all there?

Well, you heard it, did you think it was all there?

Certainly not in the Mahler . . .

Well, can you imagine what it was like in Stravinsky and Haydn? Maybe there were playing styles I couldn't get to grips with . . .

Or as you said of some other orchestras, a style you couldn't unpick . . .

Absolutely. That was the trouble. I had to ask for it to be unpicked and that's what they weren't used to.

Does it make you want to go back and try again or give the whole thing up?

My first reaction was to say, 'fair enough, no hard feelings but let's leave it'. I said this to the manager at the end of the time and then there was an enomous flurry of activity and I was rung at 11.30 p.m. by the chairman of the orchestral committee asking to come over and see me the next morning. I don't think anyone has ever said to them before that without any prejudice they would rather not come back again. I think that was a bit of a shock to them, and their pride, and I think they wanted to try again. But life is not endless, and there are many things I don't have time to do. Do I want to battle with all that again? It's not even as if they are underprivileged: they have plenty of conductors whom I admire much more than I admire myself!

I think I'm still mulling it over. It does strike me that perhaps as I get a bit older I make it more difficult for orchestras to play for me instead of more easy. I thought that as time goes on you learn more about how to cope. But now I feel I have to demand more and I find the compromises more difficult to achieve.

A close colleague of Rattle's has another perspective on the Amsterdam experience: 'The arrogance of that orchestra! They can't be bothered to play and then at the end they turn sweet and say they'd like to give him another chance. How patronizing! Why should *he* give *them* another chance!'

Rattle's relationships with orchestras abroad have not been universally sunny. It is interesting that the problems seem to have increased rather than diminished since he has been at Birmingham: as he has said elsewhere, perhaps he is now too used to an orchestra that wants to play for him and to create an occasion for him. One example of recent problems was with the Cleveland Orchestra. He had a successful first appearance with them in 1982, doing Mahler's Tenth once again, but when he returned at the end of 1984 the orchestra felt his style had changed considerably. He no longer beat as clearly, and he expected them to understand what he was doing without explaining it to them. One player told me: 'Precision is a byword in the Cleveland Orchestra and the players felt insulted. He did the Stravinsky *Symphonies of Wind Instruments* with the wind in one long line across the stage; one end couldn't hear the other end and they were very angry and very upset about the whole thing. I don't think they liked being experimented on, especially when he didn't tell them what he was trying to achieve. It was something to do with the fact that he wanted the orchestra to sense the feel and the pulse of the music. But perhaps he didn't know what the Cleveland Orchestra was taught by Lorin Maazel, who always said, 'You follow my beat and don't bother about listening to each other.' We were mystified, because the first time he came he was absolutely clear and it went well. But this time he was perhaps expecting something unrealistic. He gave the orchestra its head and it didn't know what to do with it.' Similar problems recurred when he went back there in 1987.

Rattle's experience with foreign orchestras is not as wide as might be expected of a conductor of his reputation. His first engagements abroad were arranged by Martin Campbell-White in the wake of the John Player Competition win. There were visits to some small Scandinavian orchestras in Trondheim and Sjaellands, which Rattle enjoyed. Then there was the beginning of the very successful relationship with the Rotterdam Philharmonic, who would have been happy to have had him as musical director after David Zinman left. He settled instead for a principal guest conductor post, and has always enjoyed returning to Rotterdam. The major orchestras came into view a little later, headed in the American area by the Los Angeles Philharmonic in January 1979 and followed by the Chicago Symphony that summer. On an American visit the following year he made his débuts with the San Francisco Symphony and the Toronto Symphony. The following year there was the Israel Philharmonic, then the Cleveland and Montreal Symphony orchestras and in 1983 the Boston Symphony, to which he returned in 1987. That, until the Concertgebouw Orchestra in 1986, was the sum total of the major international orchestras he had conducted.

One long-running saga has been to do with an invitation from the Berlin Philharmonic. That orchestra has asked several times for him to conduct them, but he has always offered only Mahler 10, which they – from the central European tradition which regards Deryck Cooke's attempts to complete Mahler as somehow reprehensible – have turned down. But they finally accepted Mahler 10 in principle, and Rattle agreed to go in November 1987: there were still problems over rehearsal schedules, however, and in the end they compromised with Mahler's Sixth Symphony, a work the orchestra knows far better than Mahler's Tenth. Martin Campbell-White was holding his breath to see if this important and long-awaited encounter would be more successful than Rattle's early visit to Berlin in 1976 to conduct the RIAS orchestra, for which he recalled that Rattle received reviews which were so bad he dare not translate them for him.

A distinctly unhappy encounter among the orchestras Rattle has guest conducted was with the Israel Philharmonic in December 1981:

SIMON RATTLE: It was a horrendous experience. Circumstances conspired, and in every possible way it didn't work. There was snow in England and everything closed down, so I arrived there two days late. I was going to do Mahler 10 in the first programme, but as there were only two rehearsals left we had to change round the programme, so the first time I met this orchestra was conducting Brahms 2. I might have been able to get away with that a week later – I'd done the piece very successfully with the Philharmonia and was very happy with it – but it never would occur to me to go for the first time to an orchestra and do Brahms 2, even now. There was no time at all. I had brought the Prokofiev *Romeo and Juliet* which I was going to give myself the first ten days there to learn, and we had to do that straightaway.

I really didn't know it, and I think they thought I was just a joke. They are up there, as another conductor said to me, with the hardest orchestras in the world to conduct. There's lots of noise the whole time. It was not a happy experience, and I was very lonely and miserable.

Potential music director: Rattle in his first appearances with the Los Angeles Philharmonic, which created such enthusiasm that Ernest Fleischmann was anxious to attract him as successor to Carlo Maria Guilini. Rattle turned down the offer (*photos*: Los Angeles Philharmonic)

If guest conducting has brought Rattle a fair number of unfortunate experiences, it has also brought him some happy ones – with orchestras with which he has been able to build a more than temporary relationship. Best of all, the Los Angeles Philharmonic, the first American orchestra he visited, responded to him so warmly that when Carlo Maria Giulini left, the orchestra and their manager Ernest Fleischmann wanted Rattle as music director there. It must have been a difficult post to refuse, given the exceptional conditions and the financial security it would have offered.

Ernest Fleischmann was formerly manager of the London Symphony Orchestra; he was recently tipped as the new director of the Paris Opera, but turned that down in order to stay in Los Angeles. Rattle says, 'To understand Ernest you have to realize that he was once a conductor. Like incredibly few people in that sort of position, he looks at things from an artistic point of view. I think he believes that if he manages the orchestra well the first violins will play better. I really love the man.'

ERNEST FLEISCHMANN: I first encountered Simon when he came to Los Angeles with the London Schools Symphony Orchestra in 1976, so he was still only twenty-one. The band wasn't so hot – we're used to really crack youth orchestras in the States – but it was clear from the way they responded to him in a very brief rehearsal that he was exceptional. So the next day I had lunch with the woman who ran the orchestra and with Simon and I said that whenever he felt ready I wanted him to make his American début with the LA Philharmonic. I knew he wouldn't do anything straightaway and it was clear that he was a sensitive and intelligent musician, very different from the average career-orientated young conductor I come across here. Rather like Esa-Pekka Salonen these days, he had a completely honest emphasis on music and not just the career, which I greatly admired.

It must have been early in 1978 that Simon agreed to come and we planned the début for January 1979, with Sibelius 5 and the Elgar *Enigma Variations*, which he'd done on that tour. There were some murmurings from the older musicians that first time, but his total command and security won them over, and it was clear we would want to have him back often. He did the Hollywood Bowl that summer, but I think the occasion that really cemented the relationship was Simon's coming at very short notice to do Shostakovich 14 when Giulini cancelled in April '81. That was one of those incidents. It was supposed to have been Giulini – a big thing to show that he didn't always do just classical repertory – with Jessye Norman and Simon Estes. First Jessye let it be known that although she was studying the piece it wouldn't be ready. Two weeks before, Giulini became ill and cancelled. I called Simon who was then on his sabbatical in Oxford and pleaded with him to come. He told me he was preparing the piece with Felicity Palmer, so I asked him to speed up the learning process. The first rehearsal was on a Tuesday afternoon: on the Monday morning I heard that Simon Estes had been in a TV gala the previous evening from the Met, and had lost his voice in the middle of it in front of millions of Americans on live television! So I called Simon again and we found a British bass who could sing it but he'd just left his wife and his score was back at his house so he had to drive through a hailstorm to retrieve it and fly straight out here on a tourist visa ... But Simon rehearsed it marvellously and created a superb performance, which was most moving.

Though I gather there were some problems with the audience?

Yes, that was one of the most shameful things that's happened since I've been in LA. People just kept getting up and leaving between the songs, and so Simon just stopped and turned round and said quietly, 'All those of you who are going to leave during this piece please leave now,' and then went on. Actually it heightened the tension.

What other highlights do you remember?

I can only tell you that I can hardly remember anything which hasn't gone well. Sibelius 4 was unbelievable; Shostakovich 10, Mahler 10, these were marvellous. There was the case of the Beethoven *Eroica* which when he first did it here was by no means formed. The first movement was very very slow and it didn't have that intensity and power which marks out all Simon's greatest performances. Mahler 10 we took to New York and that was Simon's début there. I take grave issue with the critics who disliked it because I just don't think New York critics are able to distinguish an orchestra playing with the special commitment which they brought to it. I thought it was one of the greatest things he ever did and was in tears at the end.

It must have been a blow for you when Simon decided not to come as music director ...

It was a blow, both musically and personally. It was such an obvious progression and I'm sure it would have worked well, but it was hardly surprising knowing Simon that he decided against it. Part of the problem was living in LA when they had a new baby, and part of the thing was the demands of a music director's post in America: all the PR and so on. But Giulini did little of that and between me and Simon we could have worked that out. More important perhaps was Simon's not feeling comfortable with the classical repertory which has to be central for us: in Birmingham that's different.

There was a time when Birmingham was not going so well when I thought he might come here and I'm sure that when Sasha is grown up they'll have to look again at the whole thing, because in ten or twenty years he and the orchestra are just going to have to get together on some more permanent basis whether I'm here or not. There's a terrific synergy there which can't be ignored.

SIMON RATTLE: There were many reasons why I didn't accept but the greatest is that I have my own orchestra and my work with them is nowhere near finished. I've seen what happened in Los Angeles when Giulini left and what a crippling blow it was. Giulini was doing wonderful things with them, but when he left the orchestra it wasn't yet able to play as well for everyone as it played for him. I'm very happy with my guest role in Los Angeles. One of the things about that orchestra is that it could be one of the very greatest contemporary-music orchestras. That goes back to Zubin Mehta, who did remarkable repertory there. I heard some tapes of what they did with Pierre Boulez a couple of years ago, and that was quite extraordinary. They have a pretty good range now, I reckon.

Shostakovich 14 was a wonderful experience because two of the orchestra are Russian and one had actually played in the première. Those weeks set the seal on my friendship with the orchestra. The audience? Maybe not. They're always friendly but they just don't want to be bothered. André Previn was telling me that he had mass walk-outs during the Britten *Spring Symphony*, of all pieces, in New York and Philadelphia. And it's not just twentieth-century music: Bernard Haitink says you expect them to applaud after the third movement of the Tchaikovsky *Pathétique*, but in New York they put on their coats and left! Was it because they didn't know there was a last movement or because they knew they didn't like it?

Rattle's début in New York with the Los Angeles Philharmonic was an especially important occasion because he had turned down all previous invitations to appear there. Both the New York Philharmonic and the Metropolitan Opera had invited him, and the Met. wanted him to do Janáček's *Jenůfa*, an important work for him and one which he will certainly conduct again in the future, but 'there was no rehearsal time for the orchestra, and the performances were spread out over a ridiculous period. If I'm going to do something like that I want to do it as well as possible.' The New York Philharmonic was well known as a minefield for conductors, and Rattle determined to steer clear of it. So the two programmes he gave at the time of his thirtieth birthday in January 1985, one at Carnegie Hall and one at Avery Fisher Hall, were thus doubly important. On the whole, as Ernest Fleischmann indicated, the press were less than rapturous. Again, the choice of Mahler's Tenth may have been a problem, and it was

West Coast idyll: Rattle shows off his first (and so far only) recording with the Los
Angeles Philharmonic, of Rachmaninov's Second Symphony

prefaced by a recent work by Takemitsu, commissioned by the Los
Angeles orchestra.

'Years from now many of us will be able to say with pride that we
were there when Simon Rattle made his local conducting début,'
enthused Robert Kimball in the *New York Post*, but others were less

overt in their praise. In the *New York Times*, Donal Henahan wrote that Rattle's conducting of the Mahler 'showed that he can handle an orchestra with confidence in an immensely difficult, problematical piece and moreover can go beyond a competent reproduction of the notes into the realm of real interpretation ... He is handsome, which gives him an edge with the audience, and he is a solid technician, which appeals to orchestral musicians. His baton divides the beat with oddly clipped and jerky movements at times, which inhibits the flow of some long-lined phrases and might take some getting used to by the players. But he conducted without referring to a score and threw important cues when they were needed without unnecessary showmanship ...'

A review by Peter G. Davis in *New York* magazine irritated Rattle's agents and supporters because his criticism of the orchestra was very fierce, but of Rattle he had this to say: 'Opinions differ on just how it happened, but Simon Rattle is generally regarded as the hottest young conductor to arrive on the international scene in years, a magnetic podium presence, an innovative programmer, and a maverick personality. He is a thirty-year-old British musician who blithely rejects every glamorous offer that comes his way, makes all the "wrong" career decisions by stubbornly remaining in the provinces, and continues to watch his reputation soar. Rattle finally made his New York début in a characteristically low-key manner ... expectations ran high but both events turned out to be disappointing ... What these thoughtfully unspectacular New York concerts indicated to me is that Rattle prefers to work methodically at being the best musician he knows how to be rather than diverting his energies into over-exposure and aggressive career politicking. That sort of disarming modesty, and an earnest wish to make himself scarce, have only added to the conductor's mystique.'

Whether Rattle will wish, in the years ahead, to increase that mystique by staying away from guest conducting dates is anyone's guess. Most musicians feel that the next decade must see him going to more great orchestras and conducting them, but after the experience of the Concertgebouw at the end of 1986 it is by no means certain that he will choose to do so. In an age of conducting promiscuity, he has often declared that 'on the whole I'm in favour of monogamy'.

CHAPTER EIGHT

'300 *per cent committed to the future*'

Development in Birmingham: 1986 –

I

BEETHOVEN'S NINTH

SEPTEMBER 1986. Adrian Boult Hall, Birmingham School of Music. Something inconceivable in London is taking place here: a sectional rehearsal for violins alone of a Beethoven symphony. If you proposed this to a professional London orchestra they would probably fall off their seats laughing: they know how the Beethoven symphonies go, and all they need is an hour or two of rehearsal to polish up their well-drilled responses (and to make any small adjustments that a conductor might find necessary, though hopefully he won't find too many).

But this is Simon Rattle's first attempt at Beethoven's Ninth Symphony with the CBSO, and he is determined to start from scratch. This rehearsal hall in the School of Music is right next door to the orchestra's new offices (as someone on the staff puts it, 'it's all very nice having them so close but it does tend to get chaotic in here when they all decide to drop in'), and the string players have a closely organized afternoon of separate and joint rehearsals; only Rattle, as usual, keeps going the whole time.

Some tiny points are being explored. He is working on the decorated variations for the violins in the slow movement, trying to get them to phrase flexibly while keeping together. I am surprised by the amount of vibrato Rattle continually demands, and by the way each note must join on to the next: 'Really hold and *molto vibrato* that top note, and take your time to vibrate it before you move on. For the time being exaggerate it.' Then again, a bit later: 'Every note must be as long as possible, and make them flow a lot. I know it's impossible

174

Getting down to the nuts and bolts: Rattle rehearsing with the CBSO in the Adrian
Boult Hall

but we really must try to do both.' There's a discussion over one awkward position change. Felix Kok, the leader: 'We try to bridge that
gap as quickly as we can.' Simon: 'That's just the moment not to rush;
just the opposite – use that moment to create something expressive.'

It is very noticeable throughout this rehearsal that even at this earliest stage in the proceedings Rattle knows exactly what he wants. He
is not trying things out in a vaguely experimental way, but working
towards the very precise goal of the way he wants them to play.

Then there's a break. I ask the players how often they've done Beethoven 9 before: for most of them the answer is twice, once in a performance by Erich Schmid in the Beethoven cycle of 1979, just before
Simon's arrival, which players remember with great affection as a
highlight and a morale-booster in a very difficult period, and once,
after a last-minute cancellation by another conductor, with Michel
Tabachnik, which everyone remembers as a complete disaster. ('Just
one of those things,' recalls Rattle; 'the first week of cancellation we
could have got anyone, and the second week, which was the Beethoven 9, there was just no one around.') So there really is a feeling of
discovery in the air.

Now, with all the strings, Rattle starts on the numinous, almost unapproachable beginning of the whole symphony. He tries to get the second violins and cellos to play their open fifths with a typical mixture of precision and freedom: 'They are absolutely not accented; although I don't want to hear them separately, I do want you to play together!' And to the first violins, violas and basses with the theme: 'More on the upbeat than on the downbeat, otherwise the upbeat gets lost.' And then to the cellos, as the movement gathers strength: 'Play right through those notes. The people who hold on longer to it are *better.*'

There's a moment of raised eyebrows from the first violins when Rattle asks them to use a lot of vibrato for a chord which uses two open strings, but that's the only moment in the entire session when they score a point over him or substantially question any of his ideas. Everything is geared to projecting the string sound – perhaps a subconscious result of the previous night's performance at the Proms in the Albert Hall in London, a huge arena where projection was so necessary and a little lacking at times. So the cellos are told to join up, not to separate, passages where Beethoven marks separate bows to articulate the phrases. Even the staccatos are played through solidly

Revitalizing Beethoven:
Rattle discusses a detail in rehearsal with leader Felix Kok

and the sforzando accents are ignored in order to press on with the legato phrasing. My feeling is that the sound comes out too sustained, too even. But the way Rattle achieves certain transitions – for instance, the shading and momentary hesitation as the music moves back into the main introductory theme – is already perfectly judged.

I come back for the final orchestral rehearsal a few days later; the sound has improved immeasurably, but there is still a lot of adjusting and recalculating going on. They are now in the Town Hall, dealing with the problematical acoustics of that building. In the break Rattle is busy altering a doubling bassoon part because he doesn't think it works. Players are still raising tiny matters ('I'm sorry to be a bore, but is it on or off the string there?' Simon: 'Off but very close!'). Rattle seems just a little tetchy about these questions, because he likes to keep the momentum of the rehearsal going especially as the performance comes nearer, and there is an enormous amount to do. I still can't see how it is all going to add up – and I haven't heard the choir, who have been busy rehearsing in the evenings, or the soloists.

SIMON RATTLE: Beethoven's Ninth is one of the works I always said I wouldn't tackle until I was much, much older. But as Giulini said to me once, there comes a time when these pieces come knocking on the door telling you to conduct them. It was Kurt Sanderling who really changed my mind, because he said that it would be a struggle whenever I did it, so I should start now and it would have much more of a chance to get better. So from that point of view, if I'm likely to have to get lots of bad performances out of the way before I get anywhere with it, we may as well do them now!

I was incredibly lucky with Beethoven 9 in having a series of Scottish Chamber Orchestra performances earlier in the year. I'd been right out of action because of Ellie's illness, so there was quite a lot of time to think about it, and then I went up there and worked with an orchestra which had never played the piece before. Makes a real difference. A couple of people in the band had played it, and they found it difficult to take all the rehearsal, I think, because they knew how it went. It was very different, of course, doing it with a chamber orchestra; they added some strings but still it was light at the bottom end. But I think we made people listen freshly, and there weren't players saying all the time 'That's not what we did last time!' And I was able to sort out quite a lot of problems.

What's the really difficult thing about the symphony?

It's really the attitude that's difficult. You've just got to get yourself out of it completely. You must get away from the feeling of 'me interpreting' and let it speak. That's very intangible, I know, but it's the essential thing. There are awkward things in the score and you've not to gloss over them but leave them standing there, awkwardly. It's such a temptation to improve on what's there. As best as you can you must become the piece.

What about problems like whether to follow the metronome marks?

These things are all just dogmas: the dogma of following the metronome marks, the dogma of the squeezed note, the dogma of bowing this way or that. They're all too rigid, and if you think those things will provide you with answers about how to do the piece, you're wrong. But I think if you rehearse a very small part of the piece, as you saw us doing in those early sectionals, and insist on certain things, a certain approach to phrasing and so on, then with intelligent musicians it will spread over to the whole piece. So without sounding pretentious the thing is to get a microcosmic approach to detail which actually creates a macrocosmic approach to the whole symphony.

You need gradually to build it up: like running – I used to run, believe it or not – you don't go first for the full distance, unless you're an idiot; you build up gradually. That's what I hate about an orchestra where you're given an overall view to start with. You can't unpick it. And in London you rarely have time to unpick it anyway. I believe in building up from the very smallest bricks and making performances like that, and the nearer we get to the performance the more I want to be performing.

I find I am not good at letting things go. I mean, God, as an English conductor you really ought to be, because that's what you expect from the players: leave it to us, and it will be fine. With the London orchestras you can get a solid level of performance, but it's so predictable. I find that unless I've built it up gradually, and have a certain amount of structural order, then I don't have enough rigour to give me the freedom I need.

I certainly felt there was a stupendous gap between what you were doing in the Beethoven rehearsals and the way it came out on the night.

I'm glad you felt it: the thing in Birmingham is that if I can put across to them a conception of a piece, then they will embrace it with open arms and I don't have any worry that they'll be unwilling to create an experience in the concert. But I have hit that problem with other orchestras and I'm beginning to realize that I'm a little bit spoilt by Birmingham's readiness to cooperate. I think it's very much a bargain, in that I'm willing to put up with all sorts of technical insufficiencies, or difficulties, or things that take a little longer to get right, as long as they'll come along with me. And it works completely.

The first performance of the symphony in Birmingham is staggering. It just takes one's breath away, the sheer assurance and control with which Rattle directs it – without a score, incidentally. A couple of things don't go quite right – one of them, ironically, the section he was rehearsing in that very first session with the first violins. The scherzo is a bit frenetic. The trio does not quite join on properly. But so much else is so right as to completely quell any reservations. In *The Times* the next morning, Paul Griffiths, who had actually come to Birmingham to hear the first half's première of a symphony drawn from Debussy's *Pelléas et Mélisande* by Marius Constant, devotes his whole notice to the Beethoven. It is spot on:

> What we heard was not an 'interpretation' of the work: it was far too simple for that – too open, even too obvious – if at the same time constantly and joyously surprising. Interpretation would imply a secondary experience, whereas this had the flat authority of something primary ... I am at a loss to know how Simon Rattle achieved this immediacy, this sense of the music speaking for itself, searching and finding its own tempo (even through some extreme rallentandos), its own phrasing, even its own colouring from the strings.
>
> No doubt the secret lies somewhat in the shared sensibility of conductor and orchestra, their working so closely in harness (and how well Rattle's stay-put policy justifies itself). But the triumph is also a personal one, dependent on Rattle's ability to be desperately and personally involved and yet to be so on behalf of something much larger than himself... The music, the continuing comprehension of this music, was all that was important.

That notice summed up very precisely the remarkable results of Rattle's work with the orchestra. One other person I knew would be watching this Beethoven performance closely was Rattle's mentor, John Carewe:

JOHN CAREWE: I think for Simon this was a make or break endeavour, and it had to be a make. And I think he knew that his role model in this had to be Furtwängler. Obviously he wasn't going to do it in the same way as Furtwängler – nobody could – but he realized (and I'm sure he sifted through various recordings of the piece) that of all the conductors of this work it was Furtwängler who provided the insight.

The architectural element is so important: it builds to a point and then goes back, and what was so amazing about Simon's performance was that he managed all that. I wonder if Simon remembers what Walter Goehr said about Beethoven 9, which was so illuminating, which is that it is not poetry, or drama, or a novel, but that it is philosophy. And it is a Germanic concept of philosophy, which is that you pursue an idea to its logical conclusion, and then another and another, until in the end you have assembled a total world view. And he made it like that.

But quite apart from the philosophy, it all worked so well on a purely pragmatic level...

Certainly, but this is the essential Simon, and where all the emphasis on sectional rehearsals and string technique and so on really pays off. He is able to say quite definitely that this chord should be mezzo forte, the brass should be piano and the strings should be forte and so on; the pure mechanics, shall we say the fingering of the piano sonata, are absolutely no problem for him. So we're left with the major decisions. This was where I was bowled over when I heard him do the second of those performances earlier in the year with the Scottish Chamber Orchestra. This piece is the Everest for conductors and he had scaled it at the first attempt. And when he was so young! He displayed an intellectual command of the score which I would normally associate only with a very much older conductor. It was also astonishing, because Simon has always been reticent about programming Beethoven and hasn't always been successful when he did so, in my view.

Were there things in the performance you disagreed with?

I have to admit that I disagreed with him about the tempo of the scherzo at the first performance in Birmingham, and in discussing it with him it emerged that he was unhappy too. I was very puzzled as to *why* it was too fast and not quite articulated, and I came to the conclusion that the reason was quite simply that he was throwing away the shape of the phrase, which must go to either the third or fourth bar of every group, not just the first; you have to encourage the orchestra to notice those middle bars. And I suggested that to get that you should go a little slower. He agreed, and in the next performance I heard in Birmingham it was absolutely perfect.

He said he had a problem getting into the trio as well...

Yes, every conductor breaks his neck over that, because of all the problems with the metronome mark. I think Simon wasn't quite secure in his own mind as to how he wanted it so it ran away slightly. This is so difficult to argue, but I really believe that this is the point where anyone who takes the score literally has to be aurally paralysed. I know some conductors try to do it up to tempo but you eventually have to say that it doesn't work, whatever Beethoven may have written. And you have to be able to make the accelerando so that you just drop into the new tempo, and that's what Simon hadn't quite managed first time round. But by the third performance he had done it; quite remarkable!

One thing I felt in the rehearsals was that he was always striving for this long, sustained sound, and neglected all the accents and the sforzandi, the light and shade.

You've put your finger on something I don't think Simon has quite sorted out. Of course in this case Simon later added to this basic sound the elements that give greater clarity and character, as was clear from the performance. But it is true that he wants a most beautiful sound and hasn't always got round to realizing that sometimes it's appropriate and sometimes it's quite wrong. One of his strengths is that he gets this gorgeous string sound because he insists on them playing through every note like a German orchestra would. But now he can afford to do something with that, to relax a bit. You can't make everything sound like an old Giulini or a Karajan, though there was a period, I must say, when I thought he would. But he's moving away from that characteristic now, and I have a hope that very soon he will acquire the courage of a Bruno Walter: to attack the notes occasionally with no regard to their sonority! And it was thrilling to hear him do Mahler 6 in January [1987] at the Festival Hall and to find that he could be utterly brutal with the sound, really using it in its right context.

With their performances of Beethoven's Ninth Symphony, it would be possible to argue, the relationship between Rattle and the CBSO came of age. The initial 'ludicrously sunny' period, as Rattle describes it, lasted from 1980 to the autumn of 1982. There was one difficult season with several changes, and then on a new level the partnership grew and matured from 1983 to 1986. Many of the events of 1986 were highlights, but while some of the big achievements – the Mahler 2 and *Turangalîla* recordings, for instance – looked backwards and summarized a period of work, the Beethoven 9 pointed forward to a future which was wide open.

And for Simon Rattle, on a personal level, Beethoven's Ninth marked an engagement with one of the 'greatest' works of the repertory such as he had always said he would be extremely cautious about – and it was also a great triumph. He too was moving from the group of works which he had known and loved from his earliest days – the Mahler and Messiaen were among the earliest classical pieces he heard on record – and into the new world of pieces he had considered unapproachable.

The question that was in everyone's minds during 1986, however, was whether the partnership between the CBSO and Simon Rattle could rise on to a new plateau. Rattle had already expressed his confidence that it would, in agreeing to extend his contract to 1989, but only on the secret condition that a major development plan would be put to the Arts Council and other funders: if it was rejected he claimed he would move on in 1989. If it was accepted by early 1987 then he would renew until 1991 and perhaps beyond.

But what was the purpose of that development plan? The back-

Staying on: Rattle signs the renewal of his contract with the CBSO until 1989 with
an extension until 1991, watched by Ed Smith (chief executive), Felix Kok (leader)
and George Jonas (chairman), in November 1985

ground to that can be found only in the complex business of the
organization of Britain's orchestral music-making, and in particular
the problems facing the regional orchestras.

II

ORCHESTRAS AND MONEY

For too long Britain's regional symphony orchestras have taken a
back seat while those in London have set the pace. London's promi-
nence as an international concert centre, and particularly as a recording centre, means that it has for a long time attracted the best
international conductors. As a result, working conditions in the regional orchestras have inevitably been poorer than in London: the
players are abysmally paid; there are fewer lucrative outside engagements such as await the energetic London player; and there is less
hope of finding good conductors. The one advantage the players in
the regional orchestras have is security: they are full-time, salaried,

with contracts which provide for structured arrangements about working hours, time off, holidays and sick pay. London players, by contrast (with the exception of those in the two opera house orchestras and the BBC Symphony Orchestra), are not contracted but self-employed. They choose what work to do and usually there is a lot of it. The best players are very well off as a result, though the question does arise as to when they can possibly have time to spend their money since they work anything up 650 sessions a year to earn it. A player in a regional orchestra, by comparison, works around 400 sessions a year.

The freelance set-up has many advantages for the players. Their orchestras are self-governing – the administrators are the servants of the players – and each player can essentially choose which dates to work and which not. This is the basis of the much-criticized deputy system, which means, for example, that the Royal Philharmonic Orchestra that plays an out-of-town choral society date may bear little relation to the Royal Philharmonic Orchestra that plays the following evening at the Festival Hall. More recently, however, there have been restrictions on this freedom, such as Simon Rattle insisted on for his *Après-midi* series with the Philharmonia in 1986 (see p. 152), and the RPO has announced ambitious plans for a period of contracted work for its players.

The commercial set-up of the four London orchestras and the increasing problem of finding adequate funds for subsidy means that more of their artistic decisions than is desirable have to be commercial decisions. The most cynical situation occurs when an orchestra engages a part-time principal conductor who flies in rarely but has an extremely good recording contract with a major company. If such a figure can also be controversial, attracting bitter denunciation as well as high praise, such as the Philharmonia have found with their current principal conductor, Giuseppe Sinopoli, then so much the better. It helps to sell concert tickets and records, both of which are necessary if the partnership is to go on working. As the manager of the Philharmonia has put it, 'every concert has to be a profit centre'.

For some time these commercial considerations were balanced by artistic policies that had at least occasionally a semblance of coherence, and though there was dissatisfaction from the press, the public and the grant-giving bodies were reasonably content. But perhaps because in recent years Arts Council grants have declined severely in real terms, dissatisfaction with the unadventurous charac-

ter of the London orchestras' programming and the absence of contemporary music from their seasons has been growing. There have
been increasingly loud complaints in the press and elsewhere about
the hand-to-mouth way London's orchestras are run; the orchestras
themselves argue that they have been gradually starved of the long-
term funding they need to improve the situation. A vacuum has been
created into which Simon Rattle and the CBSO have stepped at
exactly the right moment, and what puzzles most observers is
whether it was good luck or good management that put them in the
right place at the right time.

For the roots of London's orchestral malaise (a term which would
be hotly disputed by the managements of the four independent
London orchestras, all of which claim to be great orchestras), we have
to look back at least as far as the Goodman Report of twenty years
ago. In the wake of severe financial problems for the orchestras, it recommended that all four should receive subsidy on an even-handed
basis. The London Orchestral Concert Board was set up to channel
money from the Arts Council and the Greater London Council, and
allocated it not with any artistic discrimination but strictly in proportion to the number of concerts each orchestra mounted. Thus arose a
no-win situation which has dominated London's orchestral life for
two decades.

The attempts at breaking this stalemate have been universally
unsuccessful. In 1970 the Peacock Report on Orchestral Resources in
Great Britain investigated the problem and recommended that two
London orchestras be chosen for enhanced subsidy. The proposal
was immediately dismissed as unrealistic and the Arts Council dis-
sociated itself from the idea when the report was published. In 1972
the London Philharmonic and the New Philharmonia Orchestras
planned a merger in great secrecy. A major recording contract with
Giulini, Muti, Solti and Barenboim would have been the bedrock of
the new orchestra; but there was too much to lose for the players not
included in the scheme and it was thrown out.

Then there was the 1978 saga of the 'million-pound orchestra', a
proposal by the Arts Council music panel to upgrade one of the
London orchestras in which it could offer its players a full-time contract. The argument for it, based on the premise that 'programmes
have become stultified', and that 'orchestras rarely achieve the standard of which they are potentially capable', was indisputable – Simon
Rattle among others readily agrees with this view of the London scene

– but the problems were manifold: the temperament of London players; the willingness of any orchestra to give up its independence in return for higher subsidy; and, basically, the lack of the extra million pounds from the Arts Council, even if that figure was remotely a realistic one, which it was not.

When the Barbican Centre opened in 1982, giving the London Symphony Orchestra its long-awaited residency there, the log-jam at the Festival Hall was eased but it created other problems by providing yet another location for one-off popular concerts which drew audiences still further away from adventurous programmes elsewhere. Other proposals, connected with the Greater London Council's interventionist policy at the Royal Festival Hall, came and went. The GLC itself went, in 1986. The stalemate looked unchanged.

So why is there now a sudden opportunity for Rattle and the CBSO? The explanation has its roots in a change of direction at the Arts Council over the last few years under the chairmanship of Sir William Rees-Mogg, with Luke Rittner as secretary general. The emphasis of the council's thinking has shifted away from London and towards the previously neglected regions. This should have signalled an upswing in its support for the regional symphony orchestras, but there was a major hiccup in the way. When the council published its much-publicized strategic review, *The Glory of the Garden*, in March 1984, it did indeed argue the case for regional development and for plural funding of arts ventures with local authorities and others. Its orchestral policy, however, was barmy. It announced that it would take 'whatever steps might be necessary to reduce by one' the number of orchestras in London (a move which many have thought desirable but which no one has thought of a sensible or humane way of bringing about). That unnamed orchestra would be invited to move to eastern England as part of the council's regional development plan. A more bizarre and unlikely notion it would be hard to find, for the likelihood of a hundred or so musicians being prepared to uproot themselves from the London freelance market was very small indeed. The council was soon having to admit that it had miscalculated: no London orchestra wished to move, and because the proportion of their grant received through subsidy was now so small, the council had no lever to force them. Instead it cut all their grants equally by a sum totalling £280,000, which was however made up by the GLC.

The Glory of the Garden was received with fury by the regional orchestras. Rattle himself denounced it to the press as 'one of the silliest, most artificial ideas – like '60s town planners at work – a complete lack of reality'. In a scheme which called for development in the regions, the majority of the regions were in fact to be starved of development money because it was all to be put into the eastern area of the country for the formation of an orchestra that no one was confident was needed. In an attempt to salvage the situation the council commissioned a consultative report from Neil Duncan, who was then working as one of its music officers, called 'Promoting Regional Orchestral Music' (PROM). It clung to the idea of a new orchestra for the eastern region, based either in Nottingham or Cambridge (at a likely cost of £1.18 million a year), but suggested that in any case a new strategy was needed: 'the provision of orchestral music in the regions is overdue for reappraisal and major development'. Duncan's recommendation was that a Regional Orchestral Touring Agency should be set up (ROTA, another nice acronym) 'to assist in planning, financing and coordinating concerts by orchestras on tour'. It would not promote its own concerts, but would subsidize performances by means of limited grants or guarantees.

It soon became clear that local authority support for a new orchestra of symphony strength, with the massive continuing investment that implied, was not likely to be forthcoming. Nor was it thought feasible to base a major orchestra away from a metropolitan centre such as Birmingham or Manchester. Diligent Arts Council research suggested that with poor roads it might take four hours to get from Nottingham to Norwich by car, which might reduce the touring flexibility of an orchestra. Gradually, a more piecemeal approach emerged. Another Arts Council working-party reported back and suggested the reorganization and strengthening of the Eastern Authorities Orchestral Association. After flirting with the acronym OBOE – Organizing Board for Orchestras in the East – it came down in favour of a more sober title, the Eastern Orchestral Board; the highly experienced former general manager of the BBC Symphony Orchestra, William Relton, was appointed manager.

All this post-*Glory* manoeuvring had left the Arts Council with a certain amount of egg on its collective face. Its orchestral proposals had been universally dismissed as unrealistic and fanciful. So an astute observer could have suspected that the council was looking for some way to salvage its credibility with the orchestral profession, and at the same time to do something noteworthy for regional orchestral music.

Figuring out the future: Ed Smith and Simon Rattle's collaboration dates back to their days together in Liverpool; now they are embarked on an ambitious plan for developing the CBSO to world-class status. (*photo*: Jason Chenai)

The CBSO had been watching these moves carefully. It regarded the eastern orchestra scheme as impractical but not as a threat. As Ed Smith puts it, 'If there had been the money for a new orchestra I think everyone would have been delighted. It was just putting up the scheme without there being the money that seemed silly.' But by the end of 1984 and the beginning of 1985, when the Arts Council's commitment to a regional strategy became clear in the long term, the CBSO realized that there was an opportunity to be grasped. Through careful preliminary discussion with the Arts Council they ascertained that a development plan for the orchestra would be favourably received. It was this initial support, says Ed Smith, which led them to formulate the scheme as they did. Birmingham City Council was also involved in the preliminary discussions about the shape of the scheme. 'Our plan was already under way by the time the eastern orchestra idea collapsed,' says Smith, 'so it was not just a cynical idea of capitalizing on the space created when that scheme folded.'

Already in the 1985–6 season the CBSO had begun to benefit from the development money available to the regions from the Arts Council. A small grant of £13,400 had been given to launch an incentive marketing scheme to create a new audience for the new Wednesday subscription series. It hardly seemed a major advance, because at the same time as that development grant was given with one hand, the value of the basic Arts Council grant given with the other increased by only 2 per cent and therefore fell in real terms, much to Ed Smith's annoyance. 'I am bitterly disappointed and feel the whole thing is something of a con,' he told the *Birmingham Post*. This, coupled with the news shortly afterwards that the West Midlands County Council had frozen its grant of £279,000 (a better fate than many Midlands arts organizations, however, whose grants were cut back), made life difficult for the orchestra. But the chairman, George Jonas, rejected any talk of cutting back the size of the orchestra, which he called sacrosanct and essential for the continuance of its work.

Simon Rattle went further at the press conference to launch the 1985–6 season in Birmingham: 'The kind of philosophy which says education should only be about serving industry is the kind of philosophy that says art can't be worthwhile unless it makes a profit. It is hypocritical to say that a 2 per cent increase in grant is a rise and not a cut when it is less than the rate of inflation.' Nevertheless, the orchestra persevered with its plans to add a Wednesday subscription series, and in the event it was virtually sold out at once.

So during 1986 the scheme for a development plan was conceived, in some secrecy because Ed Smith was fully aware of the problems it could cause with other orchestras. 'We had to take the position, though, that other orchestras were not our concern – not because we don't like them, or anything silly like that, but because our prime concern is the welfare of the CBSO, and nothing ventured, nothing gained.' By May 1986 the plan was ready for submission to the Arts Council, and on 21 May there was a meeting of the Arts Council's music panel to which, very unusually, Ed Smith and Simon Rattle were invited. Clients rarely have the opportunity of putting their own case verbally to the panels, and this certainly indicated a predisposition on the part of the council towards the plan.

The details of the plan were presented in the document reproduced here as Appendix 1 (see p. 214), together with a further document outlining the financial implications. The main proposals were to establish new posts in the orchestra for co-principals and associate section leaders, so that these leading players no longer had to do 100 per cent of the work in the orchestral contract; and to raise the rates of pay throughout the orchestra, ensuring that better players joined the orchestra. The latter was bound to be controversial with other orchestral managements who felt themselves starved of Arts Council funding. In the end, the problems of the plan came down to two points: the principle, and the money. On the principle, there was the matter of the imbalance such a plan would cause with the other regional orchestras, and as far as the money was concerned, there was the problem of where it was likely to come from, how much was needed, and when. The total cost of the scheme was £600,000 of which the Birmingham City Council and the Arts Council were each being approached for half.

It would scarcely be breaking traditional Arts Council confidentiality to report that most members of the music panel were thoroughly in favour of the scheme. There were reservations about the possible threat to employment in other orchestras but a general agreement that there was a strong case for rewarding excellence in line with the new Arts Council policy of positive discrimination towards the worthwhile and the developmental. But members were also baffled by where the extra £300,000 could be found at a time when the Arts Council grant was falling in real terms. There was also recognition that the other £300,000, which it was hoped would come from Birmingham City Council who had expressed interest in the scheme, was not guaranteed. It seemed certain that the timetable proposed by the CBSO, which asked for an answer by the summer and implementation to begin in the last three months of 1986, was impossible. The Arts Council would have to consider it against its other priorities for the 1987–8 grant allocation, and it yet had to be seen whether the money came out of music funds – and thus would result in cut-backs elsewhere – or from the council's overall development funds. Music had certainly received less development funding than other art-forms, and this was a case which might find favour.

The matter was left to be discussed further, and remained confidential. But on 5 October 1986 that suddenly changed. The London *Observer* published an exclusive story by Peter Watson, headlined 'SUPER-ORCHESTRA PLAN WILL RATTLE LONDON RIVALS', which revealed what the report called a 'secret plan, kept even from the members of the orchestra', to turn the City of Birmingham Symphony Orchestra into a world-class orchestra. 'It will be created by a large injection of cash by the Arts Council, among others, to enable Birmingham to retain its luminous young conductor, Simon Rattle, and to hire the best players and soloists.' One of the more remarkable

The mythical super-orchestra: the press stories that leaked the CBSO's development plans

features of the story was the strength of the endorsement the plan received from Sir William Rees-Mogg, chairman of the Arts Council: 'I am very enthusiastic about the idea. Simon Rattle is one of the greatest young conductors in the world. Birmingham audiences have been very enthusiastic – all performances are now virtually sold out. I also applaud the idea of trying to build a British orchestra so that it can rival the international greats like Chicago. I suspect, too, that it can only be done with a regional orchestra where the players are on salary. With the London orchestras, where players are paid by the session, the quality goes up and down too much. It is noticeable that Chicago and Berlin are salaried orchestras.'

The fact that no one quoted in the story denied that the intention was to create a super-orchestra in Birmingham sent shock waves through the British musical world. Everyone was aware how over-stretched the Arts Council's resources were, and how little money was available for orchestras generally. Small wonder that London's orchestral managers initially reacted violently. John Willan of the London Philharmonic Orchestra said, 'If this is the advice the Arts Council is getting from its music advisory panel, then I find that very alarming. It's a slap in the face for London's orchestras. I just don't understand why it's necessary to go out of London, which is the musical capital of the world, and use resources which are desperately needed here.' And Ian Maclay of the Royal Philharmonic Orchestra said, 'One can't help jumping to the conclusion that the Arts Council finds it fashionable to support half-baked plans in the regions when they make it the policy to reject new and interesting formats submitted by the London orchestras.'

It was only over the next few days that the truth about Birmingham's proposals began to trickle out. As it happened, the day after the revelations Simon Rattle himself was on public view in London, at the press showing of the new television series, *From East to West*. During the lunch break he skilfully parried some intelligent questioning about the scheme from Terry Grimley, arts editor of the *Birmingham Post*, who subsequently wrote the clearest piece about the scheme, accurately reflecting Rattle's feelings that the Sunday newspaper story was unhelpful in its sensationalist aspects, but never dismissing the idea that the orchestra could, one day, become a world-beater. The only reservation was about the idea that such an orchestra could be bought, or that it could be transformed overnight. Grimley wrote: 'The picture being painted is that of the CBSO being picked out for

grooming as Britain's premier orchestra, with its four London rivals
desperate to torpedo the plans. But the reality is more complex and
less dramatic, according to the man around whom the plan revolves,
the CBSO's principal conductor, Simon Rattle: "The report was
ludicrously over the top... You have only to consider that Munich
spends £4.9 million on its one orchestra and Britain spends £4.7 million on all its symphony and chamber orchestras put together to see
that there is not the sort of money around to make that dramatic a difference. We basically want a bit more to enable us to do more of what
we are doing already, to enable the players to be paid better and to
give us more rehearsal time. I will believe it all when it actually happens."'

The internal politics of the situation, however, revolved around the
setting of regional orchestra against regional orchestra, a question Ed
Smith had foreseen very clearly. Other orchestras in the country had
been campaigning for an increase in their grant – the Hallé in Manchester had achieved one in the aftermath of *The Glory of the Garden*
with a paltry £22,500 – and the Association of British Orchestras and
the Musicians' Union had been trying to publicize the appalling pay
of regional orchestra members. But they realized that the Birmingham
development plan, if it was approved by the Arts Council, would
change the whole delicate balance of power within the country's orchestral structure. If the Birmingham orchestra increased its rates of
pay, that would obviously have the most serious consequences for
other orchestras. Players might be lost to Birmingham from other
orchestras, and it would become desperately difficult to replace them.
In the Birmingham scheme, salaries for the sub-principals and the
rank-and-file strings were planned to increase by between a third and
a half – a substantial amount. The new associate section leaders, who
would be required to do only some 60 per cent of the work, would be
well paid by any standard.

The Association of British Orchestras sent a letter to Sir William
Rees-Mogg protesting vigorously that there had been no consultation
on the plan and no opportunity for the other orchestras to put their
case. Moreover, the question of salary disparity was raised as a potentially serious issue. In the orchestral world, opinions were divided as
to whether the regional orchestras were correct to feel that they were
under threat from the CBSO plan, or whether a general raising of
salary levels and an increase in all regional symphony orchestra
grants would be the inevitable long-term result of the scheme. Rees-

Mogg naturally took the latter view, and in reply to the ABO he expressed the hope that 'the CBSO development plan will presage further development in music across the board'. How this was to happen remained unclear, and the Association was sceptical. It subsequently wrote to Luke Rittner pointing out that in spite of its support in principle for the plan, for the Arts Council 'to participate in a development plan where the entire sum is to be spent on orchestra salaries of one kind or another (the majority on increasing the salaries of musicians already in the orchestra) without responding to the consequent needs of other orchestras would be wilfully to plunge these orchestras into financial difficulties of a severity which in at least some cases they will be unable to survive'. The implication was that other managers would not be able to resist the pressure to raise their salaries, but without the funds to support such a move.

Meanwhile in the media the fall-out from the leak of the development plan continued. In his published comments Ed Smith sought to remove the idea that they were trying to create an 'elite' orchestra. 'That's just an interpretation that had been put upon it. All we are trying to do is to develop the work we are doing here already, and to keep Simon Rattle here after 1989. I don't think we should just sit back and wave goodbye to Simon.'

As it became clear that it was Arts Council *development* money that was being talked about, the orchestral managers became less unfriendly. John Willan changed his tack, and was quoted in the *Guardian* two months later as saying, 'Good luck to Birmingham. The Arts Council should reward success.' Clive Gillinson of the LSO saw past the immediate threat when he said, 'I'm delighted by any new money that comes into music, but not money that is taken from elsewhere' – and that was also the attitude of Christopher Bishop of the Philharmonia, after the dust had settled.

A week after their initial story the *Observer* returned to the attack with a full-scale leader-page profile of Simon Rattle (anonymous, as is the custom, but written by Gillian Widdicombe), which at last got all the details right and included an immortal quote from one of the London orchestral managers, who said that the plan was (figuratively) 'a load of old bassoons, because everybody knows that to make the Birmingham compare with the London orchestras you'd have to fire half the orchestra, not just add a few more players'. This quote was so near to what all the London managers probably felt privately about the plan that in a subsequent *Guardian* piece one of them denied 'using those exact words' when the quote had not come from him in the first place.

The quote produced a riposte in the *Observer* letters column from Alan Davey and Stephen Parkinson, who wrote that the remarks 'highlight the arrogant complacency of the London orchestral establishment in the face of a live music scene dying in a morass of mediocre playing of unimaginative programmes. Both of us have attended concerts in London and Birmingham on a regular basis and the difference in commitment and artistic achievement is striking. To arrive in one's overpriced concert seat in London to hear more Brahms and Mozart played by a bunch of session men on autopilot is not what we were brought up on when we had the good fortune to live in Birmingham. The London orchestras have only themselves to blame when the long-overdue moment comes for one of them to be cut. I trust the anonymous manager in question will not be too bitter if it turns out to be his own orchestra that is to disappear.' (That remark has a remarkably prophetic tone in view of the 'takeover fever' that erupted in the next sensationalized orchestral press story of the year.)

On 18 October *Classical Music*'s new editor, Graeme Kay, editorialized on the situation, pointing out that 'the mythical super-orchestra is for arts pundits either a vision for the future or a hysterical delusion, depending on your point of view – the existing non-super orchestras incline in the latter direction'. He wondered whether the CBSO had 'broken ranks and stolen a march on its rivals', but having changed the metaphor to one of playing one's cards right in the subsidy game, concluded that 'CBSO manager Edward Smith should hardly be blamed for seizing the opportunity to win a trick with his development proposals at a time when funds are available where none were before'. He also raised the question, which had already occurred both to players and listeners alike, as to whether Rattle would actually carry out his threat to leave even if the plan did not go through.

A subsequent letter to *Classical Music* raised the question of whether Rattle's commitment to Birmingham was actually a good thing. 'It cannot be very healthy,' wrote a Mr A. Gordon of London NW6, 'for someone at Mr Rattle's stage in a career to have people going to such lengths to try and entice him to remain in the same job. If he stayed surely both conductor and orchestra would become stagnated and stifled by each other?' It was not surprising that that letter came from someone with an address far from Birmingham.

Meanwhile the story was being highlighted by events in London. In December André Previn in a long and complicated statement announced his departure from the music directorship of the Royal Philharmonic, saying that in the present climate in London the job was impossible for him to do well. He would continue to do as much work as before and would remain as principal conductor while Vladimir Ashkenazy, a close friend, would become music director. It was interesting that Previn discussed at great length the problems of London's orchestral music, and that every effort was made to make the change appear a positive one which would (in a vague phrase that was not fully explained) 'instigate a new era in the London musical scene'. Shortly afterwards *The Times* ran a brief story saying that Claudio Abbado would not renew his contract with the LSO in 1988, and there were rumours of his dissatisfaction with features of the London musical scene of which many in the musical world had been aware of for some time.

All this was put into perspective by a stimulating piece in the *Guardian* by Hugh Canning on 9 December, which asked the question: why is all this happening now on the orchestral front, after all these years of soldiering on, of making do? 'The answer almost certainly lies in two little but glamorous words, Simon Rattle.' Canning's analysis was perhaps questionable in that he suggested that Birmingham's solutions could be applied to London's problems, but it at least raised important issues: the London orchestras, he wrote 'deserve encouragement from the Arts Council, perhaps with an indication that the Rattle/CBSO experiment, if it happens, should be taken as a blueprint for what might be in London. The orchestras could also help themselves by redefining the role of music director, by denying these important posts to the latest darlings of the record industry, and by appointing musicians who will work fruitfully with, and fight militantly for, their own orchestras over a long period, rather as Simon Rattle has done in Birmingham.'

Not surprisingly, that article was pinned to the CBSO's orchestral notice-board when I paid a visit there in December 1986 to find out how the news of the development plan had been received by the orchestra. Players on the council of management had had an inkling about it, and others had 'had a feeling something was going on', but the extent and substance of the plan had come as a surprise. There was a division of opinion as to how necessary it was to make a major stand over development. One said, 'I think Simon's made an issue of the development because he's embarrassed at working us so hard when we get so little money. People say, "How much longer can we keep going like this?" We just don't get paid enough for the job we do, and the standard that is demanded of us now is so high.' But another player objected: 'There could have been plenty of room for development if he hadn't made an issue of it. But he thinks a major change is needed and that could bring problems as well as opportunities.'

The feeling among the orchestra members I talked to was naturally one of relief that higher salaries might make things a little easier for them: 'It would help not to have to do absolutely all the work. We're paid so little I have to do gigs and teach and paint the house myself. At least I could get someone to paint the house!' There was a feeling, too, that the increase would reflect the extraordinarily demanding work which they were now having to do consistently, day in and day out, as a result of the orchestra's current success. 'At the moment it's just a question of survival. We're working incredibly hard – not as much as we used to in hours, but really difficult work. There's more pressure, we need to practise. The repertory is being extended, and you have to work faster and faster.'

So while there was a welcome for the development plan within the orchestra, the ramifications – the possibility that some players would be elbowed aside by new highly paid members – had not begun to be felt. What was uppermost was whether Rattle would actually carry out his threat to leave if the money did not come through: 'It's crossed my mind that he's probably bluffing. This orchestra as it is now is his creation, and if he went to Amsterdam or wherever he'd be building on someone's else's work. And if he went somewhere unknown he'd have to start again from scratch.' Another opinion was: 'My feeling is that he's got far too much to lose if he stays and it *doesn't* get better. So if we don't get the money, he'll go. But at present he is still planning centuries ahead, and that's great. There is no glimmer of an idea that he's slimming down his operation here. He's 300 per cent committed to the future.'

In fact the spectre of Rattle's possible withdrawal from Birmingham loomed large in the press during January and February 1987. It irritated Rattle considerably, but it was the inevitable consequence of his having used the possible non-renewal of his Birmingham contract as a threat in order to achieve the development aims. As luck (or

Rattle in rehearsal with the CBSO, 1986

ill-luck, depending on your point of view) would have it, a new vision
appeared in London at precisely that moment. The London Philharmonic suggested to the Philharmonia that the two orchestras pool
their administrative resources, a move that might eventually lead to
the formation of a single orchestra. This new orchestra might also be
resident on the South Bank if the new South Bank Board declared
publicly what had been discussed privately: that its plans for thematic
seasons and adventurous repertoire needed a 'house' orchestra.

It did not take much imagination to see that Rattle would be talked
of as the ideal conductor of such an orchestra, and the fact that the
Philharmonia rejected the idea out of hand did not prevent speculation continuing, as the London Philharmonic had doubtless in-
tended. It also did not take much imagination to see that if Rattle
drifted from the Philharmonia to the LPO for his London
appearances (a possibility the LPO was privately keen to exploit) the
balance of power could shift considerably. Richard Morrison wrote
in *The Times*: 'If he decides not to renew his Birmingham contract,
which is the subject of a financial hassle at the moment, he is likely to
be everyone's first choice as music director of any South Bank resident orchestra. Hitherto he has done most of his London conducting
with the Philharmonia. But if the LPO is building on its Glyndebourne association with him, working towards a tacit exclusivity in
London, that could be the end of the war.'

Rattle was annoyed by these speculations, as he was by a suggestion I made in an *Observer* piece at the same time that even if he renewed in Birmingham until 1991, he might be prepared to come to
London after that if the orchestral situation there changed radically.
To Terry Grimley of the *Birmingham Post* he said, 'What I find rather
offensive about the speculation is the assumption that I would want
to go. It's part of the arrogance of the London music scene that they
assume I would jump at it. This [Birmingham] is where my life is, this
is where my work is.' However, it would be possible to argue that, as
the awkward financial negotiations over the development plan
dragged on between Birmingham City Council and the Arts Council,
a little speculation about Rattle's future would do no harm in clinch-
ing his Birmingham deal. The January 1987 deadline for the expiry of
his option to renew his contract quietly came and went. It was not
until March 1987 that anything could be finalized, and by then Rattle
was away guest conducting in America.

On 9 March it was announced that Birmingham City Council and

Rattle in rehearsal with the CBSO, 1986

the Arts Council had 'agreed jointly to fund the first phase of ambitious plans for the future development of the CBSO: the City
Council's grant would rise from £285,000 in 1986–7 to £484,000 in
1987–8, while the Arts Council's grant would rise from £775,000 to
£885,000. Hence the City Council, because of some complicated
negotiations about funding following the abolition of the local metropolitan authority in 1986, was contributing by far the larger proportion of the money.

The crucial words in the announcement were 'first phase'. The
CBSO would not receive all the money it was looking for – a
£309,000 increase rather than £600,000 – nor did it receive any
promises about whether money would be forthcoming in the future.
So in fact, far from getting enough to fund its development plan, it
would receive only half the sum – exactly what it had always said it
did not want. Moreover not all the money received could be used immediately for development. A current deficit had to be paid off, leaving just £231,000 for development.

So how would the orchestra proceed? Would it risk embarking on
the development plan without the assurance of future funding? The
chairman, George Jonas, was optimistic: 'Neither the Arts Council
nor the city could commit future finance in advance but it was clear
that goodwill was there, and provided all goes well, they will support
us.' A committee was set up, including players, to advise on the implementation of the plan: it met for the first time on 1 April, when Rattle
was still in America. Jonas said the committee would decide how to
implement the original plan within the resources available: 'it was
agreed without dissent that nothing else made sense'. Whatever the
problems, that decision was enough for Rattle to take the course
everyone expected he would, and to renew his contract in Birmingham until August 1991.

'The future is a very interesting thing in Birmingham,' says Ed Smith.
'We have a number of trump cards up our sleeve: one is Simon, of
course, but the other is an exceptionally responsive local authority
who are backing us to the hilt. They've let us have a major input to the
design of our new concert hall in their Convention Centre, and that is
not typical – look at some of the disastrous concert halls which have
been built in the last decade when advice was not sought.'

Indeed the whole story of Birmingham's new concert hall, un-
glamorously called Hall 2 of the Convention Centre, planned to open

Future home: Hall 2 of the new Birmingham Convention Centre,
the CBSO's base from 1991

in 1991, is unusual. Like the National Theatre, it has been talked about for decades – it was promised to Adrian Boult when he was conductor of the City of Birmingham Orchestra in the 1920s – but it has always been postponed. The plan on which the CBSO is now pinning its hopes is an elaborate £106 million scheme near the city centre in Broad Street. The bid for the scheme was launched with an appeal to the European Economic Community for a direct grant of up to £50 million. In January 1986 the EEC offered £37.2 million over four years, and Birmingham decided to borrow the rest against the security of the National Exhibition Centre. In March the Environment Secretary agreed the compulsory purchase order which would be neccessary to clear the twenty-five-acre site (though one existing structure, a cast-iron men's urinal, will be re-erected elsewhere). The way seemed clear for one of the most imaginative schemes of local government cooperation in recent years. Birmingham may have got nowhere with its bid for the Olympics, but through the coming together of the political parties in schemes such as this Convention Centre, it is rebuilding its future prosperity slowly but surely.

The great advantage for the orchestra in the scheme for the new hall is the freedom of choice they have had in the design. The American firm of Artec, with its acoustic consultant, Russell Johnson, who was responsible for acoustic work in the successful new halls the orchestra plays in at Northampton and Nottingham, has developed a plan along the traditional lines of the 'shoebox' shape, so satisfactory in Vienna, Amsterdam and Boston (though not so satisfactory in Birmingham Town Hall). The new hall will be acoustically variable, with motorized curtains, an acoustic canopy above the stage (which will also help in relating the space on stage to the size of the audience) and a reverberation control chamber. The aim is to give the hall both clarity and warmth, which might seem a contradiction, but Johnson is confident that it can be achieved.

The CBSO will be watching carefully. If, in addition to the country's best young conductor, and a new injection of the best young players, it also had by 1991 the country's best concert hall, what would be the limitations on its future?

Last impressions: January–March 1987

2 JANUARY 1987. The busy Liverpool Road leads through Islington
to the northern part of central London. Off that road is a secluded
street of Georgian terraced houses, a quiet cul-de-sac. It forms part of
the once elegant Barnsbury Estate, laid out by Thomas Cubitt around
1820 before he moved on to Belgravia. There has been a long period
of neglect for many of the old houses here: a recent architectural
guide mentions that their condition 'varies from gentrification to seedy decay'. But gentrification is now the order of the day in
this newly popular area, and this street is among its sprucest little
roads.

At the Rattles' house, where Christmas lights still adorn the
window-box – a nice touch – the door is opened by Simon Rattle,
Commander of the British Empire. He was awarded the CBE in the
previous day's New Year's Honours List. He still looks pretty much
like Simon Rattle without the CBE, and he laughs off the statutory
congratulations. 'My niece wants to know if she always has to call me
commander . . .' I've brought along for him a cutting from this
morning's *Financial Times*, and I'm rather surprised to find that he's
already been out to buy it. Perhaps he was tipped off. In his review of
the previous year's music-making Andrew Clements has written:
'Rattle is unquestionably now the hottest property in British music
and whether Birmingham's pre-eminence is due to his own gifts or to
a genuine raising of the standards of the orchestra under his leadership seems to be thoroughly irrelevant. Orchestral concerts of the
quality of the recent one at the Barbican, which contained Sibelius
and Brahms symphonies on a level of achievement one had forgotten
could come from a British orchestra need to be encouraged at almost
any cost.'

Teddy bears' picnic: Ellie and Sasha Rattle join Simon for a rare public appearance
to raise money for a Birmingham charity

Rattle's response is typical in its avoidance of anything that concerns him personally: 'Well that's nice for the orchestra. Come and have some coffee.' Anyone who knows the Rattles will tell you that coffee-making is a serious ritual, carried out with great deliberation by Simon himself on an ancient espresso machine that looks as if it runs off a combustion engine. Today the machine is upstairs on the landing, something of a surprise. 'Ellie's just made me a study of my own these last couple of days and Sasha has moved downstairs.' So Sasha is sleeping in the room by the kitchen (formerly his playroom), while a secretary is working on some letters on a makeshift desk in the front room (which also houses the piano and scores). Ellie is making some phone calls and I sit on the stairs while Simon completes the coffee; the cups have to be washed in the bathroom – the logistics are not quite sorted out yet.

'People say you used to be very disorganized . . .' 'Used to be?! I'm still hopeless.' 'But you are so precise about rehearsals, and timings and what you want to do and when you want to do it...' 'That's about all I can manage, that and some cooking. The rest is a mystery to me. It was years before I discovered I had to pay National Insurance contributions...' Sasha potters upstairs, having got up. We discuss Christmas presents. We tread gingerly into Simon's new study, a tiny room with a desk, already dominated by a large photo of him with Sasha at La Scala, Milan. Berlioz's *Symphonie fantastique*, which I remember is on the Birmingham schedule for February, is being worked on: the new critical edition score is being collated with Simon's old working score. There are plenty of diversions from Sasha – who is, without any question, the centre of the household – before he and Ellie go off to see a friend. Simon says goodbye for the umpteenth time: 'If you asked me quite seriously what had been the biggest influence on me I would have to say Sasha, without any bullshit at all...'

Through all the comings and goings Simon shows a fantastic ability to keep his mind on whatever is being discussed: he'll take up a thought in mid-sentence five minutes later, saying apologetically 'Sorry, I was just on hold there.' The question of the moment is, of course, the development plan for the CBSO and what will happen if it is accepted or rejected. And what will happen to Simon Rattle? The only reply he will give to that is untypically negative: 'If I left I really don't know what I would do. I wouldn't starve.' It's clear that his mind is far from leaving, and that he is totally committed to a Birmingham future. But what is really possible there?

SIMON RATTLE: I'm still not sure how far the orchestra can go. I don't know where the technical limitations will finally scupper musical intelligence. It's a case of something that's growing – they can sometimes surprise with the number of technical improvements they can make – and technical ability and musical ability sometimes go hand in hand. But if things don't change now, I know it won't work. After five more years we'll just be getting at each other's throats. It will be time for someone else to have a go.

Mightn't your plan for new, extra players disrupt the cohesion of what you've built so far?

You never know, but it's a risk we have to take. I don't see why, because I think having people of the standard of our principal cellist who leads like that has made a vast difference. I've seen it in some other orchestras too: a new face in a certain place can buoy the thing up, provide new help. Our players need a reservoir of strength so that they don't have to strive and strive – though that is part of the excitement, of

'If you asked me seriously what had been the biggest influence on me I would have to say Sasha . . .': father and son trying out the percussion in Birmingham, December 1986 (*photo* Jason Chenai)

course, but there's just too much of it at the moment. Whatever we do can only be done a step at a time. It's not quite as simple as it might be in Chicago and Cleveland, where you just decide to do a lot of sacking. That is not the way at all.

With higher salaries you might be able to lure people from around the country but will you lure them from London?

Again, I just don't know. That would be part of the problem of persuading players of the advantages of not living the gypsy sort of life they have to live in London, always on the go, on the move. People from London wouldn't know what to do with all the time we'd be able to give them. They've never worked on the Continent so they haven't seen how it works perfectly well there.

How about the problems the plans will cause for the other regional orchestras?

Of course there will be problems. But one result will be that for the first time managers will be able to demand proper rates of pay for their players, and proper conditions, humane conditions. That cannot be a bad result.

One of Simon Rattle's least favourite questions is 'What are you going to do after Birmingham?' 'Where can you go from here?' (My favourite answer to that one out of his many was 'Yeah, well we could go down the pub': the interviewer faithfully printed it.) What irritates him is the assumption that he is on his way somewhere else, that Birmingham is only a temporary resting-place en route to the real thing. His achievements with the orchestra clearly belie that, and his commitment for the next few years is certain.

This is a subject to which we return in our last conversation in March before he leaves for six weeks in America. The development plan is on the verge of being agreed; he knows it is essentially in place. But he has been incensed by the idea that what he really ought to do in the future is to come to London, and he challenges me to say whether I think a great orchestra can really be built in Birmingham, because he does. I don't, he suggests. Well, he is right to the extent that I believe it is extremely unlikely to happen in the present set-up. The CBSO can become better, maybe much better, but great? How do orchestras become great?

SIMON RATTLE: I agree, you can't tell. But you have to get there. So let's start, one step at a time. It can't be done overnight. There's a great difference between an orchestra like the Berlin Philharmonic, which is incomparably full of individual virtuosi from the front to the back of each section, and an orchestra like the Rotterdam Philharmonic which has many problems to sort out but has the potential to become great. Cleveland was not at all a good orchestra before Szell got to work on it, and it's interesting to find out there how long it took.

I believe someone has to try and do it. Does one just sit back and say that the only great orchestras are the five or six which are already there, and you spend your time going and refining that instrument, or is it more worthwhile – for the music's sake – to have built something up gradually? There are so many things that can be learnt, and absorbed, which the players can grow into, which are not to do with the question of sheer virtuosity.

People say that in London you would have a much higher level of musical and technical preparedness given to you to work on . . .

What is the best answer to that? In some ways it's true. And there is the possibility that I'm deluding myself. But the difference is really not very great. It is definitely there, but people expect the gap to be very wide, because that's how it's been in the past. It's difficult for them to appreciate that the gap is narrowing all the time. And there are so many things that are right in Birmingham that are not right in London. Of course there is potential in London, but you would have to start from a premiss that doesn't exist at the moment: that two orchestras have been put together or whatever it might be.

So much playing in London now is like a Pavlov reaction: turn it on and it happens. Of course it's remarkable, but it's not healthy. And it destroys people. I was talking to a very fine player for hours the other day: he was blustered into a London orchestra, and it's been dreadful for him. It's going to be jungle law music-making in London until something radical changes. And what I want is organic music-making. I don't believe you can build it from the top, just doing something about programmes, even just with more money. It's got to be done from the bottom with everyone knowing where they have come from.

I suppose I want to be a Frankenstein – no, I don't like that – an architect, perhaps, rather than just a make-up artist. It's because of the music. Whatever I want to build I want to build on some sort of human foundation.

*   *   *

MARCH 1987. In Boston, Massachusetts, Simon Rattle was booed. Did he conduct badly? Apparently not: all he wanted to do was rehearse. The Boston Symphony Orchestra traditionally has one of its rehearsals as an open event for friends of the orchestra, and usually the conductor plays straight through the pieces on that occasion. Not Rattle; as everything in this book indicates, he is intent on changing the way that orchestras play and will not accept simply what is offered him by the musicians. A disgruntled Boston Symphony Orchestra supporter wrote to the *Boston Globe*: 'Who does this young man think he is? He was conducting the BSO, one of the world's great orchestras, and treating the orchestra like they are a bunch of beginners. Through the evening he stopped them again and again, usually after only a few notes had been played. It made the evening long and boring for the audience, dozens of whom left early. I suspect that members of the orchestra would have liked to have left as well... Unbelievably, when the concert [sic] finally ended – and I mean finally – Rattle was greeted with loud boos, which he had earned.'

There you have in a nutshell the reason why Simon Rattle must prefer to stay at home and work with an orchestra that wants to be stopped and challenged, rather than travel the world and be expected to take what he is offered. In England the reaction to what he achieves with this approach could scarcely be more different. After a Birmingham concert of Sibelius and Brahms early in 1987, David Fanning wrote in the *Guardian*: 'There are two problems with a Simon Rattle special such as this one. First, how to drive home safely, with one's senses reeling from the power and beauty of the music. Second, how to put into words the intensity of the experience. A third problem is how to face up again to the deadly routine of certain other musical establishments. To think what Rattle might do for orchestra X or Y is to weep at the waste of potential there.'

Few people can doubt that Simon Rattle's talents will develop and mature in the future. The most negative comment I heard from anyone while preparing this book was that his present success was luck: 'I reckon there are a couple of hundred youngsters in any generation with the same talent as Simon; he just got the breaks and was in the right place at the right time.' I hope these pages prove that to be wrong: quite apart from his almost superhuman determination to conduct, Rattle could scarcely have achieved what he has without a musicality and commitment which forces itself on orchestras and audiences alike.

Most of his career lies in the future. It would be rash to predict in what direction he will turn. Few would dispute that both his conducting technique and his musical instincts place him in the front rank of musicians of his generation; yet while he is, in a reversal of the usual position, highly praised – almost a cult figure – in the classical music world in Britain, the magic does not always work abroad. So above all Rattle will want to ensure for himself the right conditions for his work. And increasingly it looks as if those conditions will be met only in Birmingham. Now that the first phase of the orchestra's development plan has been agreed, there are many hard questions to be answered about how it will be put into effect, and many imponderables about whether it will succeed. But if it does succeed, then the sky is the limit. He could stay in Birmingham until 1995, four years after the new concert hall should open, extending his contract yet again, and at the end of it all he would still be only forty.

There are other questions besides whether Rattle can maintain the musical and personal momentum which has carried him thus far, and whether he can make the CBSO a great orchestra. There is the problem of the way orchestras are run in this country, and the even more significant question of what they play, the balance of the repertory. In this, as in so much else, Rattle is a child of his time. He was not, as we have seen, brought up on the classics, but on Mahler, Stravinsky and the post-war composers. In 1986 he was still conducting and recording pieces (Mahler's Second, Messiaen's *Turangalîla*) which he had known as a boy, while at the same time taking a new and perhaps decisive step back to the classics by tackling Beethoven's Ninth Symphony for the first time. I discussed the whole question of changing taste in orchestral life and the changing emphasis of Rattle's repertory with the pianist Alfred Brendel, who visited Paris with the CBSO in 1986 and has often appeared with them over the years; Rattle frequently turns to him for advice.

ALFRED BRENDEL: Conductors these days are steeped in Mahler rather than in the classics. There is not enough chance to work as regularly on the classical repertory as conductors used to do. The regular fare of orchestras is no longer Beethoven symphonies, and although the critics may complain about continual Beethoven, it seems to me to be so important for an orchestra and for a conductor to have that firm basis of what a symphony is about and what a symphony orchestra should sound like. Much as I can understand the reluctance of conductors today to deal with Beethoven, and their desire to give it a rest, I do feel they miss out on something important.

Simon is very typical in that the Mahler symphonies seem to come easier to him at the moment than the Beethoven symphonies. (For me, Simon has put Mahler 10 on the map; he has proved once and for all that this is a very remarkable score.) They may be nearer to us and to what we feel than Beethoven. But he knows he must now go back and find the roots of this tradition. One of the reasons for the unease of conductors and orchestras with Mozart and Beethoven is the question of performance practice, of 'authentic' performances using old instruments. Interesting and stimulating as this is, it can never be the only way to play the classics. My problem as a soloist is that I can find at present a dozen conductors who can do the Schoenberg Piano Concerto well, some of them very well. As for the Beethoven concertos, I am sometimes at a loss!

It is wonderful to work out classical concertos with Simon and the CBSO because it means breaking fresh ground. Simon is the most stunningly gifted young conductor I know, and my only reservation is that he spends too much time on repertory that I regard as second-rate; surely the first-class repertory is big enough to spend one's life with. I think the time has come to identify with what is really worthwhile – he told me just recently that doing the *Choral* Symphony gave him a new measure of what music was about.

I heard a tape of the first performance of Beethoven's Ninth he gave, in Scotland, and I would like to meet another young conductor who could bring it off in such a fashion; it was truly impressive. We also

'Simon is the most stunningly gifted young conductor I know': Alfred Brendel rehearsing with Rattle in Birmingham Town Hall, 1986

talked about one of his earlier performances of the *Eroica*, and I said to Simon that I felt it was too spacious. So, it seems, did he. Stronger concentration, greater tightness, more sense of the overall shape was needed – and, I'm sure, was achieved in the next performances. Simon loves the detail and pays great attention to it, to the point where he gets over-sensitive about it (in welcome contrast to certain other conductors!). He has a marvellous ear for sound and nuance. Recently I heard him do Mozart's K503 [with Stephen Bishop-Kovacevich] with a transparency that filled me with joy.

Simon seems far more interested than most young conductors in approaching a Furtwängler-like style; as a fellow admirer, I am with him there. Of course, it takes time to assemble and accommodate all the ingredients, and to do this in a really personal way. Did the old conductors have more time? Nowadays there is so much music. I'm all for the performance of new music, and Simon does it wonderfully well: but one has to reconcile both ends. If anybody can, Simon will make them meet. I shall keep my fingers crossed.

Looking to the future: Rattle working with Birmingham schoolchildren on a project about Stravinsky's *Firebird*, which they heard him conduct at Birmingham Town Hall in July 1987

And the last word was best put by Rattle's friend, the composer Oliver Knussen:

OLIVER KNUSSEN: What Simon is doing in Birmingham is the best thing that's happened to orchestras in this country for I don't know how long. Someone taking a Stokowskian stand like that, and saying he'll grow with it, at the expense of more prestigious guest engagements, is marvellous. What Simon is quietly doing there has the potential to create a model of change for every orchestra in this country, and things certainly need changing. It's hitting the orchestras elsewhere pretty hard psychologically, and they'll be looking to Birmingham to see if the situation throws up answers to their problems. In the end it won't be a question of competition: what is going on in Birmingham will simply be artistically more satisfactory.

The conductor is growing into the repertory with the orchestra; it's unique, and it's how it should be done.

Appendix 1:
the CBSO Society Ltd development plan

Presented to the Arts Council and the
City of Birmingham

CBSO DEVELOPMENT PLAN

2 May 1986   CONFIDENTIAL

We believe that the CBSO and the City of Birmingham together provide a uniquely fertile ground in which to cultivate an orchestra of
great international prestige under the direction of a distinguished
British conductor. This paper sets out a broad development plan for
the CBSO which would turn it from a very good British regional orchestra into one of the highest international calibre which would *consistently* challenge the standards set by the world's greatest orchestras
(Concertgebouw, Vienna Philharmonic, Berlin Philharmonic, Cleveland, Chicago, etc.). Such an orchestra would be to British musical
life what the Royal Shakespeare Company is to British theatre – a
national and international cultural institution which happened to be
based in the regions rather than London.
   We believe that such an orchestra can only be brought into being by
a combination of essential factors:

1 A substantial uplift in both national and local funding;
2 An energetic and dedicated principal conductor and artistic
   adviser of the highest international calibre;
3 An involved, stimulated and committed group of orchestral
   musicians;
4 A management team which is both sound and imaginative;
5 Informed and enthusiastic support from both audiences and
   sponsors.

We believe that in the CBSO the last four prerequisites exist. In this paper we set out a case to our major funders (Arts Council and City of Birmingham) to help us finance a project which we believe will engender pride and prestige at both national and local level.

The CBSO and Simon Rattle

The dominant feature of the CBSO's growth over the past six years has undoubtedly been Simon Rattle's loyalty and commitment which has enabled both conductor and orchestra to grow together. This has brought about an ever higher performance standard, a broadening of the repertoire and a little short of spectacular growth in audience attendances (in Birmingham, even with the introduction of a new repeat programme series, audiences are averaging 98 per cent). It might be helpful to summarize the contractual position which exists between Rattle and the CBSO:

1980   Appointed for three-year period;
1981   Extended contract to 1986;
1985   Renewed contract to run from September 1986 to August 1989 (three years) with an option for a further renewal by two years to August 1991. This option to be taken by January 1987 at the latest (i.e., eight months hence).

The renewal to 1991 and beyond is dependent on the following four conditions:

1 A new concert hall for the CBSO in Birmingham;
2 The enlargement of the string sections and the employment of additional experienced string principals;
3 Improved pay and conditions for the orchestral musicians so as, first, to attract the best possible talent to Birmingham, and then to retain it rather than have the CBSO used as a stepping-stone;
4 The ability to undertake adventurous and enterprising tours and projects and explore new fields of contemporary music.

Both Simon Rattle and the CBSO have indicated that they would like to see the relationship extend even beyond 1991.

Conditions 1. and 4. are already in hand. The new concert hall is now in the planning stage and completion is anticipated by 1990. It will seat 2,200 and is being designed by the world's leading firm of concert hall designers, Artec of New York, whose track-record of success is unmatched. As well as possessing perfect acoustics for orchestral music the hall will provide a much-needed additional 500 seats over the current Birmingham Town Hall capacity. Plans for future touring, commissions of new works, educational activities involving the orchestra in a variety of projects and a commitment to the positive promotion of the best of contemporary music are already established as essential features of our future activities.

It is conditions 2. and 3. which now require our urgent attention if we are to secure Rattle's continuing long-term commitment to Birmingham and the CBSO. If the orchestra cannot, through lack of adequate funding, develop towards the goal of becoming an international body it is likely that Rattle will look abroad for the sort of standards and conditions which would enable him to achieve his ambitions. That would be another tragic loss of home-grown talent. It *could* be possible in Birmingham with the help of a forward-looking and enterprising City Council and a concerned and quality-conscious Arts Council. We cannot fund this development from our own present resources of box-office income or from sponsorship. The very nature of entering into additional employment commitments will require a more secure financial base than can be provided from either of these sources. If additional funding is not forthcoming we shall not be able to fulfil Simon Rattle's aims and we would have to tell him sooner rather than later that the task is unachievable in Birmingham. Both he and the CBSO would then need to begin planning their separate lives post 1989.

There are two elements of the personnel development plan which we believe must go hand in hand in order to achieve success:

Enlargement

The first is to appoint a new senior string player to each of the five string sections plus an additional three rank-and-file string players. The new senior string players would share the responsibilities and playing commitments with the current section leaders – and a new title of 'associate section leader' would apply to both present incumbents and these new players. We have never yet been able to compete on an equal basis with London orchestras in attracting top-quality experienced string players to Birmingham principally because the financial rewards we are currently able to offer them (about £13,000 p.a. basic for a section leader) falls far short of the sort of earnings open to such players in London. Added to that, the highly developed and lucrative freelance opportunities in London do not exist in Birmingham. We believe, however, that given the right financial conditions and the ability for such players to develop their own musical personalities outside the confines of the orchestra (which a shared responsibility role would permit) we could attract and retain those players by a healthy and vital artistic policy.

The appointment of these additional principals would, we believe, greatly enhance our performance standards. Not only would they add strength, depth and quality to the string body (something with which British orchestras often compare unfavourably with European and American competitors), but also, by their example, enable players to develop their technique to achieve the maximum of their potential. Their presence in the orchestra would also enable the high pressure of work and responsibilities which string section leaders currently undertake to be shared. This pressure is likely to become more and more acute as performance standards rise. The shared workload would enable the orchestra to respond with the sort of speed and efficiency which top calibre conductors are used to in working with the great international orchestras.

It will be vital that such an orchestra *consistently* performs at a peak of excellence which we are often but not always able to achieve at present. An important element towards achieving this standard will be as a result of the front desk players being able to devote time, energy and commitment to the job – in all the great orchestras that role is shared.

Enhancement

The second element concerns the remainder of the string body and the rest of the orchestra. We are conscious of the fact that a great orchestra is not simply reliant on front desk stars – depth, weight, strength and experience further back in the string sections are also essential. The same applies to all other sections of the orchestra (though it has to be accepted that in terms of *time* commitment, the string players are the most heavily pressed). At current salary levels nearly all the players have to supplement their CBSO earnings with teaching. An already heavy CBSO schedule is likely to become even more demanding and will require more time in study and preparation for their CBSO work. Substantially improved salary levels and a degree of flexibility in terms of a player's time commitment will be essential if we are to have success. Additionally, we believe it would in practice be impossible to engage new associate section leaders in the string sections at greatly increased salaries and improve the working schedule commitments of senior players without acknowledging and similarly improving the pay and conditions of the rest of the orchestra.

Additional development factors

This paper has emphasized the major element of development having significant immediate financial implications. There are, of course, many other areas of the orchestra's work which will need to be fostered and developed including the preparation, performance and promotion of the best of contemporary orchestral music. At the same time there is much scope for the presentation of smaller contemporary music groups drawn from within the orchestra. Under the auspices of the CBSO and utilizing the talents which we would hope to attract to Birmingham this area of work could have many spin-off advantages for both musicians and audiences. Similarly, a broadening of the orchestra's educational activities would be envisaged – not limiting that provision simply to work with the young in schools but extending into the wider community. The profile of the orchestra will need to be lifted and its self-promotion, both to attract the best players and to attract new and additional audiences, will need to be undertaken much more positively. The services of the best artists will need to be attracted and at the same time a careful eye will need to be kept on the emergence of new talent on the international scene – so often Britain has been the last to recognize and foster such talent.

We believe that these elements, albeit important, can be achieved with a relatively modest improvement in staffing levels. Increased private-sector funding will be necessary to undertake these additional activities. We believe, however, that given the commitment from our funding bodies to the major thrust of our development (increased size and quality of the orchestra) we can fund these extra activities ourselves from the additional box-office, engagement and sponsorship income we would hope to generate as a result of that improved quality.

We realize that the project we are proposing will have significant implications for the whole of the orchestral profession in the country. We acknowledge the difficulty that a positive response from the Arts Council will create in dealing with other orchestras. It is clear that the CBSO has reached a watershed. In normal circumstances, a conductor who has been with a regional orchestra for ten years (which Rattle will have been by 1989) would be expected to 'move on'. Indeed, in 'normal' circumstances that might even be desirable for all parties. The very fact that the relationship is now beginning to flourish and that there is a will by all components of the CBSO to strive for greater things together emphasizes that this is no 'normal' situation. We need now to consolidate and continue to develop this relationship. It is for that reason we plead our special case.

Bearing in mind the January 1987 deadline for Simon Rattle's decision as to his future, we believe that a time-scale along the following lines will be required:

Summer 1986	Commitment to finance the project from Arts Council and City of Birmingham;
September–December 1986	Advertising and auditioning for new players and opening of negotiations with the orchestra;
October 1986	Introduction of half the improved pay rates to existing players;
January 1987– September 1987	New appointees take up positions;
October 1987	Full implementation.

Appendix 2

A chronology of first appearances and appointments

1970	April	Liverpool Sinfonia (conducting début)
	November	Merseyside Youth Orchestra
1972	November	Royal Academy of Music (student conducting début)
1973	May	Merseyside Youth Orchestra (début as chief conductor)
	December	Royal Academy of Music (first opera performance)
1974	May	John Player Conductors Competition (first prizewinner)
	September	Bournemouth Symphony Orchestra and Sinfonietta (assistant conductor 1974–7)
1975	February	Nash Ensemble (Queen Elizabeth Hall début)
	March	Northern Sinfonia
	April	English Chamber Orchestra (début)
	May	Royal Liverpool Philharmonic Orchestra
	June	Salomon Orchestra
	September	Glyndebourne Touring Opera
		London Schools Symphony Orchestra (Royal Festival Hall début)
	October	Brighton Philharmonic Society
	November	BBC Scottish Symphony Orchestra
1976	January	Philharmonia Orchestra (Royal Festival Hall official professional début)
	March	Chelsea Opera Group
	May	City of Birmingham Symphony Orchestra (début)
	June	English Music Theatre Company
	August	London Sinfonietta (Henry Wood Proms début)
	September	London Schools Symphony Orchestra (first American tour)

	November	Scottish Chamber Orchestra
		Trondheim Symphony Orchestra
		Sjaellands Symphony Orchestra
1977	January	National Youth Orchestra (début)
	February	London Philharmonic Orchestra (début)
	April	Royal Liverpool Philharmonic Orchestra (associate conductor, 1977–80)
	May	Glyndebourne Festival Opera (début)
	July	BBC Scottish Symphony Orchestra (assistant conductor, 1977–80)
	October	London Symphony Orchestra (début)
		Radio Symphony Orchestra Berlin (RIAS début)
1978	February	Rotterdam Philharmonic Orchestra (début)
	June	Stockholm Philharmonia Orchestra (début)
	September	London Choral Society (principal conductor 1978–83)
	December	City of Birmingham Symphony Orchestra (Birmingham début)
1979	January	Los Angeles Philharmonic Orchestra (début)
	July	Chicago Symphony Orchestra (début)
1980	March	San Francisco Symphony Orchestra (début)
		Toronto Symphony Orchestra (début)
	September	CBSO (principal conductor and artistic adviser, 1980–)
1981	August	South Bank Summer Music (artistic director, 1981–3)
	September	Los Angeles Philharmonic Orchestra (principal guest conductor 1981–)
		Rotterdam Philharmonic Orchestra (principal guest conductor 1981–4)
	December	Israel Philharmonic Orchestra (début)
1982		Aldeburgh Foundation (artistic director, 1982–)
	March	Cleveland Orchestra (début)
		Montreal Symphony Orchestra (début)
1983	March	Scottish Opera (début)
	November	Boston Symphony Orchestra (début)
1985	January	Los Angeles Philharmonic Orchestra (New York début)
	November	English National Opera (début)
1986	November	Concertgebouw Orchestra (début)
1987	November	Berlin Philharmonic Orchestra (début)

Appendix 3: a conductor's diary:
January 1986–August 1987

January 1986

6   rehearsals: CBSO

7   CBSO, Town Hall, Cheltenham:
Brahms	Piano Concerto No. 1 (Bernard Roberts)
Bartók	*Concerto for Orchestra*

9, 10   rehearsals

11   CBSO, Town Hall, Birmingham:
Falla	Three dances from *The Three-Cornered Hat*
Rodrigo	*Concierto de Aranjuez* (David Russell)
Debussy	*Ibéria*
Ravel	*Bolero*

14   rehearsals

15, 16   CBSO, Town Hall, Birmingham:
Haydn	Symphony No. 70 in D
Brahms	Violin Concerto (Kyung-Wha Chung)
Bartók	*Concerto for Orchestra*

17   CBSO, Festival Hall, Corby: programme as 15 January

18   CBSO, Town Hall, Leeds:
Debussy	*Rondes de printemps*
Brahms	Violin Concerto (Kyung-Wha Chung)
Bartók	*Concerto for Orchestra*

20   rehearsals

21   CBSO, Town Hall, Birmingham:
Murail	*Time and Again* (première)
Messiaen	*Turangalîla Symphony* (Peter Donohoe, Tristan Murail)

22   CBSO, University of Warwick Arts Centre: programme as
          21 January

23   CBSO, Barbican Hall, London: programme as 21 January

24   rehearsals

28   CBSO, Town Hall, Cheltenham:

Webern	*Passacaglia*
Beethoven	Piano Concerto No. 4 (Christian Blackshaw)
Debussy	*Images*

29   CBSO, Royal Concert Hall, Nottingham:
          programme as 21 January

30, 31   CBSO, University of Warwick Arts Centre: EMI
          recording of Messiaen's *Turangalîla Symphony*

February 1986

1   recording continued

3   rehearsals: CBSO

4   CBSO, Town Hall, Birmingham:

Webern	*Passacaglia*
Beethoven	Piano Concerto No. 4 (Alfred Brendel)
Debussy	*Images*

6   CBSO, Théâtre des Champs-Elysées, Paris:
          programme as 4 February

7   CBSO, Théâtre des Champs-Elysées, Paris:

Brahms	Piano Concerto No. 1 (Alfred Brendel)
Bartók	*Concerto for Orchestra*

[*early February to early April set aside for Scottish Opera production of
Kurt Weill's* The Rise and Fall of the City of Mahagonny *cancelled because
of the illness of Simon's wife, Ellie*]

March 1986

30, 31   rehearsals: Scottish Chamber Orchestra

April 1986

1, 2   rehearsals: Scottish Chamber Orchestra

3   Scottish Chamber Orchestra, Usher Hall, Edinburgh:

Beethoven	Overture, *Leonora* No. 3
Mahler	Four songs from *Des Knaben Wunderhorn*
Beethoven	Symphony No. 9 in D minor

4   Scottish Chamber Orchestra, City Hall, Glasgow:
                       programme as 3 April

11, 12, 14   rehearsals: CBSO

15, 16   CBSO, Town Hall, Birmingham:
                      Mahler   Symphony No. 2 (*Resurrection*) (Arleen
                                      Auger, Felicity Palmer, CBSO
                                      Chorus)

19   CBSO, Town Hall, Birmingham:
                      Elgar   Pomp and Circumstance March No. 4
                      Walton   Viola Concerto (Rusen Günes)
                      Holst   *The Planets*

20, 21   rehearsals

22   CBSO, Town Hall, Cheltenham:
                      Mozart   Serenade for thirteen wind instruments
                      Mozart   Piano Concerto in C minor K491 (Radu
                                      Lupu)
                      Mozart   Symphony No. 38 in D

23   rehearsals: CBSO Chorus

24   CBSO, Town Hall, Birmingham: programme as 22 April

25   rehearsals

26   CBSO, Town Hall, Birmingham:
                      Elgar   *The Dream of Gerontius* (Janet Baker,
                                      John Mitchinson, Neil Howlett,
                                      CBSO Chorus)

27   CBSO, Watford Town Hall: EMI recording of Mahler's
                      Symphony No. 2 (Arleen Auger, Janet Baker, CBSO
                      Chorus)

28   rehearsals

29   CBSO, Town Hall, Birmingham:
                      Ravel   *Alborada del gracioso*
                      Holloway   *Seascape and Harvest* (première)
                      Brahms   Piano Concerto No. 2 (John Lill)

May 1986

1   CBSO, University of Warwick Arts Centre:
                      Mahler   Symphony No.2 (Alison Hargan, Felicity
                                      Palmer, CBSO Chorus)

4, 5, 6, 7   rehearsals: Philharmonia Orchestra

8	Philharmonia Orchestra, Royal Festival Hall, London:	
	Debussy	*Prélude à l'après-midi d'un faune*
	Ravel	*Shéhérazade* (Maria Ewing)
	Boulez	*Rituel in memoriam Bruno Maderna*
	Ravel	*Trois poèmes de Mallarmé*
	Debussy	*Ibéria*
9, 10	rehearsals	
11	Philharmonia Orchestra, Royal Festival Hall, London:	
	Ravel	*L'Éventail de Jeanne*
	Satie	*Parade*
	Duparc	Songs with orchestra (Ann Murray)
	Debussy	*Le Martyre de Saint-Sébastien* (symphonic fragments)
	Koechlin	*Les Bandar-log*
	Ravel	*La Valse*
12	Philharmonia Orchestra, La Grande Halle de la Villette, Paris:	
	Debussy	*Prelude à l'après-midi d'un faune*
	Ravel	*Shérérazade* (Maria Ewing)
	Boulez	*Rituel in memoriam Bruno Maderna*
	Koechlin	*Les Bandar-log*
	Debussy	*Ibéria*
13, 14	rehearsals	
15	Philharmonia Orchestra, Royal Festival Hall, London:	
	Ravel	*Alborada del gracioso*
	Poulenc	Concerto for two pianos (Katia and Marielle Labèque)
	Debussy	*Jeux*
	Ravel	*L'Enfant et les sortilèges* (Elise Ross and other soloists)
16	rehearsals	
17	Philharmonia Orchestra, Queen Elizabeth Hall, London:	
	Debussy	*La boîte à joujoux*
	Messiaen	*Oiseaux exotiques* (Peter Donohoe)
	Boulez	*Éclat*
	Ravel	*Ma Mère l'oye*
18	rehearsals	
19	Philharmonia Orchestra, Royal Festival Hall, London:	
	Poulenc	*La Voix Humaine* (Elisabeth Söderström)
	Messiaen	*Et exspecto resurrectionem mortuorum*
	Ravel	*Daphnis et Chloé*

21   [*Arts Council music panel meeting*]

22   rehearsals: CBSO

24   CBSO, The Dome, Brighton Festival:
            Wagner   Prelude and *Liebestod, Tristan und
                                    Isolde*
            Messiaen   *Turangalîla Symphony* (Paul Crossley,
                                    Tristan Murail)

25   CBSO, The Dome, Brighton Festival:
            Mahler   Symphony No.2 (Alison Hargan,
                                    Alfreda Hodgson, Brighton Festival
                                    Chorus)

26   CBSO, Wells Cathedral, Bath Festival:
                programme as 24 May

28   rehearsals

29   CBSO, Barbican Hall, London:
            Haydn   Symphony No. 70 in D
            Brahms   Piano Concerto No.1 (John Lill)
            Bartók   *Concerto for Orchestra*

30   CBSO, Watford Town Hall: E M I recording of Mahler's
                Symphony No.2

June 1986

1   recording continued

2–   rehearsals: Glyndebourne Festival Opera

13   rehearsals: CBSO

14   CBSO, The Maltings, Snape, Aldeburgh Festival:
            Sibelius   Symphony No.7
            Henze   *Barcarola*
            Debussy   *Images*

15–   rehearsals: Glyndebourne Festival Opera

24   rehearsals: CBSO

25   CBSO, National Exhibition Centre, Birmingham:
            Walton   March, *Orb and Sceptre*
            Rachmaninov   *Rhapsody on a Theme of Paganini* (Peter
                                    Donohoe)
            Borodin   *Polovtsian Dances* (CBSO Chorus)
            Rodrigo   *Concierto de Aranjuez* (John Williams)
            Ravel   *Boléro*

26	CBSO, Town Hall, Birmingham:
	Ravel *Alborada del gracioso*
	Beethoven Violin Concerto (Christopher Warren-Green)
	Brahms Symphony No.4
27–	rehearsals: Glyndebourne Festival Opera

July 1986

5, 10, 13, 15, 19, 23, 26, 29	Glyndebourne Festival Opera
	Gershwin *Porgy and Bess*
16, 17	rehearsals: CBSO
18	CBSO, Town Hall, Cheltenham:
	Debussy *Ibéria*
	Kraft *Interplay* (British première)
	Brahms Symphony No.4
21, 22	CBSO, Warwick Arts Centre: BBCTV recording of Henze's Symphony No.7
24	rehearsals: CBSO
25	CBSO, Royal Albert Hall, London:
	Webern *Passacaglia*
	Henze Symphony No.7 (British première)
	Beethoven Violin Concerto (Henryk Szeryng)

August 1986

1, 4, 6, 8, 10, 12, 14	Glyndebourne Festival Opera
	Gershwin *Porgy and Bess*
24	rehearsals: CBSO
25, 26	CBSO, Derngate, Northampton: BBCTV recording of Berio's *Sinfonia* (Electric Phoenix)
27	rehearsals
29	CBSO, Usher Hall, Edinburgh:
	Elgar *The Dream of Gerontius* (Janet Baker, John Mitchinson, John Shirley-Quirk, Edinburgh Festival Chorus)
30	CBSO, Usher Hall, Edinburgh:
	Berio *Sinfonia* (Electric Phoenix)
	Mahler Symphony No.2 (Felicity Lott, Janet Baker, Edinburgh Festival Chorus)

September 1986

3, 4   rehearsals

5   CBSO, Royal Hall, Nottingham:
          Elgar   *The Dream of Gerontius* (Janet Baker,
                    John Mitchinson, John Shirley-Quirk,
                    CBSO Chorus)

6, 7, 8   Great Hall, Birmingham University: EMI recording of
          Elgar's *The Dream of Gerontius* (soloists and chorus as
          September 5)

10   rehearsals

11   CBSO, Henry Wood Prom, Royal Albert Hall, London:
          Ravel   *Alborada del gracioso*
          Debussy   *Images*
          Rachmaninov   Piano Concerto No.4 (Philip Fowke)
          Sibelius   Symphony No.7

12, 15, 16   rehearsals

17   CBSO, Town Hall, Birmingham:
          Debussy–
                    Constant   *Pelléas et Mélisande Symphony* (British
                              première)
                    Beethoven   Symphony No.9 (Alison Hargan, Louise
                              Winter, David Johnston, Willard
                              White, City of Birmingham Choir)

18, 19   Adrian Boult Hall, Birmingham: Central TV recording:
          'What's New?' (Robin Holloway etc)

22   rehearsals

23   CBSO, St Asaph Cathedral:
          Haydn   Symphony No.60
          Debussy–
                    Constant   *Pelléas et Mélisande Symphony*
          Stravinsky   *Petrushka*

24   CBSO, Derngate, Northampton:
          Debussy–
                    Constant   *Pelléas et Mélisande Symphony*
                    Beethoven   Symphony No.9 (soloists and chorus as
                              September 17)

25   CBSO, Town Hall, Birmingham:
          programme as 24 September

26   rehearsals

27	CBSO winds, University of Warwick Arts Centre:
	Mozart Serenade for thirteen wind instruments
	Stravinsky *Symphonies of Wind Instruments*
	Grainger *A Lincolnshire Posy*

29	CBSO winds, Adrian Boult Hall:
	Mozart Serenade for thirteen wind instruments

30	CBSO, Town Hall, Birmingham:
	Stravinsky *Symphony in Three Movements*
	Gershwin Piano Concerto (Peter Donohoe)
	Stravinsky *Petrushka*
	Ravel *La Valse*

October 1986

2	CBSO, Barbican Hall, London:
	programme as 30 September

3, 4	CBSO, Warwick Arts Centre: EMI recording of Stravinsky's *Petrushka* and *Symphony in Three Movements*

7	rehearsals

8	CBSO, University of Warwick Arts Centre:
	Haydn Symphony No.60
	Henze *Barcarola*
	Brahms Violin Concerto (Ida Haendel)

9	CBSO, Town Hall, Birmingham: programme as 8 October

10	CBSO, Town Hall, Birmingham:
	Wagner Overture, *The Mastersingers*
	Brahms Piano Concerto No.1 (John Lill)
	Haydn Symphony No.60
	Ravel *La Valse*

20, 21, 22	rehearsals: London Sinfonietta

23	London Sinfonietta, Queen Elizabeth Hall, London:
	Tippett Concerto for double string orchestra
	Britten Serenade for tenor, horn and strings
	Tippett *Songs for Dov* (Neil Mackie)
	Britten *Variations on a Theme of Frank Bridge*

24	London Sinfonietta, University of Warwick Arts Centre:
	Tippett Concerto for double string orchestra
	Britten Serenade for tenor, horn and strings
	Tippett *Fantasia Concertante on a Theme of Corelli*

| | Britten | *Variations on a Theme of Frank Bridge* |

| 26, 27 | rehearsals: London Sinfonietta |

| 29 | London Sinfonietta, Queen Elizabeth Hall, London: |

	Tippett	*Fantasia Concertante on a theme of Corelli*
	Britten	Symphony for Cello and Orchestra (Christopher van Kampen)
	Tippett	*Ritual Dances* from *The Midsummer Marriage*
	Britten	*Four French Songs* (Jill Gomez)
	Britten	*The Young Person's Guide to the Orchestra*

November 1986

| 3, 4 | rehearsals: Concertgebouw Orchestra |

| 5 | Concertgebouw Orchestra, Concertgebouw, Amsterdam: |

	Haydn	Symphony No.60
	Ravel	*Shéhérazade* (Maria Ewing)
	Stravinsky	*Petrushka*

| 7 | Concertgebouw Orchestra, De Doelen Hall, Rotterdam: |

| | Haydn | Symphony No.60 |
| | Stravinsky | *Petrushka* |

| 8 | rehearsal |

| 9 | Concertgebouw Orchestra, Concertgebouw, Amsterdam: programme as 5 November |

| 10, 11 | rehearsals |

| 12, 13 | Concertgebouw Orchestra, Concertgebouw, Amsterdam: |

| | Mahler | Symphony No.10 (performing version by Deryck Cooke) |

| 15 | Concertgebouw Orchestra, Musikcentrum, Utrecht: programme as 12 November |

| 23 | Brighton Philharmonic Orchestra, The Dome, Brighton: |

	Berlioz	Overture, *Carnival Romain*
	Canteloube	*Songs of the Auvergne* (Elise Ross)
	Beethoven	Symphony No. 6

| 29 | rehearsals: CBSO |

| 30 | CBSO, Royal Opera House, Covent Garden (Peter Pears memorial concert) |

| | Colin Matthews | *Tribute Fanfare* (première) |
| | Mozart | *Sinfonia concertante* for violin and viola |

	(Anne-Sophie Mutter, Bruno Giuranna)
Britten	*War Requiem* (Galina Vishnevskaya, Anthony Rolfe-Johnson, John Shirley-Quirk, Philharmonia Chorus, Westminster Cathedral choristers)

December 1986

1	rehearsals

2	CBSO, Town Hall, Cheltenham:
Wagner	Overture, *The Mastersingers*
Bruch	Violin Concerto No. 1 (Oscar Shumsky)
Beethoven	Romance No. 2 for violin and orchestra
Sibelius	Symphony No. 4

3	rehearsals

4	CBSO, Town Hall, Birmingham:
Brahms	Songs for female voices, two horns and harp (CBSO Chorus)
Bruch	Violin Concerto No. 1 (Oscar Shumsky)
Beethoven	Romance No. 2 for violin and orchestra
Sibelius	Symphony No. 4

5, 8	rehearsals

9, 10	CBSO, Town Hall, Birmingham:
Sibelius	Symphony No. 6
Mozart	Piano Concerto in C, K503 (Stephen Bishop-Kovacevich)
Brahms	Symphony No. 4

11	CBSO, Barbican Hall, London: programme as 9 December

13, 14	CBSO, University of Warwick Arts Centre: EMI recording of Sibelius's Symphonies Nos. 4 and 6

16, 17	rehearsals

18	CBSO, Town Hall, Birmingham
Strauss	Festival Prelude
Delius	*On Hearing the First Cuckoo in Spring*
Knussen	*Choral*
Strauss	*The Three Kings* (Elise Ross)
Gershwin	*A Cuban Overture*
Varèse	*Offrandes* (Elise Ross)
Canteloube	*Songs of the Auvergne* (Elise Ross)
Prokofiev	*Scythian Suite*

30—   London Sinfonietta, Henry Wood Hall, London: EMI
               recording of Milhaud's *La Création du monde*,
               Bernstein's *Prelude, Fugue and Riffs*, Gershwin's
               Rhapsody in Blue (Peter Donohoe) and Stravinsky's
               Ebony Concerto (Michael Collins)

January 1987

5, 6, 7   rehearsals: Rotterdam Philharmonic Orchestra

8   Rotterdam Philharmonic Orchestra, Palais des Beaux Arts,
               Brussels:
               Schoenberg   *Five Pieces* Op.16
               Bartók   Piano Concerto No.2 (Peter Donohoe)
               Brahms   Symphony No.4

9, 11   Rotterdam PO, De Doelen Hall, Rotterdam:
               programme as 8 January

12   rehearsals

13, 14, 15   Rotterdam PO, De Doelen Hall, Rotterdam:
               Beethoven   Symphony No.6
               Shostakovich   Symphony No.5

16   Rotterdam PO, Musikcentrum, Utrecht:
               programme as 13 January

17   Rotterdam PO, Concertgebouw, Amsterdam:
               programme as 13 January

22, 23, 26   rehearsals: CBSO

27   CBSO, Royal Hall, Nottingham:
               Sibelius   Symphony No.6
               Mahler   Symphony No.6

28   CBSO, Royal Festival Hall, London:
               programme as 27 January

29   CBSO, Town Hall, Birmingham:
               Birtwistle   *Dinah and Nick's Love Song*
               Mahler   Symphony No.6

30   rehearsals

31   CBSO, Town Hall, Birmingham:
               Mahler   Symphony No.6

February 1987

2   rehearsals
3   CBSO, Town Hall, Birmingham:
               Berio   *Sinfonia* (Electric Phoenix)

	Berlioz	*Symphonie fantastique*
5, 6	CBSO, University of Warwick Arts Centre: BBCTV recording of music by Berlioz	
8, 9	CBSO, University of Warwick Arts Centre: EMI recording of Sibelius's Violin Concerto (Nigel Kennedy)	
10	CBSO, Town Hall, Cheltenham:	
	Strauss	*Don Juan*
	Elgar	Cello Concerto (Ulrich Heinen)
	Beethoven	Symphony No.6
11	rehearsals	
12	CBSO, Town Hall, Birmingham: programme as 10 February	
13	CBSO, Civic Hall, Bedworth: programme as 10 February	
16	rehearsals	
17, 18	CBSO, Town Hall, Birmingham:	
	Schoenberg	*Five Pieces* Op.16
	Brahms	Piano Concerto No.2 (André Watts)
	Sibelius	Symphony No.5
19	CBSO, Barbican Hall, London: programme as 17 February	
20	CBSO, University of Warwick Arts Centre: programme as 17 February	
21	CBSO, University of Warwick Arts Centre: EMI recording of Sibelius's Symphony No.5	
23	rehearsals	
24	CBSO, Town Hall, Cheltenham:	
	Haydn	*The Creation* (Margaret Marshall, Philip Langridge, David Thomas, CBSO Chorus)
25	CBSO, Philharmonic Hall, Liverpool: programme as 24 February	
26	CBSO, Town Hall, Birmingham: programme as 24 February	
27	[*Received honorary degree from Birmingham Polytechnic*]	

March 1987

10, 11	rehearsals: Boston Symphony Orchestra

12, 13, 14, 17   Boston Symphony Orchestra, Symphony Hall, Boston:
                  Schoenberg   *Five Pieces* Op.16
                  Sibelius   Violin Concerto (Kyung-Wha Chung)
                  Stravinsky   *Petrushka*

18   rehearsals

19, 20, 21   BSO, Symphony Hall, Boston:
                  Haydn   Symphony No.70
                  Rachmaninov   Symphony No.2

24, 25   rehearsals: Cleveland Orchestra

26, 27, 28   Cleveland Orchestra, Severance Hall, Cleveland:
                  Bartók   Piano Concerto No.2 (Peter Donohoe)
                  Rachmaninov   Symphony No.2

30, 31   rehearsals

April 1987

1   rehearsals

2, 4   Cleveland Orchestra, Severance Hall, Cleveland:
                  Haydn   *The Creation* (Lillian Watson, Anthony
                                        Rolfe-Johnson, David Thomas,
                                        Cleveland Orchestra Chorus)

6, 7, 8   rehearsals: Los Angeles Philharmonic Orchestra

9, 10, 11, 12   LAPO, Dorothy Chandler Pavilion, Los Angeles:
                  Haydn   *The Creation* (Margaret Marshall,
                                        Jonathan Mack, David Thomas)

15   rehearsals

16, 17, 18, 19   LAPO, Dorothy Chandler Pavilion, Los Angeles:
                  Mendelssohn   Violin Concerto (Anne-Sophie Mutter)
                  Mahler   Symphony No.6

24, 25   rehearsals: CBSO

28, 29   CBSO, Town Hall, Birmingham:
                  Mahler   Symphony No.1

30   CBSO, Barbican Hall, London: programme as 28 April

May 1987

1, 4, 13, 14   rehearsals: Royal Academy of Music

15   Royal Academy of Music, London (Maurice Handford
                      memorial concert):
                  Brahms   Symphony No.1
                  Elgar   *Enigma Variations*

18	rehearsals: CBSO
19	CBSO, Town Hall, Cheltenham:

Gershwin	Overture, *Strike Up the Band*
Takemitsu	*A Flock Descends into the Pentagonal Garden*
Ravel	*La Valse*
Mahler	Symphony No. 1

20	rehearsals
21	CBSO, Assembly Rooms, Derby:

Berlioz	Overture, *Beatrice and Benedict*
Britten	*Sinfonia da Requiem*
Mahler	Symphony No. 1

23	CBSO, Town Hall, Leeds:

Gershwin	Overture, *Strike Up the Band*
Takemitsu	*A Flock Descends into the Pentagonal Garden*
Ravel	*La Valse*
Beethoven	Symphony No. 3

26	CBSO, Town Hall, Birmingham:

Bernstein	Overture, *Candide*
Sibelius	Violin Concerto (Yuzuko Horigome)
Brahms	Symphony No. 4

June 1987

1	CBSO, Memorial Hall, Matsudo, Japan: programme as 23 May
2	CBSO, Hitomi Memorial Hall, Tokyo: programme as 23 May
3	CBSO, Suntory Hall, Tokyo:

Berlioz	Overture, *Beatrice and Benedict*
Sibelius	Violin Concerto (Yuzuko Horigome)
Brahms	Symphony No. 4

5	CBSO, Numazu Shimin Bunka Center, Tokyo:

Berlioz	Overture, *Beatrice and Benedict*
Britten	*Sinfonia da Requiem*
Mahler	Symphony No. 1

6	CBSO, Bunka Kaikan, Tokyo: programme as 5 June
7	CBSO, Symphony Hall, Osaka: programme as 3 June
8	CBSO, Takamatsu, Shimin Kaikan:

Britten	*Sinfonia da Requiem*

| | Sibelius | Violin Concerto (Yuzuko Horigome) |
| | Brahms | Symphony No. 4 |

9   CBSO, Yasu Bunka Hall, near Kyoto:
         programme as 23 May

10   CBSO, Bunka Kaikan, Tokyo:
         programme as 5 June

19–   rehearsals: Glyndebourne Festival Opera

25, 26   rehearsals: CBSO

27   CBSO, St Edmundsbury Cathedral, Bury St Edmunds,
         (Aldeburgh Festival):

| | Britten | *Sinfonia da Requeim* |
| | Beethoven | Symphony No.9 (Harolyn Blackwell, Marietta Simpson, Damon Evans, Bruce Hubbard, CBSO Chorus) |

July 1987

2, 3   rehearsals: CBSO

4   CBSO, Lichfield Cathedral, (Lichfield Festival):

	Sibelius	Symphony No.6
	Sibelius	Violin Concerto (Nigel Kennedy)
	Sibelius	Symphony No.5

6–   rehearsals: Glyndebourne Festival Opera

9   CBSO, Town Hall, Birmingham (CBSO Prom):

	Tchaikovsky	*Nutcracker Suite*
	Shostakovich	*Age of Gold Suite*
	Stravinsky	*The Firebird*

22, 29, 30   Glyndebourne Festival Opera

| | Ravel | *L'Enfant et les sortilèges* |
| | Ravel | *L'Heure espagnole* |

26, 27, 28, 29,   rehearsals: Orchestra of the Age of Enlightenment
30, 31

28   [*investiture of CBE, Buckingham Palace*]

August 1987

2, 4   Orchestra of the Age of Enlightenment, Queen Elizabeth
         Hall, London:

| | Mozart | *Idomeneo* |

7, 10, 11, 13,   Glyndebourne Festival Opera
15, 17, 19

| | Ravel | *L'Enfant et les sortilèges* |
| | Ravel | *L'Heure espagnole* |

Discography

Ravel: *Chansons madécasses; Trois poèmes de Mallarmé*
Felicity Palmer (soprano), Nash Ensemble (Recorded St John's, Smith Square, 25 May 1975) Argo ZRG 834

Stravinsky: *Symphonies of Wind Instruments: Three Japanese Lyrics*
Jane Manning (soprano), Nash Ensemble (Recorded BBC Studios, Maida Vale, 13–14 February 1977) Chandos ABR 1048 (in *Stravinsky: a Tapestry*)

Schoenberg: *Pierrot lunaire*
Webern: *Concerto for Nine Instruments*, Op.24
Jane Manning (soprano), Nash Ensemble (Recorded BBC Studios, Maida Vale, 22–3 February 1977) Chandos ABR 1046 (originally for the Open University)

Stravinsky: *Pulcinella*, Suites Nos.1 & 2
Northern Sinfonia (Recorded Northern Sinfonia Centre, Newcastle, 28–9 March 1977 and 3–4 January 1978) EMI ASD 3604

Stravinsky: *The Rite of Spring*
National Youth Orchestra of Great Britain (Recorded Goldsmith's College, London, 14–15 April 1977) Enigma MID 5001; ASV ACM 2030

Prokofiev: Piano Concerto No.1; *Romeo and Juliet* (excerpts)
Ravel: Piano Concerto in D; *Pavane pour un infante défunte*
Andrei Gavrilov (piano), London Symphony Orchestra (Recorded EMI Studios, Abbey Road, London, 7–9 July 1977) EMI ASD 3571

Maxwell Davies: Symphony No.1
Philharmonia Orchestra (Recorded Kingsway Hall, London, 10, 11, 15 August 1978) Decca HEAD 21

Mahler: Symphony No. 10 (Deryck Cooke performing edition, second version with additional revisions for this recording by Simon Rattle and Berthold Goldschmidt)
Bournemouth Symphony Orchestra (Recorded Guildhall, Southampton, 10–12 June 1980) EMI SLS 5206

Holst: Suite, *The Planets*
Philharmonia Orchestra (Recorded Kingsway Hall, London, 29–30 December 1980) EMI ASD 4047

Janáček: *Glagolitic Mass*
Felicity Palmer, Ameral Gunson, John Mitchinson, Malcolm King, Jane Parker-Smith (organ), CBSO Chorus, CBSO (Recorded Great Hall, Birmingham University, 9–10 January 1981) EMI ASD 4066

Sibelius: Symphony No. 5; *Night Ride and Sunrise*
Philharmonia Orchestra (Recorded 9–10 October 1981) EMI ASD 4168

Liszt: Piano Concerto No. 1
Saint-Saëns: Piano Concerto No. 2
Cécile Ousset (piano), CBSO (Recorded University of Warwick Arts Centre 25–6 March 1982) EMI ASD 4307

Britten: *Young Apollo: Canadian Carnival; Four French Songs; Scottish Ballad*
Philip Fowke, Peter Donohoe (pianos), Jill Gomez (soprano), CBSO (Recorded Cheltenham Town Hall 22–3 April 1982) EMI ASD 4177

Weill: *The Seven Deadly Sins*
Elise Ross (soprano), CBSO (Recorded Town Hall, Birmingham, 7 September 1982) EMI ASD 4402

Rachmaninov: *Three Symphonic Dances; Vocalise*
CBSO (Recorded The Maltings, Snape, 24 October 1982 (*Dances*), Birmingham University Great Hall, 28 February 1983 (*Vocalise*))
EMI ASD 1436111

Janáček: *Taras Bulba; Sinfonietta*
Philharmonia Orchestra (Recorded Abbey Road Studios, 17–18 November 1982) EMI ASD 4066

Britten: *War Requiem*
Elisabeth Södeström, Robert Tear, Thomas Allen, CBSO Chorus, Boys of Christ Church Cathedral, Oxford, CBSO (Recorded Great Hall, Birmingham University, 27 February, 1, 4 March 1983)
HMV SLS 1077573

Vaughan Williams: *Songs of Travel; On Wenlock Edge*
Thomas Allen, Robert Tear, CBSO (Recorded Town Hall, Birmingham,
26–7 May 1983) EMI EL 27 0059 1

Mahler: *Das klagende Lied* (complete original version)
Helena Döse, Alfreda Hodgson, Robert Tear, Sean Rea, CBSO Chorus,
CBSO (Recorded Town Hall, Birmingham, 12–13 October 1983, 24 June
1984) EMI EL 27 0136 1

Rachmaninov: Symphony No. 2, Los Angeles PO (Recorded Dorothy
Chandler Pavilion, LA, 2–3 January 1984) EL 2700 521

Rachmaninov: Piano Concerto No.2; *Rhapsody on a Theme of Paganini*
Cécile Ousset (piano), CBSO (Recorded Town Hall, Birmingham, 24–5
June 1983 (recording not issued); University of Warwick Arts Centre, 3–4
May 1984) EMI EL 27 0103 1

Britten: *Sinfonia da Requiem; An American Overture; An Occasional
Overture; Suite on English Folk Tunes (A Time There Was ...)*
CBSO (Recorded University of Warwick Arts Centre, 23–4 May 1984)
EMI EL 27 0263 1

Brahms, orchestrated by **Schoenberg:** Piano Quartet in G minor
CBSO (Recorded The Maltings, Snape, 19 June 1984) EMI EL 27 0169 1

Sibelius: Symphony No.2; *Scene with Cranes (Kuolema)*
CBSO (Recorded University of Warwick Arts Centre, 21–2 June 1984)
EMI EL 27 0160 1

Nielsen: Symphony No.4 *(The Inextinguishable); Pan and Syrinx*
CBSO (Recorded University of Warwick Arts Centre, 13–14 September
1984) EMI EL 27 0260 1

Sibelius: Symphony No.1; *The Oceanides*
CBSO (Recorded University of Warwick Arts Centre, 7, 8, 13 December
1984) EMI EL 27 0309 1

Shostakovich: Symphony No. 10
Philharmonia Orchestra (Recorded Abbey Road Studios, 3–4 April 1985)
EMI EL 27 0315 1

Bartók: Concerto for two pianos, percussion and orchestra
Katia and Marielle Labèque (pianos), Sylvio Gualda and Jean-Pierre Drouet
(percussion), CBSO (Recorded University of Warwick Arts Centre, 20–1
September 1985) EMI EL 27 0418 1

Sibelius: Symphony No.3; Symphony No.7
CBSO(Recorded University of Warwick Arts Centre, 10–11 October 1985)
EMI EL 27 0496 1

Messiaen: *Turangalîla Symphony*
Peter Donohoe (piano), Tristan Murail (ondes martenot), CBSO (Recorded
University of Warwick Arts Centre, 30–1 January, 1 February 1986)
EMI EL 27 0468 3

Mahler: Symphony No.2
Arleen Auger, Janet Baker, CBSO Chorus, CBSO (Recorded Watford
Town Hall, 27 April, 30 May, 1 June 1986) EMI EL 27 0598 3

Elgar: *The Dream of Gerontius*
Janet Baker, John Mitchinson, John Shirley-Quirk, CBSO Chorus, CBSO
(Recorded Great Hall, Birmingham University, 7–9 September 1986)
EMI EX 749 549 1

Milhaud: *La Création du monde*
Gershwin: *Rhapsody in Blue*
Stravinsky: *Ebony Concerto*
Bernstein: *Prelude, Fugue and Riffs*
Arrangements for the Paul Whiteman Band
London Sinfonietta, Peter Donohoe (piano), Michael Collins (clarinet)
(Recorded Abbey Road Studios, 30 January–2 February 1987)
EMI EL 747 9911

Stravinsky: *Petrushka* (1947 version); *Symphony in Three Movements*
CBSO (Recorded University of Warwick Arts Centre, 3–4 October 1986)
EMI EL 749 053 1

Sibelius: Symphony No.4: Symphony No.6
CBSO (Recorded University of Warwick Arts Centre, 13–14 December
1986)

Sibelius: Symphony No.5; Violin Concerto
Nigel Kennedy (violin), CBSO (Recorded University of Warwick Arts
Centre, 8 February (Concerto), 21 February 1987 (Symphony)

Index

This is principally a list of names. Composer references are only included, when there is a substantive mention in the text.

Abbado, Claudio, 47, 142, 195
Age of Enlightenment, Orchestra of the, 161
Aldeburgh Festival, 4, 62, 92, 137–8
Alden, David, 141, 156
Allen, Thomas, 77
Alvin Ailey Dance Theatre, 45
Aprahamian, Felix, 52
Arnold, Geoffrey, 33
Arnold, Malcolm, 35, 37
Arrau, Claudio, 2
Artec, 202
Arts Council, 57, 135, 146, 149, 153, 181, 183–93, 195, 198–200
Ashkenazy, Vladimir, 195
Association of British Orchestras (ABO), 192–3
Aston University, 16
Atherton, David, 47
Auger, Arleen, 134
Avon, Lord, 32
Ax, Emanuel, 124, 127

Bailey, Dennis, 127
Bailey, Derek, 91
Baillie, Alexander, 91
Baker, Arthur, 102–3
Baker, Janet, 127
Ballardie, Quintin, 59
Barbican Hall, 22, 73, 185, 203
Barenboim, Daniel, 62, 184
Baskerville, John, 15
Bath Festival, 21, 113
Baumann, Hermann, 127
BBC (British Broadcasting Corporation), 7, 45, 65, 67–8, 82, 86, 88, 89, 91, 93, 108
BBC Scottish Symphony Orchestra, 3, 11, 64–8

BBC Symphony Orchestra, 35, 45, 67, 108, 183, 186
BBC Welsh Symphony Orchestra, 7
Beaumont, Anthony, 46
Bedford, Steuart, 43
Beecham, Thomas, 107, 129
Berglund, Paavo, 48, 121, 128
Berio, Luciano, 86–7, 88, 92
Berlin Festival, 133
Berlin Philharmonic Orchestra, 1, 80, 109, 118, 167, 191, 207
Birkenhead Music Society, 35
Birmingham City Council, 103, 107, 187, 189, 198–200
Birmingham International Convention Centre, 16, 200–2
Birmingham Festival, 106
Birmingham School of Music, 18, 174
Birmingham Town Hall, 18, 22, 23, 106, 107, 177
Bishop, Christopher, 146, 147, 149, 152–3, 193, 202
Bishop-Kovacevich, Stephen, 114, 212
Blackwell, Harolyn, 156
Blades, James, 42
Blenkinsop, David, 56
Bluecoat School, Liverpool, 27
Blyth, Alan, 52, 62, 93
Boston Symphony Orchestra, 162, 208–9
Boulez, Pierre, 7, 20, 41, 45, 47, 64, 93, 116, 143, 171
Boult, Sir Adrian, 18, 52, 107–8, 109, 201
Boulton, Matthew, 15
Bournemouth Sinfonietta, 48, 54–9, 64, 104
Bournemouth Symphony Orchestra, 48, 54–9, 64, 76, 108, 113, 125
Braga, Robert, 37

Brendel, Alfred, 120, 134, 136, 210–12
Brighton Festival, 56, 72, 73, 146
Britten, Benjamin, 77, 79, 81, 84, 89, 110,
    122, 137, 138, 140, 141
Brooke, Gwydion, 60
Brown, Iona, 120, 127
Burrows, Denise, 38
Burton, Humphrey, 89

Cairns, David, 145
Caley, Ian, 120
Calgary Philharmonic Orchestra, 54
Campbell-White, Martin, 47–8, 53, 55, 59,
    60, 62, 63, 64, 69, 142, 148, 158, 162, 164,
    166, 167
Canning, Hugh, 195
Capital Radio, 145
Carewe, John, 6–11, 42, 48, 57, 64, 79, 140,
    150, 179–81
Carpenter, Clinton, 147
CBS, 85
CBSO (City of Birmingham Symphony
    Orchestra), 2, 3, 4, 5, 12, 16–23, 30, 38,
    45, 64, 71, 72–5, 77, 79, 81, 82–5, 86–9,
    91, 92, 99, 102–36, 137, 138, 143, 146,
    174–81, 184, 185, 187–202, 203–13
CBSO Proms, 105, 117
Celibidache, Sergiu, 54
Central Television, 89, 91, 93
Chappell, Herbert, 89
Chelsea Opera Group, 62, 156
Chicago Symphony Orchestra, 167, 191, 207
Chung, Kyung-Wha, 127, 134
Clements, Andrew, 118, 126, 203–4
Cleveland Symphony Orchestra, 99, 166,
    167, 207, 208
Clifford, Julian, 107
Cohen, Robert, 130
Cole, Hugo, 61
Concertgebouw Orchestra, 75, 162, 164–6,
    167, 173
Conlon, James, 121
Contemporary Music Network (Arts
    Council), 57
Cooke, Deryck, 59, 76, 162, 164, 167
Cooper, Imogen, 120
Copley, John, 43
Corsaro, Frank, 155
Costa, Michael, 106
Crichton, Ronald, 52, 60
Cronkite, Walter, 32
Crossley, Paul, 114, 140, 143
Cubitt, Thomas, 203

Curzon, Clifford, 146

Dalby, Martin, 65–7
Dartington Summer School, 1, 62, 137
Davey, Alan, 194
Davies, Philippa, 44
Davis, Andrew, 47, 60, 71, 146
Davis, Colin, 138
Davis, Peter G., 173
Dean, Stafford, 122
Del Mar, Norman, 48
Deutsch, Max, 7, 9
Dickie, Brian, 48, 155–6, 158–60
Donohoe, Peter, 51, 79, 120, 130, 134, 148
Döse, Helena, 81, 124
Driver, Paul, 129
Drummond, John, 67
Duncan, Neil, 186
Dupré, Desmond, 25
Dutch, David, 41–2
Dutch, Elspeth, 42

Eastern Orchestral Board, 186
Edinburgh Festival, 41, 130, 146
Edwards, Terry, 87
EEC (European Economic Community), 201
Elder, Mark, 46, 121, 138
Electric Phoenix, 86–7
EMI, 73, 75–7, 79–81, 82, 91, 125, 127, 141,
    145, 146, 150
English Bach Festival, 2, 110
English Chamber Orchestra, 59
English Music Theatre, 62
English National Opera, 121, 138, 155
Estes, Simon, 169–70
Ewing, Maria, 134, 148, 162

Fanning, David, 209
Feeney Trust, 19
Ferrara, Franco, 54
Fiedler, Arthur, 32
Finch, Hilary, 161
Fischer-Dieskau, Dietrich, 55
Fleischmann, Ernest, 63, 71, 169–71
Fowke, Philip, 2–4, 45, 69, 114, 116
Freedman, Amelia, 55
Frémaux, Louis, 77, 102–4, 105, 109, 110,
    112
From East to West (television documentary),
    88, 89, 91–2, 191
Fujikawa, Mayumi, 114, 122
Furtwängler, Wilhelm, 7, 101, 179, 212

Gardner, John, 42
Gavin, Barrie, 86–7, 88, 89, 91–3
Gavrilov, Andrei, 77
Gibson, Sir Alexander, 68
Gilbert, Anthony, 45
Giles, Cathy, 50
Gillinson, Clive, 193
Giulini, Carlo Maria, 113, 169, 170, 172,
    177, 181, 184
Glasgow Schools Symphony Orchestra, 9
Glory of the Garden, The (Arts Council
    paper), 185–6, 192
Glyndebourne Festival Opera, 4, 6, 33, 43,
    44, 48, 51, 54, 62, 70, 85, 137, 138,
    154–61, 198
Glyndebourne Touring Opera, 104
Godovsky, Leopold, 33
Goehr, Alexander, 142
Goehr, Walter, 7, 9, 57, 179
Gomez, Jill, 79, 140
Goodall, Reginald, 131
Goodman Report, 184
Gordon, A., 194
Grainger, Percy, 88, 93
Granada Television, 91
Graves, Francis, 22–3
Gray, Linda Esther, 56
Gray, Stephen, 20, 47, 54, 69, 71
Grayson, Barrie, 112
Greene, Gordon, 4, 42
Greenfield, Edward, 129, 145, 161
Grier, Christopher, 118
Griffiths, Paul, 118, 129, 145, 160, 161, 179
Griller, Sidney, 42
Grimley, Terry, 191, 198
Grinke, Frederick, 42
Grove, John, 42
Groves, Sir Charles, 20, 21, 30, 32, 37, 48, 68
Gulbenkian Foundation, 46
Gunson, Ameral, 114, 120, 148

Haendel, Ida, 120
Haitink, Bernard, 158, 159, 161, 171
Hall, Carol, 87
Hall, Sir Peter, 155, 159
Hall, Peter, 148
Hallé Orchestra, 108, 192
Handford, Maurice, 54
Hannan, Eilene, 124
Hansom, Joseph, 17
Harewood, Earl of, 155
Hargan, Alison, 114
Harnoncourt, Nikolaus, 75, 99, 161

Harold Holt Ltd, 47, 48, 53
Harrell, Lynn, 114, 124
Harris, Dinah, 148
Harrison, Max, 61
Head, Michael, 43
Heath, Edward, 63
Heifetz, Jascha, 33
Hemsley, Thomas, 120
Henahan, Donal, 173
Henderson, Gavin, 145, 146
Henderson, Robert, 61, 136, 150
Henry Wood Promenade Concerts, 3, 4, 18,
    20, 28, 29, 41, 62–3, 68, 88, 92, 118, 122,
    136, 141, 145, 148, 176
Henze, Hans Werner, 88, 92
Herford, Henry, 130, 148
Herincx, Raimund, 148
Heward, Leslie, 108
Heyworth, Peter, 126
Hickox, Richard, 50
Hodgson, Alfreda, 114, 120
Holliger, Heinz, 58, 120, 130
Holliger, Ursula, 120
Holloway, Robin, 126
Hurst, George, 33, 50, 58

Imai, Nobuko, 122, 130
Israel Philharmonic Orchestra, 167

Jenkins, Bill, 30, 33, 35, 45
Jenkins, Lyndon, 107, 108, 109–10, 117,
    122, 125, 128
John Player International Conductor's
    Award, 10, 48–9, 53, 68, 89, 158, 166
Johnson, Russell, 202
Johnston, Robert, 120
Jonas, George, 17, 103–5, 119, 188, 200
Joyce, James, 44, 87, 113
Judd, James, 46

Karajan, Herbert von, 80, 181
Katsaris, Cyprien, 110
Kay, Graeme, 194
Kennedy, Michael, 108
Kenton, Stan, 21
Kim, Young Uck, 127
Kimball, Robert, 172–3
King, Malcolm, 114
King, Mary, 130, 148
King-Smith, Beresford, 16–17, 105–6, 107
Klemperer, Otto, 9, 99
Knussen, Oliver, 4–6, 89, 137, 143, 146, 213
Kok, Felix, 116, 175

Kraemer, Nicholas, 99, 135

Labèque, Katia, 148
Labèque, Marielle, 148
Lalandi, Lina, 110
Langridge, Philip, 122
Lewis, Anthony, 35
Lill, John, 134
Liverpool College, 30, 33, 37, 38, 39, 40
Liverpool Concert Orchestra, 35
Liverpool Mozart Orchestra, 7, 41
Liverpool Schools Junior Orchestra, 30
Liverpool Sinfonia, 38, 41
Liverpool Spastic Fellowship, 37
Liverpool Youth Music Committee, 35
Lloyd-Jones, David, 43
Loader, Sally, 29
London Choral Society, 137
London Orchestral Concert Board, 184
London Philharmonic Orchestra (LPO), 55,
   79, 82, 150–1, 153, 160, 184, 191, 198
London Schools Symphony Orchestra, 60, 63,
   169
London Sinfonietta, 4, 5, 48, 54, 56, 62, 63,
   70, 79, 137, 139–43, 153
London Symphony Orchestra (LSO), 22, 73,
   77, 109, 169, 185, 193, 195
Loppert, Max, 160
Loriod, Yvonne, 120
Los Angeles Philharmonic Orchestra, 63, 71,
   77, 99, 116, 156, 167, 169–73
Lott, Felicity, 43
Loughran, James, 68
Loveland, Kenneth, 117
Lovett, Leon, 45
Lupu, Radu, 127, 135

Ma, Yo-Yo, 124, 127, 133
Maazel, Lorin, 146, 166
McGrath, Roderick, 46
Maclay, Ian, 191
Malko, Nikolai, 108
Mancini, Henry, 38
Marshall, Margaret, 122
Martin, Frank, 130
Matthews, Appleby, 107
Matthews, David, 68, 92, 140, 146
Maxwell Davies, Sir Peter, 10, 56, 66, 145,
   146
Mayer, Sir Robert, 60
Mehta, Zubin, 171
Merseyside Concert Orchestra, 38, 41
Merseyside Youth Orchestra (MYO), 3, 4,

28, 30, 35, 38, 45, 46, 47, 50, 51, 54
Messiaen, Olivier, 7, 18–19, 20, 21–2, 83–4,
   121, 122, 135, 143, 181, 210
Metropolitan Opera, New York, 25, 170, 171
Metters, Colin, 46, 50
Milanova, Stoika, 114
Miles, Maurice, 37, 42
Miller, Douglas, 33
Milnes, Rodney, 62
Mitchell, Donald, 92
Mitchinson, John, 114, 120, 124, 134
Montgomery, Kenneth, 48, 159
Montreal Symphony Orchestra, 167
Moore, Bob, 86
Morrison, Richard, 198
Mulholland, Raymond, 30
Murail, Tristan, 19, 20, 22, 134
Murdoch, William, 15
Murray, Ann, 148
Murray, David, 70, 73, 82–5, 118, 161
Musicians' Union, 68, 192
Muti, Riccardo, 146, 150, 152, 184

Nash Ensemble, 54, 55–6, 59
National Exhibition Centre, 16, 201–2
National Theatre, 202
National Youth Orchestra (NYO), 12, 41, 44,
   47, 64
Newborough School, Liverpool, 28
New London Chamber Orchestra, 44
New Philharmonia Orchestra, *see*
   Philharmonia Orchestra
New York Philharmonic Orchestra, 20, 171
New Opera Company, 45
Norman, Jessye, 92, 148, 169–70
Norris, Geoffrey, 35
Northcott, Bayan, 126, 146
Northern Sinfonia, 55, 76, 79
Nunn, Trevor, 154, 155, 156, 157

Oakley, Annie, 30
Oliver, Alexander, 130
Orchestre National de Paris, 109
Orwell, George, 26
Ousset, Cécile, 77
Overton, Bill, 35

Palmer, Felicity, 59, 114, 134, 170
Panufnik, Andrzej, 108–9
Paris Autumn Festival, 133
Paris Opera, 169
Parkinson, Stephen, 194
Pay, Anthony, 55, 142
Peacock Report, 184

Pears, Sir Peter, 137
Percussionists Anomymous, 38
Pernod Award, 38
Pettitt, Stephen J., 60, 141, 150
Philharmonia Orchestra, 12, 18, 21, 48, 54,
 57, 60, 61, 62, 66, 76, 77, 79, 99, 109, 127,
 137, 145–53, 160, 167, 183, 184, 193, 198
Ponsonby, Robert, 67
Porter, Andrew, 129
Pound, Ezra, 44
Pountney, David, 155
Previn, André, 84, 95, 171, 195
Priestley, Josiah, 14
Pritchard, John, 32
Purser, John, 65, 66

Ramsay, Pat, 67
Rattle, Denis, 1, 24–35, 50, 58
Rattle, Elise (Ellie), *see* Ross, Elise
Rattle, Pauline, 1, 25–6, 30, 40, 71
Rattle, Sasha, 4, 79, 170, 204–5
Rattle, Susan, 1, 25, 27, 28–9, 40
Rees, Judith, 87
Rees-Mogg, Sir William, 185, 191, 192–3
Reich, Steve, 92
Relton, William, 186
Rendall, David, 43
Reynish, Timothy, 46
RIAS orchestra, 167
Richter, Hans, 106
Rickenbacher, Karl Anton, 65
Ridley, Anthony, 37
Rignold, Hugo, 109
Rittner, Luke, 185, 193
Ross, Elise, 4, 77, 91, 113, 114, 120, 130,
 134, 142, 148, 177, 204–5
Rotterdam Philharmonic Orchestra, 71, 124,
 164, 166, 208
Royal Academy of Music, 3, 4, 9, 10, 28, 37,
 40, 41, 42–8, 51–2, 54, 69, 73, 99, 142,
 158
Royal Academy of Music Chamber
 Orchestra, 48
Royal Liverpool Philharmonic Orchestra, 20,
 28, 30–2, 37, 38–9, 45–6, 47, 54, 65, 68,
 70, 109, 158
Royal Opera House, Covent Garden, 70, 138,
 159
Royal Philharmonic Orchestra (RPO), 59, 71,
 109, 183, 191, 195
Royal Shakespeare Company, 154, 155

Sadler's Wells, 43, 45, 62

Salomon Orchestra, 59–60
Salonen, Esa-Pekka, 18, 85, 98, 150, 153, 169
Sanderling, Kurt, 121, 177
San Francisco Symphony Orchestra, 167
Schenker, Heinrich, 99
Schmid, Erich, 104, 175
Schwarz, Rudolf, 101, 103, 105, 108
Scottish Chamber Orchestra, 63, 131, 177,
 180
Seaman, Christopher, 68
Sendak, Maurice, 160
Shawe-Taylor, Desmond, 126
Sheady, Mike, 81
Shirley-Quirk, John, 134
Simon, Geoffrey, 50
Sinopoli, Giuseppe, 152, 153, 183
Sjaellands Symphony Orchestra, 64, 166
Smaczny, Jan, 161
Smith, Edward, 38–9, 45–6, 50–1, 86, 103,
 104–5, 110, 112, 113–14, 116, 120–1,
 128, 187, 188, 192, 193, 194, 200
Snowman, Nicholas, 153
Söderström, Elisabeth, 148
Solti, Sir Georg, 184
South Bank Board, 198
South Bank Summer Music, 6, 91, 118, 121,
 122, 127, 129, 141, 157
Spiegl, Emma, 27
Spiegl, Fritz, 27–8, 39
Stevenson, Adlai, 32
Stockley, William, 106
Streets, John, 43–4, 46–7, 54
Swingle Singers, 87
Sydney Opera House, 33
Szekely, Julianna, 116
Szell, George, 99, 208
Szeryng, Henryk, 130

Tabachnik, Michel, 175
Taplin, Frank, 24–5
Tear, Robert, 77, 81
Tennstedt, Klaus, 82
Thomson, Virgil, 155
Tierney, Neil, 37–8, 46, 70
Tinsley, Pauline, 70
Toronto Symphony Orchestra, 167
Trondheim Symphony Orchestra, 64, 166
Tschaikov, Basil (Nick), 48, 145

Vakarelis, Janis, 124
Vásáry, Tamás, 120
Vickers, Jon, 92
Vyner, Michael, 5, 48, 140

Walden, Peter, 124, 130
Wallace, John, 147
Walsh, Stephen, 59–60
Ward, John, 28, 29, 37, 38, 41
Warren, Eva, 38
Watson, Peter, 189
Watt, James, 14
Wedgwood, Sir Josiah, 14–15
Weingartner, Felix, 108
Weldon, George, 103, 105, 108
Weller, Walter, 68, 71
Wells, H. G., 26
West Midlands County Council, 188
White, Willard, 69, 119, 127, 134, 156
Whiteman, Paul, 79, 141
Widdicombe, Gillian, 57, 193

Willan, John, 79–82, 84, 127, 150–1, 191, 193
Williams, Howard, 46
Williams, John, 130
Williams, Laverne, 119
Wood, Sir Henry, 106–7
Woodage, Wesley, 35
Wordsworth, Barry, 46

Yazaki, Hikotaro, 50
Yentob, Alan, 93

Zinman, David, 71, 166
Zollman, Ronald, 50
Zukerman, Pinchas, 59